PERFECT RIGOR

Books by Masha Gessen

Blood Matters: From Inherited Illness to Designer Babies, How the World and I Found Ourselves in the Future of the Gene

Ester and Ruzya: How My Grandmothers Survived Hitler's War and Stalin's Peace

Dead Again: The Russian Intelligentsia After Communism

In the Here and There, by Valeria Narbikova (as translator)

Half a Revolution: Contemporary Fiction by Russian Women (as editor and translator)

Perfect Rigor: A Genius and the Mathematical Breakthrough of the Century

PERFECT RIGOR

A Genius *and the* Mathematical
Breakthrough *of the* Century

||||||||||||||||||||||||||||||||||||||||||||||||||||||||||||||||||||||||||||||||||||||||

MASHA GESSEN

HOUGHTON MIFFLIN HARCOURT • BOSTON / NEW YORK • 2009

For information about permission to reproduce selections from this book,
write to Permissions, Houghton Mifflin Harcourt Publishing Company,
215 Park Avenue South, New York, New York 10003.

www.hmhbooks.com

Library of Congress Cataloging-in-Publication Data
Gessen, Masha.
Perfect rigor : a genius and the mathematical breakthrough
of the century / Masha Gessen.
p. cm.
Includes bibliographical references and index.
ISBN 978-0-15-101406-4
1. Perelman, Grigori, 1966–   2. Mathematicians—Russian (Federation)—
Biography.   3. Poincaré conjecture.   I. Title.
QA29.P6727G47   2009
510.92–dc22 [B]   2009014742

Book design by Brian Moore

Printed in the United States of America

DOC 10 9 8 7 6 5 4 3 2

Contents

A Problem for a Million Dollars

Numbers cast a magic spell over all of us, but mathematicians are especially skilled at imbuing figures with meaning. In the year 2000, a group of the world's leading mathematicians gathered in Paris for a meeting that they believed would be momentous. They would use this occasion to take stock of their field. They would discuss the sheer beauty of mathematics—a value that would be understood and appreciated by everyone present. They would take the time to reward one another with praise and, most critical, to dream. They would together try to envision the elegance, the substance, the importance of future mathematical accomplishments.

The Millennium Meeting had been convened by the Clay Mathematics Institute, a nonprofit organization founded by Boston-area businessman Landon Clay and his wife, Lavinia, for the purposes of popularizing mathematical ideas and encouraging their professional exploration. In the two years of its existence, the institute had set up a beautiful office in a building just outside Harvard Square in Cambridge, Massachusetts, and had handed out a few research awards. Now it had an ambitious plan for the future of mathematics, "to record the problems of the twentieth century that resisted challenge most successfully and that we would most like to see resolved," as Andrew Wiles, the British number theorist who had famously conquered Fermat's Last Theorem, put it. "We don't know how they'll be solved or when: it may be five years or it may be a hundred years. But we believe that somehow by solving these problems we will open up whole new vistas of mathematical discoveries and landscapes."

As though setting up a mathematical fairy tale, the Clay Institute named seven problems—a magic number in many folk traditions—and assigned the fantastical value of one million dollars for each one's solution. The reigning kings of mathematics gave lectures summarizing the problems. Michael Francis Atiyah, one of the previous century's most influential mathematicians, began by outlining the Poincaré Conjecture, formulated by Henri Poincaré in 1904. The problem was a classic of mathematical topology. "It's been worked on by many famous mathematicians, and it's still unsolved," stated Atiyah. "There have been many false proofs. Many people have tried and have made mistakes. Sometimes they discovered the mistakes themselves, sometimes their friends discovered the mistakes." The audience, which no doubt contained at least a couple of people who had made mistakes while tackling the Poincaré, laughed.

Atiyah suggested that the solution to the problem might come from physics. "This is a kind of clue—hint—by the teacher who cannot solve the problem to the student who is trying to solve it," he joked. Several members of the audience were indeed working on problems that they hoped might move mathematics closer to a victory over the Poincaré. But no one thought a solution was near.

True, some mathematicians conceal their preoccupations when they're working on famous problems—as Wiles had done while he was working on Fermat's Last—but generally they stay abreast of one another's research. And though putative proofs of the Poincaré Conjecture had appeared more or less annually, the last major breakthrough dated back almost twenty years, to 1982, when the American Richard Hamilton laid out a blueprint for solving the problem. He had found, however, that his own plan for the solution—what mathematicians call a program—was too difficult to follow, and no one else had offered a credible alternative. The Poincaré Conjecture, like Clay's other Millennium Problems, might never be solved.

Solving any one of these problems would be nothing short of a heroic feat. Each had claimed decades of research time, and many a mathematician had gone to the grave having failed to solve the problem with which he or she had struggled for years. "The Clay Mathematics Institute really wants to send a clear message, which is that mathematics is mainly valuable because of these immensely difficult problems, which are like the Mount Everest or the Mount Himalaya of mathematics," said the French mathematician Alain Connes, another twentieth-century giant. "And if we reach the peak, first of all, it will be extremely difficult—we might even pay the price of our lives or something like that. But what is true is that when we reach the peak, the view from there will be fantastic."

As unlikely as it was that anyone would solve a Millennium Problem in the foreseeable future, the Clay Institute nonetheless laid out a clear plan for giving each award. The rules stipulated that the solution to the problem would have to be presented in a refereed journal, which was, of course, standard practice. After publication, a two-year waiting period would begin, allowing the world mathematics community to examine the solution and arrive at a consensus on its veracity and authorship. Then a committee would be appointed to make a final recommendation on the award. Only after it had done so would the institute hand over the million dollars. Wiles estimated that it would take at least five years to arrive at the first solution—assuming that any of the problems was actually solved—so the procedure did not seem at all cumbersome.

Just two years later, in November 2002, a Russian mathematician posted his proof of the Poincaré Conjecture on the Internet. He was not the first person to claim he'd solved the Poincaré—he was not even the only Russian to post a putative proof of the conjecture on the Internet *that year*—but his proof turned out to be right.

And then things did not go according to plan—not the Clay Institute's plan or any other plan that might have struck a mathematician as reasonable. Grigory Perelman, the Russian, did not publish his work in a refereed journal. He did not agree to vet or even to review the explications of his proof written by others. He refused numerous job offers from the world's best universities. He refused to accept the Fields Medal, mathematics' highest honor, which would have been awarded to him in 2006. And then he essentially withdrew from not only the world's mathematical conversation but also most of his fellow humans' conversation.

Perelman's peculiar behavior attracted the sort of attention to the Poincaré Conjecture and its proof that perhaps no other story of mathematics ever had. The unprecedented magnitude of the award that apparently awaited him helped heat up interest too, as did a sudden plagiarism controversy in which a pair of Chinese mathematicians claimed they deserved the credit for proving the Poincaré. The more people talked about Perelman, the more he seemed to recede from view; eventually, even people who had once known him well said that he had "disappeared," although he continued to live in the St. Petersburg apartment that had been his home for many years. He did occasionally pick up the phone there—but only to make it clear that he wanted the world to consider him gone.

When I set out to write this book, I wanted to find answers to three questions: Why was Perelman able to solve the conjecture; that is, what was it about his mind that set him apart from all the mathematicians who had come before? Why did he then abandon mathematics and, to a large extent, the world? Would he refuse to accept the Clay prize money, which he deserved and most certainly could use, and if so, why?

This book was not written the way biographies usually are. I did not have extended interviews with Perelman. In fact, I had no conversations with him at all. By the time I started working on this project, he had cut off communication with all journalists and most people. That made my job more difficult—I had to imagine a person I had literally never met—but also more interesting: it was an investigation. Fortunately, most people who had been close to him and to the Poincaré Conjecture story agreed to talk to me. In fact, at times I thought it was easier than writing a book about a cooperating subject, because I had no allegiance to Perelman's own narrative and his vision of himself—except to try to figure out what it was.

1

Escape into the Imagination

S ANYONE WHO has attended grade school knows, mathematics is unlike anything else in the universe. Virtually every human being has experienced that sense of epiphany when an abstraction suddenly makes sense. And while grade-school arithmetic is to mathematics roughly what a spelling bee is to the art of novel writing, the desire to understand patterns—and the childlike thrill of making an inscrutable or disobedient pattern conform to a set of logical rules—is the driving force of all mathematics.

Much of the thrill lies in the singular nature of the solution. There is only one right answer, which is why most mathematicians hold their field to be hard, exact, pure, and fundamental, even if it cannot precisely be called a science. The truth of science is tested by experiment. The truth of mathematics is tested by argument, which makes it more like philosophy, or, even better, the law, a discipline that also assumes the existence of a single truth. While the other hard sciences live in the laboratory or in the field, tended to by an army of technicians, mathematics lives in the mind. Its lifeblood is the thought process that keeps a mathematician turning in his sleep and waking with a jolt to an idea, and the conversation that alters, corrects, or affirms the idea.

"The mathematician needs no laboratories or supplies," wrote the Russian number theorist Alexander Khinchin. "A piece of paper, a pencil, and creative powers form the foundation of his work. If this is supplemented with the opportunity to use a more or less decent library and a dose of scientific enthusiasm (which nearly every mathematician possesses), then no amount of destruction can stop the creative work." The other sciences as they have been practiced since the early twentieth century are, by their very natures, collective pursuits; mathematics is a solitary process, but the mathematician is always addressing another similarly occupied mind. The tools of that conversation—the rooms where those essential arguments take place—are conferences, journals, and, in our day, the Internet.

That Russia produced some of the twentieth century's greatest mathematicians is, plainly, a miracle. Mathematics was antithetical to the Soviet way of everything. It promoted argument; it studied patterns in a country that controlled its citizens by forcing them to inhabit a shifting, unpredictable reality; it placed a premium on logic and consistency in a culture that thrived on rhetoric and fear; it required highly specialized knowledge to understand, making the mathematical conversation a code that was indecipherable to an outsider; and worst of all, mathematics laid claim to singular and knowable truths when the regime had staked its legitimacy on its own singular truth. All of this is what made mathematics in the Soviet Union uniquely appealing to those whose minds demanded consistency and logic, unattainable in virtually any other area of study. It is also what made mathematics and mathematicians suspect. Explaining what makes mathematics as important and as beautiful as mathematicians know it to be, the Russian algebraist Mikhail Tsfasman said, "Mathematics is uniquely suited to teaching one to distinguish right from wrong, the proven from the unproven, the probable from the improbable. It also teaches us to distinguish that which is probable and probably true from that which, while apparently probable, is an obvious lie. This is a part of mathematical culture that the [Russian] society at large so sorely lacks."

It stands to reason that the Soviet human rights movement was founded by a mathematician. Alexander Yesenin-Volpin, a logic theorist, organized the first demonstration in Moscow in December 1965. The movement's slogans were based on Soviet law, and its founders made a single demand: they called on the Soviet authorities to obey the country's written law. In other words, they demanded logic and consistency; this was a transgression, for which Yesenin-Volpin was incarcerated in prisons and psychiatric wards for a total of fourteen years and ultimately forced to leave the country.

Soviet scholarship, and Soviet scholars, existed to serve the Soviet state. In May 1927, less than ten years after the October Revolution, the Central Committee inserted into the bylaws of the USSR's Academy of Sciences a clause specifying just this. A member of the Academy may be stripped of his status, the clause stated, "if his activities are apparently aimed at harming the USSR." From that point on, every member of the Academy was presumed guilty of aiming to harm the USSR. Public hearings involving historians, literary scholars, and chemists ended with the scholars publicly disgraced, stripped of their academic regalia, and, frequently, jailed on treason charges. Entire fields of study—most notably genetics—were destroyed for apparently coming into conflict with Soviet ideology. Joseph Stalin personally ruled scholarship. He even published his own scientific papers, thereby setting the research agenda in a given field for years to come. His article on linguistics, for example, relieved comparative language study of a cloud of suspicion that had hung over it and condemned, among other things, the study of class distinctions in language as well as the whole field of semantics. Stalin personally promoted a crusading enemy of genetics, Trofim Lysenko, and apparently coauthored Lysenko's talk that led to an outright ban of the study of genetics in the Soviet Union.

What saved Russian mathematics from destruction by decree was a combination of three almost entirely unrelated factors. First, Russian mathematics happened to be uncommonly strong right when it might have suffered the most. Second, mathematics proved too obscure for the sort of meddling the Soviet leader most liked to exercise. And third, at a critical moment it proved immensely useful to the State.

In the 1920s and '30s, Moscow boasted a robust mathematical community; groundbreaking work was being done in topology, probability theory, number theory, functional analysis, differential equations, and other fields that formed the foundation of twentieth-century mathematics. Mathematics is cheap, and this helped: when the natural sciences perished for lack of equipment and even of heated space in which to work, the mathematicians made do with their pencils and their conversations. "A lack of contemporary literature was, to some extent, compensated by ceaseless scientific communication, which it was possible to organize and support in those years," wrote Khinchin about that period. An entire crop of young mathematicians, many of whom had received part of their education abroad, became fast-track professors and members of the Academy in those years.

The older generation of mathematicians—those who had made their careers before the revolution—were, naturally, suspect. One of them, Dimitri Egorov, the leading light of Russian mathematics at the turn of the twentieth century, was arrested and in 1931 died in internal exile. His crimes: he was religious and made no secret of it, and he resisted attempts to ideologize mathematics—for example, trying (unsuccessfully) to sidetrack a letter of salutation sent from a mathematicians' congress to a Party congress. Egorov's vocal supporters were cleansed from the leadership of Moscow mathematical institutions, but by the standards of the day, this was more of a warning than a purge: no area of study was banned, and no general line was imposed by the Kremlin. Mathematicians would have been well advised to brace for a bigger blow.

In the 1930s, a mathematical show trial was all set to go forward. Egorov's junior partner in leading the Moscow mathematical community was his first student, Nikolai Luzin, a charismatic teacher himself whose numerous students called their circle Luzitania, as though it were a magical country, or perhaps a secret brotherhood united by a common imagination. Mathematics, when taught by the right kind of visionary, does lend itself to secret societies. As most mathematicians are quick to point out, there are only a handful of people in the world who understand what the mathematicians are talking about. When these people happen to talk to one another—or, better yet, form a group that learns and lives in sync—it can be exhilarating.

"Luzin's militant idealism," wrote a colleague who denounced Luzin, "is amply expressed by the following quote from his report to the Academy on his trip abroad: 'It seems the set of natural numbers is not an absolutely objective formation. It seems it is a function of the mind of the mathematician who happens to be speaking of a set of natural numbers at the given moment. It seems there are, among the problems of arithmetic, those that absolutely cannot be solved.'"

The denunciation was masterful: the addressee did not need to know anything about mathematics and would certainly know that solipsism, subjectivity, and uncertainty were utterly un-Soviet qualities. In July 1936 a public campaign against the famous mathematician was launched in the daily *Pravda*, where Luzin was exposed as "an enemy wearing a Soviet mask."

The campaign against Luzin continued with newspaper articles, community meetings, and five days of hearings by an emergency committee formed by the Academy of Sciences. Newspaper articles exposed Luzin and other mathematicians as enemies because they published their work abroad. In other words, events unfolded in accordance with the standard show-trial scenario. But then the process seemed to fizzle out: Luzin publicly repented and was severely reprimanded although allowed to remain a member of the Academy. A criminal investigation into his alleged treason was quietly allowed to die.

Researchers who have studied the Luzin case believe it was Stalin himself who ultimately decided to stop the campaign. The reason, they think, is that mathematics is useless for propaganda. "The ideological analysis of the case would have devolved to a discussion of the mathematician's understanding of a natural number set, which seemed like a far cry from sabotage, which, in the Soviet collective consciousness, was rather associated with coal mine explosions or killer doctors," wrote Sergei Demidov and Vladimir Isakov, two mathematicians who teamed up to study the case when this became possible, in the 1990s. "Such a discussion would better be conducted using material more conducive to propaganda, such as, say, biology and Darwin's theory of evolution, which the great leader himself was fond of discussing. That would have touched on topics that were ideologically charged and easily understood: monkeys, people, society, and life itself. That's so much more promising than the natural number set or the function of a real variable."

Luzin and Russian mathematics were very, very lucky.

Mathematics survived the attack but was permanently hobbled. In the end, Luzin was publicly disgraced and dressed down for practicing mathematics: publishing in international journals, maintaining contacts with colleagues abroad, taking part in the conversation that is the life of mathematics. The message of the Luzin hearings, heeded by Soviet mathematicians well into the 1960s and, to a significant extent, until the collapse of the Soviet Union, was this: Stay behind the Iron Curtain. Pretend Soviet mathematics is not just the world's most progressive mathematics—this was its official tag line—but the world's only mathematics. As a result, Soviet and Western mathematicians, unaware of one another's endeavors, worked on the same problems, resulting in a number of double-named concepts such as the Chaitin-Kolmogorov complexities and the Cook-Levin theorem. (In both cases the eventual coauthors worked independently of each other.) A top Soviet mathematician, Lev Pontryagin, recalled in his memoir that during his first trip abroad, in 1958—five years after Stalin's death—when he was fifty years old and world famous among mathematicians, he had had to keep asking colleagues if his latest result was actually new; he did not really have another way of knowing.

"It was in the 1960s that a couple of people were allowed to go to France for half a year or a year," recalled Sergei Gelfand, a Russian mathematician who now runs the American Mathematics Society's publishing program. "When they went and came back, it was very useful for all of Soviet mathematics, because they were able to communicate there and to realize, and make others realize, that even the most talented of people, when they keep cooking in their own pot behind the Iron Curtain, they don't have the full picture. They have to speak with others, and they have to read the work of others, and it cut both ways: I know American mathematicians who studied Russian just to be able to read Soviet mathematics journals." Indeed, there is a generation of American mathematicians who are more likely than not to possess a reading knowledge of mathematical Russian—a rather specialized skill even for a native Russian speaker; Jim Carlson, president of the Clay Mathematics Institute, is one of them. Gelfand himself left Russia in the early 1990s because he was drafted by the American Mathematics Society to fill the knowledge gap that had formed during the years of the Soviet reign over mathematics: he coordinated the translation and publication in the United States of Russian mathematicians' accumulated work.

So some of what Khinchin described as the tools of a mathematician's labor—"a more or less decent library" and "ceaseless scientific communication"—were stripped from Soviet mathematicians. They still had the main prerequisites, though—"a piece of paper, a pencil, and creative powers"—and, most important, they had one another: mathematicians as a group slipped by the first rounds of purges because mathematics was too obscure for propaganda. Over the nearly four decades of Stalin's reign, however, it would turn out that nothing was too obscure for destruction. Mathematics' turn would surely have come if it weren't for the fact that at a crucial point in twentieth-century history, mathematics left the realm of abstract conversation and suddenly made itself indispensable. What ultimately saved Soviet mathematicians and Soviet mathematics was World War II and the arms race that followed it.

Nazi Germany invaded the Soviet Union on June 22, 1941. Three weeks later, the Soviet air force was gone: bombed out of existence in the airfields before most of the planes ever took off. The Russian military set about retrofitting civilian airplanes for use as bombers. The problem was, the civilian airplanes were significantly slower than the military ones, rendering moot everything the military knew about aim. A mathematician was needed to recalculate speeds and distances so the air force could hit its targets. In fact, a small army of mathematicians was needed. The greatest Russian mathematician of the twentieth century, Andrei Kolmogorov, returned to Moscow from the academics' wartime haven in Tatarstan and led a classroom full of students armed with adding machines in recalculating the Red Army's bombing and artillery tables. When this work was done, he set about creating a new system of statistical control and prediction for the Soviet military.

At the beginning of World War II, Kolmogorov was thirty-eight years old, already a member of the Presidium of the Soviet Academy of Sciences—making him one of a handful of the most influential academics in the empire—and world famous for his work in probability theory. He was also an unusually prolific teacher: by the end of his life he had served as an adviser on seventy-nine dissertations and had spearheaded both the math olympiads system and the Soviet mathematics-school culture. But during the war, Kolmogorov put his scientific career on hold to serve the Soviet state directly—proving in the process that mathematicians were essential to the State's very survival.

The Soviet Union declared victory—and the end of what it called the Great Patriotic War—on May 9, 1945. In August, the United States dropped atomic bombs on the Japanese cities of Hiroshima and Nagasaki. Stalin kept his silence for months afterward. When he finally spoke publicly, following his so-called re-election in February 1946, it was to promise the people of his country that the Soviet Union would surpass the West in developing its atomic capability. The effort to assemble an army of physicists and mathematicians to match the Manhattan Project's had by that time been under way for at least a year; young scholars had been recalled from the frontlines and even released from prisons in order to join the race for the bomb.

Following the war, the Soviet Union invested heavily in high-tech military research, building more than forty entire cities where scientists and mathematicians worked in secret. The urgency of the mobilization indeed recalled the Manhattan Project—only it was much, much bigger and lasted much longer. Estimates of the number of people engaged in the Soviet arms effort in the second half of the century are notoriously inaccurate, but they range as high as twelve million, with a couple million of them employed by military research institutions. For many years, a newly graduated young mathematician or physicist was more likely to be assigned to defense-related research than to a civilian institution. These jobs spelled nearly total scientific isolation: for defense employees, burdened by security clearances whether or not they actually had access to sensitive military information, any contact with foreigners was considered not just suspect but treasonous. In addition, some of these jobs required moving to the research towns, which provided comfortably cloistered social environments but no possibility for outside intellectual contact. The mathematician's pencil and paper could be useless tools in the absence of an ongoing mathematical conversation. So the Soviet Union managed to hide some of its best mathematical minds away, in plain sight.

Following Stalin's death, in 1953, the country shifted its stance on its relationship to the rest of the world: now the Soviet Union was to be not only feared but respected. So while it fell to most mathematicians to help build bombs and rockets, it fell to a select few to build prestige. Very slowly, in the late 1950s, the Iron Curtain began to open a tiny crack—not quite enough to facilitate much-needed conversation between Soviet and non-Soviet mathematicians but enough to show off some of Soviet mathematics' proudest achievements.

By the 1970s, a Soviet mathematics establishment had taken shape. It was a totalitarian system within a totalitarian system. It provided its members with not only work and money but also apartments, food, and transportation; it determined where they lived and when, where, and how they traveled for work or pleasure. To those in the fold, it was a controlling and strict but caring mother: her children were well nourished and nurtured, an undeniably privileged group compared with the rest of the country. When basic goods were scarce, official mathematicians and other scientists could shop at specially designated stores, which tended to be better stocked and less crowded than those open to the general public. Since for most of the Soviet century there was no such thing as a private apartment, regular Soviet citizens received their dwellings from the State; members of the science establishment were assigned apartments by their institutions, and these apartments tended to be larger and better located than their compatriots'. Finally, one of the rarest privileges in the life of a Soviet citizen—foreign travel—was available to members of the mathematics establishment. It was the Academy of Sciences, with the Party and the State security organizations watching over it, that decided if a mathematician could accept, say, an invitation to address a scholarly conference, who would accompany him on the trip, how long the trip would last, and, in many instances, where he would stay. For example, in 1970, the first Soviet winner of the Fields Medal, Sergei Novikov, was not allowed to travel to Nice to accept his award. He received it a year later, when the International Mathematical Union met in Moscow.

Even for members of the mathematical establishment, though, resources were always scarce. There were always fewer good apartments than there were people who desired them, and there were always more people wanting to travel to a conference than would be allowed to go. So it was a vicious, backstabbing little world, shaped by intrigue, denunciations, and unfair competition. The barriers to entry into this club were prohibitively high: a mathematician had to be ideologically reliable and personally loyal not only to the Party but to existing members of the establishment, and Jews and women had next to no chance of getting in.

One could easily be expelled by the establishment for misbehaving. This happened with Kolmogorov's student Eugene Dynkin, who fostered an atmosphere of unconscionable liberalism at a specialized mathematics school he ran in Moscow. Another of Kolmogorov's students, Leonid Levin, describes being ostracized for associating with dissidents. "I became a burden for everyone to whom I was connected," he wrote in a memoir. "I would not be hired by any serious research institution, and I felt I didn't even have the right to attend seminars, since participants had been instructed to inform [the authorities] whenever I appeared. My Moscow existence began to seem pointless." Both Dynkin and Levin emigrated. It must have been soon after Levin's arrival in the United States that he learned that a problem he had been describing at Moscow mathematics seminars (building in part on Kolmogorov's work on complexities) was the same problem U.S. computer scientist Stephen Cook had defined. Cook and Levin, who became a professor at Boston University, are considered coinventors of the NP-completeness theorem, also known as the Cook-Levin theorem; it forms the foundation of one of the seven Millennium Problems that the Clay Mathematics Institute is offering a million dollars to solve. The theorem says, in essence, that some problems are easy to formulate but require so many computations that a machine capable of solving them cannot exist.

And then there were those who almost never became members of the establishment: those who happened to be born Jewish or female, those who had had the wrong advisers at their universities, and those who could not force themselves to join the Party. "There were people who realized that they would never be admitted to the Academy and that the most they could hope for was being able to defend their doctoral dissertation at some institute in Minsk, if they could secure connections there," said Sergei Gelfand, the American Mathematics Society publisher, who happens to be the son of one of Russia's top twentieth-century mathematicians, Israel Gelfand, a student of Kolmogorov's. "These people attended seminars at the university and were officially on the staff of some research institute, say, of the timber industry. They did very good math, and at a certain point they even started having contacts abroad and could even get published occasionally in the West—it was hard, and they had to prove that they were not divulging state secrets, but it was possible. Some mathematicians came from the West, some even came for an extended stay because they realized there were a lot of talented people. This was unofficial mathematics."

One of the people who came for an extended stay was Dusa McDuff, then a British algebraist (and now a professor emeritus at the State University of New York at Stony Brook). She studied with the older Gelfand for six months and credits this experience with opening her eyes to both the way mathematics ought to be practiced—in part through continuous conversation with other mathematicians—and to what mathematics really is. "It was a wonderful education, in which reading Pushkin's *Mozart and Salieri* played as important a role as learning about Lie groups or reading Cartan and Eilenberg. Gelfand amazed me by talking of mathematics as though it were poetry. He once said about a long paper bristling with formulas that it contained the vague beginnings of an idea which he could only hint at and which he had never managed to bring out more clearly. I had always thought of mathematics as being much more straightforward: a formula is a formula, and an algebra is an algebra, but Gelfand found hedgehogs lurking in the rows of his spectral sequences!"

On paper, the jobs that members of the mathematical counterculture held were generally undemanding and unrewarding, in keeping with the best-known formula of Soviet labor: "We pretend to work, and they pretend to pay us." The mathematicians received modest salaries that grew little over a lifetime but that were enough to cover basic needs and allow them to spend their time on real research. "There was no such thing as thinking that you had to focus your work in some one narrow area because you have to write faster because you had to get tenure," said Gelfand. "Mathematics was almost a hobby. So you could spend your time doing things that would not be useful to anyone for the nearest decade." Mathematicians called it "math for math's sake," intentionally drawing a parallel between themselves and artists who toiled for art's sake. There was no material reward in this—no tenure, no money, no apartments, no foreign travel; all they stood to gain by doing brilliant work was the respect of their peers. Conversely, if they competed unfairly, they stood to lose the respect of their colleagues while gaining nothing. In other words, the alternative mathematics establishment in the Soviet Union was very much unlike anything else anywhere in the real world: it was a pure meritocracy where intellectual achievement was its own reward.

In after-hours lectures and seminars, the mathematical conversation in the Soviet Union was reborn, and the appeal of mathematics to a mind in search of challenge, logic, and consistency once again became evident. "In the post-Stalin Soviet Union it was one of the most natural ways for a freethinking intellectual to seek self-realization," said Grigory Shabat, a well-known Moscow mathematician. "If I had been free to choose any profession, I would have become a literary critic. But I wanted to work, not spend my life fighting the censors." Mathematics held out the promise that one could not only do intellectual work without State interference (if also without its support) but also find something not available anywhere else in late-Soviet society: a knowable singular truth. "Mathematicians are people possessed of a special intellectual honesty," Shabat continued. "If two mathematicians are making contradictory claims, then one of them is right and the other one is wrong. And they will definitely figure it out, and the one who was wrong will definitely admit that he was mistaken." The search for that truth could take long years—but in the late Soviet Union, time stood still, which meant that the inhabitants of the alternative mathematics universe had all the time they needed.

2

How to Make a Mathematician

I N THE MID-1960S Professor Garold Natanson offered a graduate-study spot to a student of his, a woman named Lubov. One did not make this sort of offer lightly: female graduate students were notoriously unreliable, prone to pregnancy and other distracting pursuits. In addition, this particular student was Jewish, which meant that securing a spot for her would have required Professor Natanson to scheme, strategize, and call in favors: in the eyes of the system, Jews were even more unreliable than women, and convoluted discriminatory anti-Semitic practices carried the force of unwritten law. Natanson, a Jew himself, taught at the Herzen Pedagogical Institute, which ranked second to Leningrad State University and so was allowed to accept Jews as students and teachers—within reason, or what passed for it in the postwar Soviet Union. The student was older—she was nearing thirty, which placed her well beyond the usual Russian marrying-and-having-children threshold, so Natanson could be justified in assuming that she had resolved to devote her life entirely to mathematics.

Natanson was not entirely off the mark: the woman was indeed wholly devoted to mathematics. But she turned down his generous offer. She explained that she had recently married and planned to start a family, and with that she accepted a job teaching mathematics at a trade school and disappeared from the Leningrad mathematical scene for more than ten years.

Ten or twelve years was nothing in Soviet time. There was a bit of new housing construction in Leningrad, and some families were able to leave the crowded and crumbling city center for the new concrete towers on its outskirts. Clothing and food continued to be in short supply and of regrettable quality, but industrial production picked up a bit, so some of the new suburban dwellers could actually buy basic semiautomatic washing machines and television sets for their apartments. The televisions claimed to be black-and-white but showed mostly shades of gray, thereby providing an accurate visual reflection of reality. Other than that, little changed. Natanson continued to teach at the Herzen, which itself grew only more crowded and crumbling. His former student Lubov found him in his office. She was older and a bit heavier. She reported that she had indeed had a baby all those years ago, and now this baby was a schoolboy who exhibited a talent for mathematics. He had taken part in a district math competition in one of those newly constructed concrete suburbs where they now lived, and he had done well. In the timeless scheme of Russian mathematics, he was ready to take up where his mother had left off.

It all must have made perfect sense to Natanson. He himself hailed from a mathematical dynasty: his father, Isidor Natanson, was the author of the definitive Russian calculus textbook and had also taught at the Herzen, until his death, in 1963. Lubov's boy was entering fifth grade—the age at which he could begin appropriately rigorous mathematical study in a system that had been constructed over the years for the making of mathematicians. Natanson had his eye on a young mathematics coach to whom he could direct the boy and his mother.

So began the education of Grigory Perelman.

Competitive mathematics is more like a sport than most people imagine. It has its coaches, its clubs, its practice sessions, and, of course, its competitions. Natural ability is necessary but entirely insufficient for success: the talented child needs to have the right coach, the right team, the right kind of family support, and, most important, the will to win. At the beginning, it is nearly impossible to tell the difference between future stars and those who will be good but never great.

Grisha Perelman arrived at the math club of the Leningrad Palace of Pioneers in the fall of 1976, an ugly duckling among ugly ducklings. He was pudgy and awkward. He played the violin; his mother, who had studied not only mathematics but also the violin when she was a child, had engaged a private teacher when Grisha was very young. When he tried to explain a solution to a math problem, words seemed to get tangled at the tip of his tongue, where too many of them collected too quickly, froze momentarily, and then tumbled out, all jumbled up. He was precocious—a year younger than the other children at his grade level—but one of the other kids at the club was even younger: Alexander Golovanov had packed two grades into every year of school and would be finishing high school at thirteen. Three other boys beat Grisha in competitions for the first few years in the club. At least one more—Boris Sudakov, a round, animated, curious boy whose parents happened to know Grisha's family—showed more natural ability than Grisha. Sudakov and Golovanov both carried the marks of brilliance: they seemed always to be rushing forward and bubbling over. They naturally fought for dominance in any room, and mathematics was simply one of many things that got them excited, one of the ways to apply their excellent minds, and one of the tools to showcase their uniqueness. Next to them, Grisha was the interested but quiet partner, almost a mirror; he was a joy for them to bounce their ideas off, but he himself rarely seemed to exhibit the same need. He formed relationships with the math problems; these relationships were deep but also, it seemed, deeply private: most of his conversations appeared to be mathematical and to take place inside his head. A casual visitor to the club would not have singled him out from the other boys. Indeed, even among the people who met him many years later, not one that I encountered described him as brilliant; no one thought he sparkled or shone. People described him, rather, as very, very smart and very, very precise in his thinking.

Just what manner of thinking this was remained something of a mystery. Crudely speaking, mathematicians fall into two categories: the algebraists, who find it easiest to reduce all problems to sets of numbers and variables, and the geometers, who understand the world through shapes. Where one group sees this:

$$a^2 + b^2 = c^2$$

the other sees this:

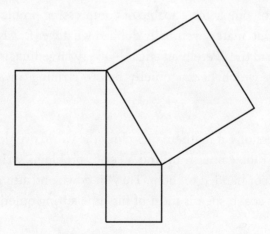

Golovanov, who studied and occasionally competed alongside Perelman for more than ten years, tagged him as an unambiguous geometer: Perelman had a geometry problem solved in the time it took Golovanov to grasp the question. This was because Golovanov was an algebraist. Sudakov, who spent about six years studying and occasionally competing with Perelman, claimed Perelman reduced every problem to a formula. This, it appears, was because Sudakov was a geometer: his favorite proof of the classic theorem above was an entirely graphical one, requiring no formulas and no language to demonstrate. In other words, each of them was convinced Perelman's mind was profoundly different from his own. Neither had any hard evidence. Perelman did his thinking almost entirely inside his head, neither writing nor sketching on scrap paper. He did a lot of other things—he hummed, moaned, threw a Ping-Pong ball against the desk, rocked back and forth, knocked out a rhythm on the desk with his pen, rubbed his thighs until his pant legs shone, and then rubbed his hands together—a sign that the solution would now be written down, fully formed. For the rest of his career, even after he chose to work with shapes, he never dazzled colleagues with his geometric imagination, but he almost never failed to impress them with the single-minded precision with which he plowed through problems. His brain seemed to be a universal math compactor, capable of compressing problems to their essence. Club mates eventually dubbed whatever it was he had inside his head the "Perelman stick"—a very large imaginary instrument with which he sat quietly before striking an always-fatal blow.

Practice sessions at mathematics clubs the world over look roughly the same. Kids come in to find a set of problems written on the blackboard or handed to them. They sit down and attempt to solve them. The coach spends most of his time sitting quietly; teaching assistants check in with the students occasionally, sometimes prodding them with questions, sometimes trying to nudge them in different directions.

To a Soviet child, the afterschool math club was a miracle. For one thing, it was not school. Every morning Soviet children all over the country left their identical concrete apartment blocks a little after eight and walked to their identical concrete school buildings to sit in their identical classrooms with the walls painted yellow and with identical portraits of bearded dead men on the walls—Dostoyevsky and Tolstoy in the literature classrooms, Mendeleev in the chemistry classroom, and Lenin everywhere. Their teachers marked attendance in identical class journals and reached for identical textbooks that they used to impart a perfectly uniform education to their charges, of whom they demanded uniformity in return. My own first-grade teacher, in a neighborhood on the outskirts of Moscow that looked just like Perelman's neighborhood on the outskirts of Leningrad, actually made me pretend my reading skills were as poor as the other children's, enforcing her own vision of conforming to grade level. The first time I spent an afternoon solving math problems—around the same time Perelman was doing it, four hundred miles to the north—I sat for what seemed like an eternity, holding a pencil over a drawing of some shape. I do not remember the problem, but I remember that the solution required transposing the shape. I sat, unable to touch my pencil to paper, until a teaching assistant came by and asked me a very basic question, something like "What might you do?"

"I might transpose it, like this," I answered.

"So do it," he said.

Apparently, this was a place where I was expected to think for myself. A wave of embarrassment covered me; I hunched over my piece of paper, sketched out the solution in a couple of minutes, and felt a wave of relief so total that I think I became a math junkie on the spot. I did not drop the habit until I was in college (and was actually busted for illegally replacing a required humanities course with advanced calculus). The joy of feeling my brain rev up, rush toward a solution, reach it, and be affirmed for it felt like love, truth, hope, and justice all handed to me at once.

The particular math club where Perelman landed was a barebones operation. The coach with whom old Natanson decided to place his protégé by proxy was a tall, freckle-faced, light-haired loudmouthed man named Sergei Rukshin. He had one very important distinguishing characteristic: he was nineteen years old. He had no experience leading a club; he had no teaching assistants. What he did have was outsize ambition and a fear of failure to match. By day, he was an undergraduate at Leningrad State University; two afternoons a week, he put on a suit and tie and impersonated an adult math-club coach at the Palace of Pioneers.

In the quiet, dignified mathematics counterculture of Leningrad, Rukshin was an outsider. He had grown up in a town near Leningrad, a troubled kid like any troubled kid anywhere in the world. By the age of fifteen, he had racked up several minor juvenile offenses, and the only thing he liked to do was box. He was on a clear path to trade school, then the military, followed by a short life of drink and violence—like most Russian men of his generation. The prospect terrified his parents so much that they begged and pleaded and possibly bribed until a miracle happened and their son got a spot at a mathematical high school in the city. There, another miracle happened: Rukshin fell in love with mathematics and turned all his creative, aggressive, and competitive energies toward it. He tried to compete in mathematics olympiads, but he was outmatched by peers who had been training for years. Still, he believed he knew how to win; he just could not do it himself. He formed a team of schoolchildren who were just a year younger than he and trained them, and they did better than he had. He started training upperclassmen all over Leningrad. Then he became a teaching assistant at the Palace of Pioneers, and barely a year later, when the coach with whom he had been apprenticing left for a job assignment in a different city, he became a coach himself.

Like any young teacher, he was a little scared of his students. His first group included Perelman, Golovanov, Sudakov, and several other boys, all of whom were just a few years younger than he but poised to become successful competitive mathematicians. The only way he could prove he deserved to be their teacher was by becoming the best mathematics coach the world had ever seen.

Which is exactly what he did. In the decades since, his students have taken more than seventy International Mathematical Olympiad medals, including more than forty gold ones; in the past two decades, about half of the competitors Russia has put forward have come from Rukshin's now-sprawling club, where they were trained by either him or one of his students, who use his unparalleled training method.

What exactly made his method unparalleled was not entirely clear. "I still don't understand what he did," admitted Sudakov, now an overweight and balding computer scientist living in Jerusalem, "even though I know a thing or two about the psychology of these things. We would come in and sit down and we would get our problem sets. We would solve them. Rukshin would be sitting there at his desk. When somebody solved one of the problems, [that student] would go over to Rukshin's desk and explain his solution and they would discuss it. There! That's all there was to it. Eh?" Sudakov looked at me across the table of a Jerusalem café, triumphant.

"That's what everyone does," I responded, as expected.

"Exactly! That's what I'm talking about!" Sudakov fidgeted happily as he talked.

I observed practice sessions at the club Rukshin still ran a quarter century later. It was now called the Mathematics Education Center; it included a couple of hundred children eleven and older. Just like Perelman's group, they spent two afternoons a week at the club. At the end of each session—which lasted two hours at the lower grade levels and could stretch into the night for upperclassmen—the students got a list of problems to take home. Rukshin claimed that one of his unique strategies was adapting the list of problems to the class during the course of the session: the instructor had to go in with several possible lists and choose among them depending on what he learned about the students' progress over the next couple of hours. Three days later, the students brought in their solutions, which, one by one, they explained to teaching assistants for the first hour of the session. In the second hour, the instructor went over all correct solutions at the blackboard. As they grew older, the students gradually transitioned to explaining their own solutions at the blackboard themselves, in front of the entire group.

I watched the younger kids struggle with the following problem: "There are six people in the classroom. Prove that among them there must be either three people who do not know one another or three people who all know one another." Teaching assistants encouraged them to start with the following diagram:

Two of the half dozen children working on the problem managed to doodle their way to the fact that the diagram can develop in one of three possible ways:

,   , or

The challenge, to which two children successfully rose, was to explain that this was a graphical—and therefore irrefutable—way to show that there must be at least three people who either all know or all do not know one another. Listening to the children struggle to put this into words, battling an entire short lifetime of inarticulateness, was painful.

Mathematicians know this as the Party Problem; in its general form, it asks how many people must be invited to a party so that at least m will know one another or at least n will not know one another. The Party Problem refers back to Ramsey theory, a system of theorems devised by the British mathematician Frank Ramsey. Most Ramsey-type problems look at the number of elements required to ensure a particular condition will hold. How many children must a woman have to ensure that she has at least two of the same gender? Three. How many people must be present at a party to ensure that at least three of them all know or all do not know one another? Six. How many pigeons must there be to ensure that at least one pigeonhole houses two or more pigeons? One more than there are pigeonholes.

The Mathematics Education Center children—some of them, at least—would learn about Ramsey theory in time. For the moment, they had to learn to express a way of looking at the world that would ultimately make them interested in Ramsey theory and in other methods of observing order in a chaotic environment. To most individuals, children in a classroom or guests at a party are just people. To others, they are the elements of an order and their relationships the parts of a pattern. These others are mathematicians. Most mathematics teachers seem to believe some children are born with the inclination to seek patterns. These children must be identified and taught to nurture this skill, the peculiar ability to see triangles and hexagons where others see only a party.

"That's my biggest know-how," Rukshin told me. "I discovered this thirty years ago: every child must be heard out on every problem he thinks he has solved." Other math clubs had children present their solutions to the class—which meant that the first correct solution ended the discussion. Rukshin's policy was to engage every child in a separate conversation about that child's particular successes, difficulties, and mistakes. This was perhaps the most labor-intensive instruction method ever invented; it meant that none of the children and none of the instructors could coast at any time. "In the end we teach children to talk," said Rukshin, "and we teach the instructors to understand the students' incoherent speech and direct them. Rather, I should say, to understand their incoherent speech and their incoherent ideas."

As I listened to Rukshin and watched him teach, I struggled to place the feeling his club sessions communicated. What made them different—more emotionally engaged but also more tense than any other math, chess, or sports practice session I had ever seen? It took months for my mind to locate the analogy: these sessions felt most like group therapy. The trick really was to get *every* child to present his or her solution to the *entire* group. Mathematics was the most important thing in these children's lives; Rukshin would not have it any other way. They spent most of their free time thinking about the problems they had been given, investing all the emotion and energy they had—not unlike a conscientious twelve-stepper who stayed connected with the program between meetings by writing out the steps. Then, at the meetings, the children laid bare their minds before the people that mattered most to them by telling the stories of their solutions in front of the entire group.

Did this explain Rukshin's unprecedented coaching success? Like many insecure people, Rukshin tended to oscillate between self-effacement and self-aggrandizement, now telling me that he was no more than a mediocre mathematician himself, now telling me for the fifth time in three days that he had been offered a job with the Ministry of Education in Moscow (he turned it down). Similarly, he told me several times that his teaching methods could be reproduced, and had been, to rather spectacular results: his students made money by training math competitors all over the former Soviet bloc. But other times he told me he was a magician, and these were the times he seemed most sincere. "There are several stages of teaching," he said. "There are the student, apprenticeship stages, like in the medieval guild. Then there are the craftsman, the master—these are the stages of mastery. Then there is the art stage. But there is a stage beyond the art stage. This is the witchcraft stage. A sort of magic. It's a question of charisma and all sorts of other things."

It may also have been that Rukshin was more driven than any coach before or since. He did some research work in mathematics, but mathematics seemed to be almost a sideline of his life's work: creating world-class mathematics competitors. That kind of single-minded passion can look and feel very much like magic.

Magicians need willing, impressionable subjects to work their craft. Rukshin, who was so wrong for the job of mathematics teacher for so many external reasons, cast about not just for the most likely child genius but also for the best way to prove he could make a mathematician out of a child. He focused his attention not on the loudest boy, or the quickest-thinking boy, or the most fiercely competitive boy, but on the most obviously absorbent boy.

Rukshin claims not to have appreciated the power of Perelman's mind right away. He had helped judge some of the district competitions in Leningrad in 1976, reading through many sheets of graph paper with ten- to twelve-year-olds' solutions to math problems. He was on the lookout for kids who might amount to something mathematically; the unwritten rules of math clubs allowed them to recruit but not poach, so an unknown like Rukshin had to look for kids early and aggressively. Perelman's set of solutions went on the list; the child's answers were correct, and he arrived at them in ways that were sometimes unexpected. Rukshin saw nothing in those solution sets that would have placed the child head and shoulders above the rest, but he saw solid promise. So when Professor Natanson called and said the child's name, Rukshin recognized it. And when he finally saw the boy, he recognized in him the promise of something bigger than a good mathematician: the fulfillment of Rukshin's ambition to be the best math coach who had ever lived. Adjusting his judgment of Perelman so quickly must have required something of a leap of faith for Rukshin, but it also promised the reward of making a singular discovery—that a child who seemed as capable as dozens of others would surpass them all.

"When everyone is studying math and there is one person who can learn much better than others, then he inevitably receives more attention: the teacher comes to the home, he tells him things." Alexander Golovanov spoke from experience: not only had he spent years studying mathematics alongside Perelman, but he had spent most of his adult life coaching children and teenagers for mathematics competitions. He was Rukshin's anointed heir. And now he explained to me just what it meant to have a favorite student, or to be one. As in any human relationship, love can engender commitment, which can engender investment, which in turn deepens the commitment and perhaps even the love. "So that is one definition of a favorite pupil, and Grisha was that: a favorite pupil because he had been given more. Another aspect, a very important one, is that anyone who teaches [competitive mathematics] has a very clear idea of how much he has done—what he can and cannot take credit for. Say, there are kids who have been to the [all-Russian] olympiad three or four times—and I can say that if I hadn't taught them, they would have made it two rather than three times. So I wasn't the main reason. And then there are people about whom I can say that yes, I was the main reason. That doesn't mean they were pathetic and I put a brain in their heads. What it means is love. And what I think is that Rukshin feels that way about Grisha. And I also think he is right." There was a third aspect too, said Golovanov, one that had to do with pure closeness. Rukshin was a hypochondriac whom the erudite Golovanov compared to Voltaire. Over the months when I was in contact with Rukshin, he spent no less than a third of his time in hospitals. "So there was one time when Rukshin was going blind," Golovanov remembered. "It was during summer camp, and he and Grisha were sharing a room." Perelman was then a university student working as a teaching assistant to Rukshin. "And one morning Rukshin said he'd felt great joy upon awakening because he saw Grisha lying in the other bed. And there was no telling what pleased him more: that he could see in general or that he could see Grisha in particular."

At some point, the care and teaching of Perelman became the thing that gave meaning to Rukshin's life; Rukshin, for his part, strove to insert meanings into Perelman's head. He got Grisha to quit the violin—and the derision with which he spoke of it almost thirty years later impressed me. "It's the shtetl dream." He scowled. "Learn the fiddle and play at weddings and funerals."

Like every competitive sports coach, Rukshin disliked it when his boys spent their time doing anything else. He claimed that he'd kicked Alexander Khalifman, the future chess world champion, out of his club for failing to choose math over chess. And like many coaches, he claimed his sport was the fairest, truest, and most beautiful sport of all. Also like many coaches, he saw it as his mission to shape not only his students' competitive skills but their entire personalities. When they grew older, Rukshin hounded any boy who was sighted doing something as undignified and distracting as kissing a girl—and he caught them with such regularity that the boys began to suspect he had spies shadowing them. Perelman never disappointed his teacher in this way; as Rukshin repeatedly told me, "He was never interested in girls."

Two evenings a week Rukshin, accompanied by his math boys and a couple of girls, walked from the Palace of Pioneers to the Vitebsk Railroad Station, where he and Grisha boarded the same train. Rukshin, who had married very early, lived with his wife and mother-in-law outside the city in the historic town of Pushkin; Grisha lived with his mother, father, and baby sister on the far southern outskirts of the city, in a dreary concrete apartment block in the Kupchino neighborhood. Rukshin and his pupil rode the subway together to Kupchino, which was the last stop, where Grisha would get off and walk home and Rukshin would switch to a commuter train with hard wooden seats and ride another twenty minutes to Pushkin. Along the way, Rukshin discovered things about Grisha. He learned, for example, that Grisha would not untie the earpieces of his fur hat while riding the subway. "It's not just that he would not take the hat off," recalled Rukshin. "He would not even untie the ears, saying that his mother would kill him because she told him never to untie the hat or he'd catch cold." The subway car was generally heated to normal room temperature, but the compactor in Grisha's brain left no room for the nuance of circumstance. Rules were rules.

When Rukshin criticized Grisha for not reading enough—Rukshin saw it as his duty to introduce the children not only to mathematics but to literature and music—Grisha asked why he should be reading books. To Rukshin's argument that reading was "interesting," Grisha responded that anything that needed to be read would be included on the school's required-reading list. Rukshin had better luck with music. When Grisha came to the club, his taste was limited to clear and precise classical instrumental music, generally with a violin solo. While solving a problem, he often engaged in what his club mates alternately called "howling" and "acoustic terror," but when he was asked, Grisha explained that he was humming Camille Saint-Saëns' *Introduction and Rondo Capriccioso*, a composition for violin and orchestra remarkable for both its clarity and the prominence of a virtuoso violin soloist. However, at one of the summer camps, Rukshin succeeded in interesting his pupil in vocal music, through which Grisha proceeded to move systematically: he accepted the lower-range voices first, then gradually moved through to the sopranos, but he drew the line at Rukshin's attempt to introduce him to the singing of castrati, which he deemed "unnatural" and therefore "uninteresting."

Far from being disappointed in his student, Rukshin seemed to rejoice in Perelman's lopsided nature. In this love pairing of teacher and student, each continuously got to be the other's better half. Perelman could be the competitor Rukshin never was, while Rukshin could interact with the outside world on Perelman's behalf and shield his student from it at the same time. They—or, rather, Rukshin—created situations in which they complemented each other in more practical ways too. At summer camp, where fifteen-year-old Perelman lived away from his mother for the first time in his life, Rukshin took care of his day-to-day needs. Personal hygiene was tricky, but Rukshin occasionally managed to get Perelman to change his socks and underwear and pack the soiled items away in a plastic bag, since he refused to wash them—as, often, he refused to wash himself. He also refused to go swimming with the rest of the boys, both because he disliked the water and, more important, because he did not see the point of such a nonintellectual and noncompetitive pastime (he did play Ping-Pong, and was very good at it, and very competitive). So Rukshin used him as an extension of himself: Rukshin got in the water with the children and swam in the deep end, using his own body to mark the line the children were not allowed to cross; Perelman sat on the shore and kept a constant head count, making sure no one went missing. As time went on, Rukshin found other ways to use Perelman's brain as a more efficient extension of his own. As a university student, for example, Perelman would sift through thousands of math problems to select problem sets for training. "It's work that I could have done and spent, say, t amount of time on it," Rukshin told me. "Grisha did it in t over five. Now these problem sets are club classics and no one remembers at this point what was done by me and what was done by Perelman."

It was a match made in mathematical heaven.

3

A Beautiful School

AS PERELMAN MATURED, he learned to take the words that bunched up in his mouth and combine them to form sentences—beautiful, precise, correct sentences—but his narrative remained tangled and personal. The reigning star of the club for the first three or four years, a boy named Alexander Levin, would, said Rukshin, "explain his solution with the idea of helping people understand how to solve these sorts of problems. Perelman told the story of his own personal communication with this particular problem. Imagine the difference between a doctor filling out a medical history and the patient's mother talking about sitting by her child's bedside, wiping his brow and listening to his labored breathing. So did Grisha tell the story of his own journey through the problem. And if the solution could have been different or even shorter, Grisha would still only tell the story of how he had solved it. After he talked, I often had to go up to the blackboard and point out what was important and what could have been cut or simplified—not because he did not see it himself but because he was not the one who would do it."

It is remarkable that Perelman learned to explain as well as he did. Imagine how unmanageable everyday language is for someone given to understanding things literally. Language is not just a frustratingly imprecise way of trying to navigate the world but also a willfully and outrageously inaccurate one. The psychologist and linguist Steven Pinker observed that "language describes space in a way that is unlike anything known to geometry, and it can sometimes leave listeners up in the air, at sea, or in the dark as to where things are." In speech, noted Pinker, objects have primary and secondary dimensions, ranked by importance. A road is imagined as one-dimensional, as is a river or a ribbon—all of them consist of length only, like a segment in geometry. "A *layer* or a *slab* has two primary dimensions, defining a surface," continued Pinker, "and a bounded secondary dimension, its thickness. A *tube* or a *beam* has a single primary dimension, its length, and two secondary dimensions, plumping out its cross-section."

Even greater trouble with language begins when we split up objects into their contents and their boundaries. We describe a stripe as the boundary of a plate, and we portray both objects as two-dimensional, and to a literal mind, all of this is wrong: the stripe is not the actual boundary of the plate (the plate's edge is), and the plate has three dimensions. At the same time, words like *end* and *edge* are used to denote shapes that have anywhere from zero to three dimensions. What is worse, the sloppy way of describing objects coexists in language with an extreme wealth of names for actual shapes. There may be as many as ten thousand shape-names in English; and in all human languages, the number of shape nouns far exceeds the ability to define them. To a literal mind, this is an outrage: how can we use words for things that we not only cannot define properly but insist on defining incorrectly?

Take the Möbius strip, the length of ribbon famously twisted before being reconnected to itself. Language is stumped by the Möbius strip. Does something move *along* the strip, as with a one-dimensional object; *around* the strip, as with a two-dimensional object; or, as in the title of a 2006 animated film, *"thru"* the strip—suggesting a three-dimensional object? For a literal mind, salvation lies in the geometry that lives in the imagination—where every shape is clearly defined. In fact, geometry as it is studied in secondary school, with its basic theorems and its precise measurements, represents a marked improvement over everyday speech, but it is topology that is the quintessence of geometrical clarity. Not coincidentally, the Möbius strip, which evades casual understanding, is among the earliest known objects of topological inquiry. *Clearly defined,* in the case of topology, does not mean that every shape can easily be visualized. Quite the opposite: it means that every shape has only those qualities that its definition grants it. A shape has a certain number of dimensions; it may be bounded; it may or may not be smooth; and it may or may not be simply connected, which is to say, it may or may not have holes. An object in topology may be a sphere—that is, all of its constituting points are an equal distance from the center—but a topologist notes that the essential qualities of a sphere do not change if the sphere is dented; the sphere can easily be reshaped, so its temporary change in imaginary appearance may be disregarded. Not so if a hole appears in the sphere: the sphere is no longer a sphere but a torus, an object with a different relationship to that which surrounds it and one that cannot easily be reconstituted as a sphere. The topological universe has no use for silly riddles like those of which Pinker is fond: "What can you put in a bucket to make it lighter?" "A hole!" This is not funny to the literal mind. You cannot *put* a hole anywhere. Moreover, a hole—or an additional hole—means the shape is no longer what it was; the bucket would not be made lighter because it would no longer be a bucket.

Normally, even mathematicians do not begin to study topology until they have entered college; the discipline has traditionally been considered too abstract to present to children. But a mind like Grisha Perelman's, an undeniably mathematical mind that was at the same time neither visual nor numeric—a mind that thought in systems, that traded in definitions—was a mind born for topology. Starting roughly when Perelman was in eighth grade (when he was around thirteen), visiting lecturers at the math club sometimes taught a class in topology. Topology called to Perelman from beyond the more traditional geometry he had already navigated, the same way the lights of Broadway call to the child who moves the audience to tears in a middle-school production of *Annie*. Grisha Perelman would grow up to live in the universe of topology. He would master all its rules and definitions. He would be a lawyer in the court of shapes, eventually able to argue precisely and articulately why a three-dimensional, simply connected closed object would always be a sphere. Rukshin would light Perelman's way there; he came to Perelman as an emissary from his mathematical future, and his implicit promise was that he would make Perelman's life in Leningrad as safe and as ordered as his life in the imagination.

For this, there was Leningrad's Specialized Mathematics School Number 239.

The summer Grisha Perelman turned fourteen, he took the train from Kupchino to Pushkin every morning and spent the day being tutored by Rukshin in the English language. The plan was to cover four years' worth of English in one summer so that in September Perelman could enter Leningrad's Specialized Mathematics and Physics School Number 239. This was the shortest path to engaging with mathematics fully, with minimal outside disturbances.

The strange story of the specialized math schools goes back to Andrei Kolmogorov. Having been so essential to the war effort dur-

ing World War II, Kolmogorov alone among the top Soviet mathematicians avoided being drafted into the postwar military effort.
His students always wondered why—and the only likely explanation seems to be Kolmogorov's homosexuality. His lifelong partner,
with whom he shared a home starting in 1929, was the topologist
Pavel Alexandrov. Five years after the couple started living together, the Soviet Union criminalized male homosexuality, but
Kolmogorov and Alexandrov, who exercised minimal discre-
tion—they called each other "friends" but made no secret of the
life-shaping nature of their relationship—apparently had no trouble with the law. The academic world accepted them as a pair, if
not a couple: they generally requested academic appointments together, booked their accommodations together at Academy of Sciences resorts, and made donations to military relief efforts together. In his last interview, recorded for a documentary film about
his life, the eighty-year-old Kolmogorov asked the filmmaker to use
Johann Sebastian Bach's Double Violin Concerto—a baroque composition based on the interplay of two violins—when showing the
home he had made with Alexandrov.

Whatever the reason, his not being a part of the military effort left Kolmogorov free to devote his considerable energies to
creating the world for mathematicians that he had envisioned
since he was a young man. Kolmogorov and Alexandrov both hailed
from Luzitania, Luzin's magic land of mathematics, and they
sought to re-create it at their dacha outside of Moscow, where they
would invite their students for days of walking, cross-country skiing, listening to music, and discussing their mathematical projects.

"The way our graduate group interacted with Kolmogorov was
almost classically Greek," said one of the countless memoirs published by his students; virtually everyone who had contact with
Kolmogorov seemed to have been moved to write about him.

"Through the woods or along the shore of the Klyazma River the muscular mathematician would be moving briskly, on foot or on skis, surrounded by young people. The shy students would be rushing behind him. He talked almost without stopping—although, unlike perhaps the ancient Greeks, he talked less of mathematics and more of other things." Kolmogorov believed that a mathematician who aspired to greatness had to be well versed in music, the visual arts, and poetry, and—no less important—he had to be sound of body. Another of Kolmogorov's students wrote in his memoir that he was singled out by the teacher for wrestling well.

The mix of influences that shaped Kolmogorov's idea of a good mathematical education would have been an odd combination anywhere, but in the Soviet Union in the middle of the twentieth century, it was extraordinary almost beyond belief. Kolmogorov hailed from a wealthy Russian family that founded a school of its own in Yaroslavl, a town about a hundred and fifty miles north of Moscow. There they published a children's newspaper to which Kolmogorov, along with other family members, contributed. Here is a math problem he authored at the age of five: How many different patterns can you create with thread while sewing on a four-hole button? Don't try solving this one until you have some time; I know two professional mathematicians, both students of Kolmogorov's, who each came up with a different response.

In 1922, Kolmogorov—nineteen, a student at Moscow University, and already an emerging mathematician in his own right—started teaching mathematics at an experimental school in Moscow. Incredibly, the school was modeled after the Dalton School, the famous New York City institution immortalized by, among others, Woody Allen in the film *Manhattan*. The Dalton Plan, which lay at the foundation of both the Dalton School and the Potylikha Exemplary Experimental School where Kolmogorov taught, called for an individual instruction plan for every student. Each child would map out his own path for the month and proceed to work independently. "So every student spent most of his school time at his desk, or going to the small school libraries to get a book, or writing something," Kolmogorov recalled in his final interview. "The instructor would be sitting in the corner, reading, and the students would approach him in turn to show what they had done." This might have been the first sighting of the figure of the instructor reading quietly behind his desk; decades later, the math-club coach would take up this position.

It was always a boys' club. Kolmogorov himself referred to his students affectionately as "my boys," reporting to Alexandrov, in a letter from a trip taken with his students in 1965, "In just three hours at an elevation of 2400 meters all my boys got so badly sunburned (parading around in their swimming trunks or without them) that they could barely sleep for two nights following." The casual happy homoeroticism of Kolmogorov's view of his students seemed to come from an entirely different time and place. Before the Iron Curtain sealed off the Soviet Union from the rest of the world, Kolmogorov and Alexandrov had done some traveling. Alexandrov, who was seven years older, had traveled extensively before the two met, but the pair spent the 1930–1931 academic year abroad, some of it together. They started out in Berlin, where all culture, and gay culture in particular, was flourishing. They imported all they could: books, music, ideas. "Interesting that this idea of a truly beloved friend seems to be purely Aryan: The Greeks and the Germans seem always to have had it," Alexandrov wrote to Kolmogorov in 1931, a few years before the reference to Aryans would have had a different connotation. "The theory of a lone friend is a difficult one to fulfill in the contemporary world," Kolmogorov lamented in response. "The wife will always have pretensions to that role, but it would be too sad to consent to this. In Aristotle's times, these two sides of the issue never came into contact:

The wife was one thing, and the friend quite another." Kolmogorov brought back from Germany collections of verse by Goethe, who would always be his favorite poet. In all their letters to each other, Kolmogorov and Alexandrov included detailed reports of concerts attended and music heard, and when vinyl records became available, they started collecting them. Alexandrov hosted weekly classical-music evenings at the university; he would play records and lecture on the music and the composers; after Alexandrov's death, Kolmogorov—already nearing eighty and crippled by Parkinson's disease—took over as host.

Classical music and male bonding, mathematics and sports, poetry and ideas added up to Kolmogorov's vision of the ideal man and the ideal school. At the age of forty, Kolmogorov wrote up a plan "of how to become a great man should I have sufficient desire and diligence." The plan called for completing his research work by the age of sixty and devoting the rest of his life to teaching secondary school. He followed the plan: in the 1950s he enjoyed a second creative flowering, publishing as prolifically as he had in his thirties—very unusual for a mathematician—and then he stopped and turned his full attention to teaching children.

In 1935, Kolmogorov and Alexandrov organized the first Moscow mathematical competition for children, helping to lay the foundation for what would eventually become the International Mathematical Olympiad. A quarter century later, Kolmogorov teamed up with Isaak Kikoin, an unofficial kingpin of Soviet nuclear physics who had run similar competitions in physics. Since the only value the State seemed to assign their sciences was military, the two conspired to make Soviet leaders believe that elite, specialized math-and-physics high schools could supply the country with the brains it needed to win the arms race. The project was championed by a young Central Committee member named Leonid Brezhnev—then five years away from becoming the Soviet leader. The Soviet of Ministers issued a decree creating the school in August 1963, and it opened in December of that year. Half a dozen similar schools soon opened in Moscow, Leningrad, and Novosibirsk. Kolmogorov's students ran most of them, and he personally oversaw the shaping of the curriculum.

That August, Kolmogorov organized a summer mathematics school in a town outside of Moscow. Forty-six high-school seniors who had done well in the All-Russian Mathematical Olympiad attended. Kolmogorov and his graduate students taught workshops, lectured the boys in mathematics, and took them hiking in the surrounding woods. In the end, nineteen boys were chosen to attend the new mathematics-and-physics boarding school in Moscow.

They landed in a strange new world. Kolmogorov, who had been dreaming up the school for forty years, had developed not only a method of individual instruction based on the Dalton Plan but an entirely new curriculum. Lectures in mathematics—a number of them presented by Kolmogorov himself—aimed to introduce ideas from the world of real research while taking into account the students' varied backgrounds, for Kolmogorov emphasized choosing students who exhibited the presence of what he called "a spark from God" rather than a thorough knowledge of high-school mathematics. In addition, the boarding school was probably the only one in the Soviet Union that offered a high-school course in the history of antiquity. The curriculum also included more hours of physical education instruction than regular Soviet schools did. Finally, Kolmogorov himself lectured the students in music, the visual arts, and ancient Russian architecture. He also took the boys on boating, hiking, and skiing trips. "We liked the trips and the poems," one of the students wrote in a memoir. "And few of us understood the music: that required at least some background. Fortunately, [Kolmogorov] kept quiet on the importance of the social sciences." In other words, Kolmogorov not only rushed to impress his students with his version of Renaissance values but also shielded them from the Marxist indoctrination to which they had been subjected in secondary school and which they would be forced to endure once again at the university.

Kolmogorov's goal was not just to create a handful of elite institutions for talented mathematicians but also to teach real mathematics to as many children as could learn it. He developed a curriculum that took schoolchildren out of the business of adding and subtracting and getting confused, and into the business of thinking about mathematics in clear and interesting ways. He oversaw a curriculum-reform effort that introduced the use of simple algebraic equations with variables and of computers as early as possible. In addition, Kolmogorov sought to revamp the secondary-school understanding of geometry, opening the way to comprehending non-Euclidean ideas. In the mid-1970s I attended one of the schools chosen to try out the new textbooks (this was not a specialized math school but an "experimental" school open to a much broader range of children). It must have been in third grade that I shocked my father, a computer scientist, with my understanding of the concept of congruence. It made perfect sense to me: two triangles, for example, were considered congruent if they were exactly the same in every way. The word *equal*, which older textbooks had used, was clearly less precise.

Bizarrely, it was the subject of introducing congruence to schoolchildren that forced Kolmogorov's first serious confrontation with the Soviet system—something he had avoided for decades, through luck and care. In December 1978 the seventy-five-year-old Kolmogorov was dressed down at a general meeting of the mathematics section of the Soviet Academy of Sciences. One after another, Kolmogorov's colleagues rose to criticize him for the term *congruence,* for a difficult new definition of *vectors* used in the textbooks he oversaw, and for the introduction of set theory as the cornerstone of the math curriculum. These, the speakers claimed, were examples of a larger failing: the reform—and its authors—were evidently anti-Soviet. "These things can provoke nothing but disgust," opined Lev Pontryagin, one of the leading Soviet mathematicians. "This is a disaster. This is a political phenomenon." Newspaper denunciations followed: authors of the curriculum reform were exposed as having "fallen under a foreign influence of bourgeois ideology" of set theory. They had a point. Education reform just then under way in the United States and, indeed, throughout the Western hemisphere mirrored Kolmogorov's efforts. The New Math movement brought actual mathematicians into active involvement in secondary schools; set theory was introduced in early grades and formed a basis for teaching all of mathematics. The Harvard psychologist Jerome Bruner observed at the time that it had "the effect of freshening [the student's] eye to the possibility of discovery." At the third-grade level, mathematics finally became accessible enough to be dragged through the pages of the Soviet newspapers—and Kolmogorov was exposed as what he most certainly was: an agent of Western cultural influence in the Soviet Union.

The aging Kolmogorov never recovered from the scandal. His health deteriorated catastrophically; he developed Parkinson's and lost his sight and, eventually, speech. Some of his students believed the illnesses were set off by the public disgrace and by a head trauma that resulted from what may have been an attack: walking through a university building, Kolmogorov was struck by a heavy door that he thought might have been swung deliberately by someone he then saw rushing away. As long as Kolmogorov was able, and perhaps a little longer, he continued to lecture at the boarding school. He died at eighty-four, speechless, blind, and motionless, but surrounded by his students, who for the preceding couple of years had taken turns providing round-the-clock care at his house.

The ideological conflict that made Kolmogorov's proposed reforms impossible was real. His plan called for dividing high-school students into groups depending on their interest and abilities in mathematics, allowing the most talented and motivated to get farther faster. The entire Soviet system of secondary education was based on the concept of uniformity: everyone was to be taught the same thing at the same time, using the same textbooks. But the Soviet Union still craved international prestige—in fact, that need became more and more pronounced as the technological rivalries of the second half of the century heated up. Just as the world of adult mathematics had to cultivate a certain number of geniuses to showcase at international conferences, so a small world of talented children had to be allowed to exist in a sort of greenhouse setting, if only for the country to field competitors at international math and physics olympiads. And just as it was in the world of adult mathematicians, in the world of student mathematicians, the space for comfortable existence was too small to accommodate all whose talents warranted inclusion; to get in, a Jewish child had to be twice as good as a non-Jewish child and four times as good as the child of an apparatchik.

Possibly because there were so few schools, they were all fairly similar, shaped in the Kolmogorov mold of increased emphasis not only on math and physics but also on music, poetry, and hiking— in no small part because Kolmogorov's students influenced most of these schools directly. They were all subject to heightened scrutiny: Kolmogorov's boarding school was visited frequently by ideology inspectors, who became especially vigilant following the denunciation of his curriculum reform. School supporters were often called upon to defend it before the authorities, who claimed that "elite education is not allowable in our society"; Moscow's School 2 was apparently the object of many denunciations—written by concerned parents and outraged Soviet-issue teachers—that eventually had its cofounders fired; and School 239 lost some of its most popular teachers to KGB pressure while its principal was frequently reprimanded for admitting too many Jewish children (according to historical lore, two out of four Leningrad math schools were shut down in the 1970s for having too many Jewish students). And the feature that united all the math schools was the sheer concentration of student brainpower, teacher talent, and intellectual urgency: the children had only two or three years to spend at the school, which was always on the verge of being discovered and shut down by the authorities.

The selection of teachers assembled at these schools matched that of the best Soviet universities. In fact, for the most part, they were the same people. Kolmogorov brought his students to teach at his school, and those students, in turn, drafted their own students. Some teachers came because their children attended the school; some were strong-armed for the same reason. School 2 graduates recalled that when members of Moscow's intellectual elite flocked to the school, the director set the price of admission: those parents who were college instructors had to offer electives at the school. As a result, the school's bulletin boards overflowed with announcements of elective courses offered by some of the top names in various fields—more than thirty courses at one time. Clearly, if there had been more schools like these, the concentration of outstanding instructors at them would not have been so high. By trying to keep the number of schools low, the Soviet authorities had in fact created hotbeds of freethinking.

"What made the school different was that the students' talents and intellectual achievements made them more popular and significant," remembered a Boston computer scientist who graduated from a Leningrad math school in 1972. In the world outside the school, peers respected one another for athletic achievements while the establishment rewarded proletarian provenance or Komsomol (the Communist youth organization) eagerness. Inside the school, the ideological demands of the outside world were flouted:

some schools allowed students not to wear uniforms (though they were still required to put on a jacket and tie and keep their hair cropped); some teachers read forbidden works of literature aloud in class (though they avoided naming the author or the work). "What can be more beneficial at sixteen or seventeen than not having to lie?" author Mikhail Berg wrote in a memoir of his years at a Leningrad math school. "You had an interview, you were admitted, and you became a member of a community in which the percentage of anything Soviet was many times lower than outside of it. You had to pay for the opportunity to breathe in this microclimate: Every day, spine bent, you had to deliver gifts to the altar of the idols—the two sisters Mathematics and Physics and their mother, Logic. Mathematics and rigid logic simply left no space for ideology: It could mix with logic no more than water can mix with kerosene." Granted, these were still Soviet schools, complete with Komsomol organizations, denunciations, and "primary military training" classes, but compared with the rest of the country, the boundaries placed on speech and thought had been broadened so much as to seem almost nonexistent. The schools managed to create a bubble that resisted the pressure of the Soviet state. It protected both the students who paid mathematical dues in order to gain a measure of intellectual freedom, like Berg, and those who paid intellectual dues—studying antiquity, for example—in order to gain the freedom to study mathematics, like Perelman.

The schools taught children not only how to think but also that thinking was rewarded—and rewarded fairly. In other words, they reared people who were very ill-suited for life in the Soviet Union —or, one could argue, for life in the real world anywhere. The schools produced freethinking snobs. A graduate of Kolmogorov's boarding school recalled studying with Yuli Kim, one of the Soviet Union's best-known dissident singer-songwriters, who taught literature at the school (until his firing was forced by the KGB in

1968): "Because of him, we felt like gods: We lived our lives and had our accomplishments, and we had our own Orpheus to sing our praises."

The Soviet system, fine-tuned to all shades of difference, rejected these kids and put every possible obstacle in their way once they graduated. The year I would have graduated from math school in Moscow (had my family not emigrated to the United States), none of the graduates would be admitted to Moscow University's Mechanics and Mathematics department—and the teachers made a point of warning us about this. Leningrad's School 239, most of whose graduates were convinced—some say rightly—that they could easily sleep through their freshman year at any university and still ace the exams, saw so few of its students allowed into Leningrad University that it had to forge a relationship with a second-tier college that would take its kids, overeducated and overconfident as they were. They may have believed they were gods, but when they emerged from high school, they found themselves outside the well-organized and well-guarded mainstream of Soviet mathematics. Not all of them—perhaps not even a majority—would become mathematicians, but those who did were destined for the very strange world of the alternative mathematics subculture.

Kolmogorov himself was no stranger to the official mathematics establishment. He was eccentric for an insider, protected in large part by his larger-than-life standing in international mathematics, earned early and maintained with apparent ease for decades. Still, he spent months and years of his life negotiating teaching hours and salary increases and apartments for assorted members of the Academy. He was, by all accounts, extremely careful in what he said and did—and he made no secret of his fear of the secret police (and indeed hinted at a cooperative relationship with them)—

but in 1957 he was fired as dean of Moscow University's Mechanics and Mathematics department following dissident rumblings among his students.

Daily exigencies of life within the establishment notwithstanding, Kolmogorov held to the ideals he passed on to his students. He parted with his ideas with famous ease: after doing a few weeks' work on the foundation of a problem, he would give it to one of his students, who might spend months or a lifetime working on it. He claimed little interest in the authorship of solutions as long as the great problems of mathematics were indeed solved. In other words, even when he was recognized and celebrated by the establishment as the greatest Russian mathematician of his age, he espoused every ideal of the Soviet mathematical counterculture. His numerous students were that culture's leaders, and Kolmogorov himself its guiding light.

His vision was gospel to his students and their students and their students' many students. Kolmogorov had envisioned a world without dishonesty or backstabbing, without women and other undue distractions, with only math and beautiful music and just rewards for all; several generations of Russian mathematical boys believed in it. Wrote Mikhail Berg: "Many of us would have wanted to take the school with us after graduation, like a turtle's armor, because we could feel comfortable only within the confines of its precise and logically understandable rules."

A life within the confines of logical and understandable rules was what Rukshin offered Perelman in exchange for the heroic feat of learning English in a summer. For his part, Rukshin would get to realize his own project. Math clubs are to math schools what after-school band practice is to the High School of Performing Arts: one is a respite from the rest of school life but might produce brilliant professionals; the other offers total immersion and a vision of the future. They are two different, if related, worlds. Now, if Rukshin had his way, the two worlds would meld. For the first time in the history of Leningrad math clubs, virtually all suitably aged members of the club would go to high school together. Ordinarily, they had to apply—and be accepted—to receive their last two years of secondary education at either of the two Leningrad math schools, and they were spread among different classes so as not to skew math instruction too much in any particular class. It was generally expected that the club mathematicians, like professional athletes among talented amateurs, would spend some of their time at the math schools being bored and waiting for others to catch up. Rukshin had a radically different idea: create a class that consisted mostly of math-club members, add some kids from a physics club, fill it out with the help of other exceptionally gifted and motivated children, and—most important, he thought—keep everyone else out. No one who was not obsessed with mathematics, or at least with the sciences, should be allowed into the class "lest the rot catches on and spreads" was how Rukshin put it to me a quarter of a century later. When he was in a more generous mood, he explained that he'd wanted his charges to be surrounded by other kids with similar interests, since "there wasn't an Eton School for them." Plus, there were organizational issues: "They could all come to the club together, it wouldn't be like one was getting out of school at one and another at four. I could make arrangements with their teachers regarding what they would be studying in mathematics and physics at school and what I would cover at the club. And concerted action is always better where it comes to gifted kids. Many of them were black sheep, and this way they could have a teacher who would shield them the same way I did." Once the coach, and his math club, became the center of these children's lives, he was not going to budge.

The only snag in the plan to create a bigger and better cocoon for Perelman and his ilk was the foreign-language issue. Soviet schools generally offered either English, German, or French starting in fifth grade, and transferring from school to school was contingent on a language match. School 239 offered English and, if enough students required it, German; Perelman had been studying French for four years. Rukshin claimed his own English was bad and to illustrate this offered, "My knowledge of English leaves very much to be desired," pronounced with the queen of England's accent. This was vintage Rukshin: either his English was excellent and he was just fishing for compliments, or his English was as poor as he claimed but he had memorized that one phrase. Whatever the case, it was Rukshin and his bizarre English-learning project that took over Perelman's life the summer he turned fourteen.

Perelman's mother allowed her son to submit to this taxing regimen without protest, as she had done with all of Rukshin's demands—even though this meant keeping the family, which now included a toddler named Lena, in the city for the summer instead of going to the dacha like all the other Leningrad families that belonged to what might have been called the Soviet middle class. Rukshin's own mother-in-law, he said, was furious: "Not only had her daughter married a poor mathematician but now he was dragging his Young Pioneers home." Since they were not welcome in the apartment, Rukshin and Perelman spent their days walking the numerous scenic pathways in the town's huge historical parks, first following textbooks and then teaching themselves conversational English by conversing in it. Once again, Rukshin proved to be an outstanding coach. At the end of the summer, Perelman was fit to study at School 239. Years later, he wrote in excellent English, not only correct but idiomatic—and while that was partly a result of the couple of years he'd spent in the United States as a postdoc, it rested on the foundation he received from Rukshin during those walks in the parks.

Now all of Rukshin's "black sheep" could go to school together. Twenty-seven years later I spoke with a Russian Israeli psychologist who was married to Boris Sudakov, one of Perelman's club mates and, later, classmates. Boris had suggested I talk to her because she had seen something off balance in Perelman when he visited Israel in the mid-1990s. I wondered if she'd noticed something then that had been a portent of his later oddness. "Come on," she said, apparently irritated. "I'd seen Boris's other classmates, and they are all like that. Weird. It's like they are made of different stuff." The literal translation of the Russian expression she used is "made of different dough," which is particularly appropriate for the pudgy, pale boys who grew up into pale, doughy men.

Collecting these kids in a single classroom struck many of the teachers at School 239 as a crazy idea. "They'd speak up at the meetings, they'd say that it would just be too hard," recalled current principal Tamara Yefimova, who had been the vice principal back in those days. "I mean, there was this boy, for example, he was so talented, and his teacher would come to me almost in tears, and I'd ask the boy what happened, and he'd say, 'Tamara Borisovna, I left home on time, but then I just got to thinking.' And they were just like that, so difficult to understand: they'd be sitting in the back of the class, she'd be saying her thing, and who knows what they were doing back there, maybe thinking again." The principal, a short, stout woman with a crewcut, looked and sounded more like everyone's favorite gym teacher than the head of an elite school that imagined itself to be a Russian Dalton or Eton. In her youth she had run a secondary school on a military base someplace she still tried not to name. She had been sent down to School 239 by the Party to keep watch over the school's exceedingly liberal atmosphere and was apparently accepted there as a reasonable evil: She clearly possessed a genuine admiration for the intellectuals she found herself commanding. She finessed the endless Party inspections to which the school was subjected, and she succeeded in accomplishing things none of her more cultivated predecessors had pulled off—like repairing the leaky roof and restoring the school's magnificent auditorium. But her support for a math-club class apparently struck some of the teachers as a misguided expression of her fondness for intellectualism; she claimed that several teachers actually left in protest. Still, in September 1980, the first club class entered School 239.

Some people are born to be schoolteachers. I have met a few, and they are an unusual breed: supremely sensitive, thin-skinned like the children or adolescents to whose needs they are so finely attuned, yet secure in the understanding that their best students will develop into adults who are smarter and altogether better educated than they are. Valery Ryzhik was born, in 1937, to teach mathematics. He was twenty-five when he started teaching at School 239, where he helped create the mathematics curriculum, and he had been teaching mathematics for twenty-eight years when, over his vocal objections, he was handed the club class of Rukshin's creation. His job was to teach them math and also to serve as the class teacher, something like a homeroom teacher at an American high school.

Ryzhik had the idea that teaching School 239's average students —who had been top students at other schools, but not the exceptionally gifted sort—was best accomplished by teaching the very best students in such a manner that the rest got pulled along. Students recalled that in ordinary years he picked five top students at the start of the school year and focused all his attention on them while the others learned by watching. "There would be inspectors criticizing me for not working with the average kids," Ryzhik recalled in 2008, when he had been a practicing schoolteacher for nearly half a century. "And I would say, The issue is not working with the average kids; the issue is working with the gifted kids —and that's really hard, because, for one thing, they are all different. Another is, if you teach them in a way that's not interesting for them, they can tolerate it for a day or two and then they get bored and start wondering what they are doing at this school. And that can't happen. You have to make their eyes light up, and I can't explain to you how you do that."

Having a group of ten exceptionally gifted students thrown at him along with twenty-five other adolescents presented Ryzhik with an apparently insurmountable challenge. The club kids were all different. Alexander Golovanov, the wunderkind, sat up front "and wouldn't let anyone get a word in," Ryzhik remembered. "Such a little boy." Grisha Perelman sat in the back. He never spoke up unless a solution or an explanation required a correction. "And then he would raise his hand." Ryzhik mimicked the movement, lifting his hand off his desk only slightly. "You could hardly see it. His was the final word." Still, Perelman never did what other exceptional students did: he never let himself grow distracted and, say, fiddle with a different problem during class. He sat and listened to discussions that were of no pragmatic use to him; rules were rules, and if one came to class, one listened.

Ryzhik had met kids like Perelman before. "We got someone like that every year," he told me. "What's curious is that they were all marked by an extraordinary modesty, a schoolchild's reserve. There is never any conceit, and I think that's one of the necessary conditions for something extraordinary in the future. I have seen kids like Golovanov too, but I've never known them to do something outstanding in mathematics—they stop at the professorial level. The ones who make it beyond are a different kind of person." With his trained teacher's eye, Ryzhik spotted an awe-inspiring student.

Ryzhik attempted to form a personal relationship with Perelman—partly at the request of Grisha's mother. She came in early in the school year to ask Ryzhik to try to ensure two things: that Grisha ate something while at school and that he tied his shoelaces. A Western mother might have bought her son slip-on shoes to wear, but Soviet stores offered no such option for the absent-minded schoolchild. Ryzhik never succeeded at either task: Perelman walked around with his laces flopping about, and he would not eat. "Maybe he could not get distracted," suggested Ryzhik. "Maybe his entire nervous system was so tuned to the learning process that he could not stray from it. Or maybe it was a blood pressure issue—he might have felt that if he ate, his thinking would not be as precise." Another possibility was that school food was too varied for Perelman; the cafeteria had a different menu for each day of the week. In the math-club group, every boy had his own pronounced food preference. So in the afternoons, when they made the walk from the school to the Palace of Pioneers, they made quick pit stops for the refueling of each club member. Naturally, Perelman's system was the simplest and the fastest: he would go to the bakery on Liteyniy Prospect, less than halfway between the school and the club, and buy a Leningrad loaf, a large piece of wheat bread with raisins on the inside and crushed peanuts on top. Perelman did not eat peanuts, so Golovanov would scrape them off and eat them. Sometimes the ebullient Golovanov would try to help himself to the raisins also, whereupon Perelman would slap his hand hard.

Mondays Perelman would stay at school after class and play chess in Ryzhik's chess club. They played fast chess, a game that is believed to require more intuition than calculation, but Perelman did very well, even winning twice against Ryzhik himself—probably because what chess players call intuition is in fact the ability to grasp complex systems in a single take, which was exactly Perelman's strength. But in all the weekly afternoons together, the tactful and awestruck Ryzhik never tried to venture into more personal territory with Perelman, never broached a subject that reached beyond school, chess, and mathematics. Nor did he choose him as one of the students he regularly addressed in the classroom; rather, he kept him as his "command reserve," as he put it, for particularly difficult problems.

To the general troops, Ryzhik tried to be an all-encompassing leader. On Sundays—the only day of leisure for Soviet schoolchildren at the time—he would take his class out of the city for hikes and orientation races. Summers, he would take groups of children on weeks-long trips in difficult terrain in the Caucasian mountains or the Siberian forests. Perelman never went. Ryzhik believed this was because he was a homebody, though he apparently did submit to the requisite math-school culture hikes organized by Rukshin for his club kids; his out-of-school self belonged to Rukshin. Both Rukshin and Ryzhik practiced the Kolmogorovian approach: while dragging the children on long and grueling walks, they tried to shape them into the human beings they wanted to see—with Rukshin focusing more on literature, music, and all-around erudition, and Ryzhik on chivalry, honesty, responsibility, and other universal values. Ryzhik had been doing this for more than twenty years, but with the club class of 1982, he felt he failed.

"The class split into two groups," recalled Ryzhik. "One was a group of learners, and the other had different values. And I never did manage to connect them." The math-club boys formed the heart of the learners' contingent. During one of the Sunday hikes in their second and final year at School 239, one of the math-club students got a nonclub classmate involved in a chemistry experiment. He handed him a substance but failed to warn him it was highly explosive if heated. When the boy approached the campfire, the stuff blew up in his hand, severing it at the wrist. "The boy survived—thank god for that," said Ryzhik. "And then I recall I had a talk with the kids. I remember it well. I said, 'Imagine we are on a trip. And say, we have set up camp somewhere for the night. And say there is a lake there, and I do not like the look of the lake and I judge the approach to be unsafe, so I tell you not to go there without my oversight under any circumstances. And now imagine that one of you has decided to go for a swim during the night anyway. Who will wake me up to tell me what's happening?' No one! And I said, 'Do you see what's happening? A child might die! You may not understand this, but I do. And still, based on this silly child-corporate-value system of yours, you are going to keep quiet. That means that story with the explosion taught you nothing. You still don't get it.'"

Rukshin's club-class experiment upset the delicate balance that existed at School 239 and at other math schools, as well as in the adult Soviet world, where the mathematics counterculture was allowed to exist quietly so long as it did not take its ideas to the streets. In Ryzhik's class, the usual rules of nonconfrontation between the geniuses and the rest no longer applied: the genius contingent was too large, too male, and too adolescent for that. It was war, and Ryzhik was right in thinking he had failed to convince the students it was wrong. A quarter of a century later, the student who had slipped his classmate the bomb referred to the incident occasionally in his blog, recalling it with a clear lack of remorse. There is no single explanation for what happened. Perhaps Rukshin's boys perceived their classmates as representatives of the system that had humiliated them at other schools; perhaps they had already grown to perceive anyone outside their small circle as the enemy. In any case, as always happens in war, the two sides saw each other as less than human. Ryzhik discontinued the hikes following this conversation. The following year, he cut his class time down to one day a week so he could focus on finishing a geometry textbook that he had been test-driving with his students. The year after, when he tried to return to full-time teaching at School

239, Ryzhik was turned away, apparently because the principal had come under increased pressure to cut the number of Jewish teachers.

By the time I met Ryzhik, he was seventy, teaching again—at a new elite physics-and-math school—playing chess in the afternoons, and given to looking back kindly on his life, which had been lived largely in the shadow of the Soviet compromise. He had been denied entry to Leningrad University because he was Jewish. "They did not even manage to find a problem I couldn't solve: I sat for three hours after the exam was over, I solved them all, and still they failed me. I was just a boy. I went home and cried." He graduated from Herzen, the second-tier college, and was later cut from its faculty because there were too many Jews. He never managed to defend his doctoral dissertation, which was based on the geometry textbook he coauthored and was criticized for violating every rule of Soviet teaching methodology. In the hours I spent with him, the only regret he expressed concerned his failure to bring together the very strange experiment of a class in which Grisha Perelman had been his student.

The drama of this teacher surely passed Perelman by, as did most of what surrounded him at School 239. He never attended the literary Tuesdays, which contained poetry and generally reached beyond the mandatory school reading list. He probably did not follow the story when the School 239 principal Viktor Radionov was fired amid charges of pedophilia. He was surely oblivious to the countless ideological inspections, which required the teachers and the more attuned students to be on their best Soviet-school behavior, which came naturally to Perelman anyway. He almost certainly never posted a question on the supposedly anonymous question-and-answer board run by the history teacher Pyotr Ostrovsky, who impressed students with his willingness to entertain even risky political questions and who was later exposed as a KGB informant who tracked down those tricky questioners and denounced them and their parents.

While careers teetered and entire lives were ruined, and while some children thrived in the liberal math-school atmosphere and others labored anxiously to keep up, Perelman studied mathematics. A classmate recalled seeing Perelman and Golovanov stop about halfway between the underground station and the school to write formulas frantically on the sidewalk in front of what happened to be the U.S. consulate. In all likelihood, Perelman did not notice the consulate, or the popular movie theater that was housed in the church building to which the school was adjacent, or the school's grand semicircular marble staircase and the white marble boards with the names of national olympiad prize takers, on which Perelman's own name would eventually appear in gold. To his classmates, he appeared a sort of math angel: he sounded his voice only if a solution required his intervention; looked forward to Sundays, sighing happily and saying that he could "finally solve some problems in peace"; and if asked patiently explained any math issue to any of his classmates though apparently utterly unable to conceive of anyone not comprehending such a simple thing. His classmates repaid him with kindness: they recalled his civility and his mathematics, and none ever mentioned to me that he walked around with his shoelaces undone—not a particularly uncommon occurrence at the school anyway—or that by the time he was in his last year of school, his fingernails were so long they curled.

Other School 239 graduates thanked the school for opening their minds; for teaching them that intelligence, erudition, and civility were rewarded; and for giving them a head start in their higher education. If it ever occurred to Perelman to thank anyone for something so intangible, he should have thanked School 239 for leaving him alone. One suspects that Rukshin's entire clubclass design worked for only two people: Rukshin and Perelman. It was destructive for other kids, and it was tragic for Ryzhik, but it allowed the symbiosis of Perelman and Rukshin to continue unchallenged and Perelman's view of the world to remain undisturbed—but also unexpanded. Like all protective bubbles, the environment of the math school served not only to shield but also to isolate its inhabitants. It ensured that Perelman's relentlessly logical approach to life was never challenged, allowing him to concentrate on mathematics to the exclusion of—literally—almost everything else. It let him avoid confronting the fact that he lived among humans, each with his or her own ideas and thoughts, to say nothing of emotions and desires. Many gifted children realize with a start as they mature that the world of ideas and the world of people compete for their attention and their energy. Many make a difficult choice in favor of one or the other. Not only did School 239 spare Perelman the choice; it kept him from noticing that the tension between people and mathematics even existed.

4

A Perfect Score

SOMETIME DURING THE FINAL year of school, Ryzhik would have difficult, delicate talks with some of his students' parents. He would ask them to think about their child's chances for university admission. Ryzhik, who himself had cried when he was turned away for being Jewish, endeavored to warn parents who he felt had not given the issue enough thought. There were subtleties in the admission process, of which he was acutely aware. Leningrad University's Mathematics and Mechanics department had a quota of two Jews admitted per year, which was enforced strictly but not zealously: unlike its Moscow counterpart, the Mathmech, as it was known, did not delve into the family histories of applicants in an effort to root out hidden Jewish relatives. At the same time, Mathmech turned away non-Jewish applicants burdened with Jewish-sounding surnames.

"I had a student named Filipovich," recalled Ryzhik. "It's not a Jewish name, but it might sound Jewish, so just in case, they did not accept her. Olga Filipovich got run over by the system." Parents had to be warned and then directed to schools with more liberal admissions policies, if need be. Ryzhik had two rules: he did not talk to the students directly about this, preferring that they learn the facts from their parents, and he talked to the parents only when he judged it absolutely necessary. He said he hated meddling, and he surely must have hated acting as the unwilling agent of an absurd and cruel system of discrimination. But when he had to, he engaged the parents in what he called "a standard conversation: that you have to be mindful of what you are doing to spot the child, and you have to have a plan for what you are going to do if it doesn't work out. And how are you going to explain this to the child? I had been through it all myself."

The children in question were not that young—Soviet schools generally graduated seventeen-year-olds—but the stakes were indeed too high for many adolescents to understand and to handle. The Soviet system of college admissions was based on a set of four or five exams, generally a combination of oral and written formats, for which the applicant had to be physically present at the college. Therefore, a high-school graduate could apply to two colleges, at most, in one summer. If he was male and he failed to gain admission, he would be drafted into the military. When Perelman was graduating, the Soviet Union was in the third year of its war in Afghanistan; roughly eighty thousand conscripts were serving there at any given time, and conscription was what every parent feared most.

For a Jewish adolescent who was exceptionally gifted in mathematics, there were only three available college strategies: choose a college other than Leningrad University, with less discriminatory admissions policies; bank on being one of only two Jews accepted in a given year; or become a member of the Soviet team at the International Mathematical Olympiad—members of the team, which numbered four to eight people each year, were admitted to the colleges of their choice without having to take the entrance exams. Boris Sudakov, a boy Rukshin had believed was no less naturally talented than Perelman but who had performed erratically in competitions, chose the first strategy. Alexander Levin, the reigning number two at the math club, chose the second strategy. By the time Perelman was in his last year of secondary school, he had one silver and one gold medal from the All-Soviet Math Olympiad to his name, and it seemed a certainty to him and to everyone around him that he would travel to the international competition and return triumphant, assured of a place at the Mathmech. It was a relief for Ryzhik, who was particularly loath to meddle in the life of a student he respected so highly, especially since trying to prove the anti-Semitic nature of admissions policies to either Grisha or his mother might very well have been an impossible task. Lubov Perelman, it seemed, had an extraordinary gift for denying the obvious, and she had passed this gift along to her child.

The basic questions of parenthood—what to tell your child, when, and how much—are tinged with fear in a totalitarian society, where dissidence is punished. What if the child says the wrong thing at the wrong time, exposing the family to danger? My own parents, active consumers and sometime producers of samizdat, chose to give me unfettered access to information, occasionally admonishing me to keep my mouth shut. On several occasions I spilled more than I should have, and this fortunately went unnoticed—but while I am ever grateful to my parents for treating me like an adult, the risk they took was probably unwise. Most other parents kept to a policy of never exposing their children to anything that could not be safely repeated at school. Lubov Perelman seems to have pursued an even more radical strategy: she taught her son that the world worked exactly as it should.

"He never believed there was anti-Semitism in the Soviet Union," Rukshin told me on a couple of occasions, repeating this observation with the kind of joyous wonder with which he had informed me that Grisha was never interested in girls, as though the denial of anti-Semitism too were evidence of Perelman's unparalleled purity.

When I asked Golovanov, who also happened to be Jewish, whether this was true, he was uncharacteristically stumped. No, he had never discussed the topic with Perelman, but how could anyone in his right mind believe there was no anti-Semitism in the Soviet Union? "He was not stupid," Golovanov assured me.

How can one not believe in something as evident as Soviet anti-Semitism? This raises two other questions: What is belief? And what is evidence? Soviet anti-Semitism was not quantifiable. Nor was it absolute: for example, the number of Jews accepted to Mathmech appeared to vary from year to year. Never was discrimination practiced so openly as to be articulated: when a Jew was turned down for a job or for university admission, a reason other than the person's Jewishness was generally cited. When Perelman was thirteen, all the boys who took prizes at the Leningrad citywide math olympiad at his grade level were Rukshin students and Jewish; the surnames of prize takers and honorable-mention recipients included Alterman, Levin, Perelman, and Tsemekhman. This was worse than just four Jewish boys; this was four *obviously* Jewish boys. As Rukshin remembered it, the university professor who chaired the city jury that year, himself a Jew, looked at the list and sighed. "We ought to have fewer of these sorts of winners."

Starting in the eighth grade, those who took first and second places in the city olympiad would advance to another round of competition to select the city representative for the national competition. Predictably, the winners that year came from Rukshin's club: Alexander Vasilyev and Nikolai Shubin took first place; Perelman, along with two more boys and a girl from Rukshin's club, took second place. The rules dictated that the six teenagers advance to the selection round, but all six were Jewish. Still, the names of the two top-prize takers were not as obviously Jewish as Perelman was: Vasilyev was a Slavic surname, and Shubin, while Jewish, did not sound quite as offensive as Perelman did to those who were offended by the Jewishness of others. So, apparently in an attempt to avoid reprimands, the organizers suggested scrapping the selection round and simply sending either Vasilyev or Shubin to the nationals. Rukshin waged a fight to have a selection tour and to have Perelman take part in it. Rukshin's ambitions as coach melded with his indignation on behalf of his favorite student, and he succeeded —almost: the organizers agreed to hold a selection round, but only between top scorers Shubin and Vasilyev. "I pleaded, I swore, I screamed, and I threatened," recalled Rukshin. In the end Perelman was not allowed to compete, but the organizers said he could attend the selection round to practice solving problems if he so wished.

Except that Perelman did not want to attend the selection round. "He kept saying, 'But I really didn't solve as many problems as Shubin and Vasilyev,'" said Rukshin. "I mean, if ever the Soviet regime could rear a Jewish boy who believed that man was always rewarded in accordance with his accomplishments, here he was." Finally, Rukshin strong-armed Perelman into attending, and Perelman ended up solving seven out of seven problems—the next-best result was three out of seven—and going to the nationals. Rukshin chalked up another strategic victory in the battle against anti-Semitism even as Perelman demonstrated that the existence of anti-Semitism could not be proved. So why should he believe in it? That would be like believing an object was a sphere just because it looked round only to discover that it had a tiny hidden hole.

My own father had cried following his first round of university admissions exams, just as Ryzhik had. My mother had walked out of her exam when she saw the word *Jewess* in black ink next to her name on a sheet of paper on the examiner's desk. Both of my parents had been warned about anti-Semitic admissions policies and had decided to trust their abilities to break through. As long as I can remember, they talked of the prospect of my own college entrance exams with dread—what I now understand to be the chilling dread of trying to explain to your child that some of the world is so unfair as to make all hope futile. I know that this dread was a large part of the reason for my parents' decision to emigrate.

Lubov Perelman acted as though reality corresponded to the rules—and for the moment, reality accommodated her, albeit with a lot of help from Grisha Perelman's small phalanx of supporters.

Sometime in the fall of 1981 Alexander Abramov, the young coach of the Soviet IMO team, traveled to Leningrad to ask Rukshin who among his students would likely be joining the team. Rukshin's reputation as a brilliant coach had already been established, so it was certain he would be offering someone. He named two people: Perelman and Levin. Both were graduating from high school that year, making it the last year they were eligible to compete.

Members of the math club believed Perelman to be the undisputed and unreachable number one and Levin his distant but stable and also hardly reachable number two. City competition results bore this out, and, in the self-absorbed way of adolescents in general and members of Rukshin's club in particular, the students believed Perelman and Levin were the top two mathematics competitors in the whole huge country. In Rukshin's opinion, Levin's potential indeed equaled or even exceeded Perelman's. But in this competition, Levin had too many disadvantages. "His parents did not understand what it was to be a mathematician," explained Golovanov. "Grisha's mother understood it very well, while Levin's parents thought studying mathematics might be useful if one wanted to become an engineer." In other words, they failed to see the value of the single-minded devotion Rukshin inspired in his students. Levin's parents apparently insisted he pay as much attention to his schoolwork as to the math club. "He was too good a student at the school, consequently he did not always attend the club, and that was his silly accident, the gate that had been left open, so Alik was done in by his conscientiousness," said Golovanov, referring to the fortress gate that, legend has it, brought down Constantinople in the fifteenth century. "At the All-Soviet competition he solved all the problems with the exception of the one that had actually been solved at the club." It was a freak accident: only very, very rarely and contrary to all rules and logic was a problem used in the All-Soviet competition one that had been floated elsewhere. But since every math problem had a human author and an idea behind it, no one could guarantee uniqueness. And in this particular case, in April 1982, a problem that was offered to competitors in the All-Soviet Mathematical Olympiad was one whose solution had been written down neatly by every member of Rukshin's math club—at least, everyone who had shown up. Alexander Levin had not come to the club that particular day. He did not solve the problem in the competition, and he did not make the Soviet IMO team. And though surely this was not intended by Levin, Rukshin, or even Perelman, it was fitting; that year only Rukshin's favorite, brightest, singular student went to the IMO. Rukshin had worked for this for six years, shaping Grisha into the ideal competitor.

The Leningrad city competition looks very much like any session of a Petersburg math club: competitors sit in classrooms solving problems, and when one considers a problem solved, he raises a hand to call attention to himself; a pair of judges then escorts the competitor out of the classroom to listen to his solution and make a judgment on the spot on its quality; the competitor then returns to the classroom to either rework his solution or go on to another problem. As Rukshin recalled, at the selection round Perelman was explaining his solution to one of the problems. He had talked his way through one of the possible outcomes when the two judges who were his audience turned to leave, saying that his solution was correct. "Wait!" he shouted, grabbing one of them by the tail of his suit jacket. "There are three more possible outcomes."

Two key Perelman traits were displayed here. One was that, as Rukshin put it, "he was deliriously honest even at moments when what was important was that he could have saved time." *Delirious* is a wonderful word, conjuring up the drive of someone organically incapable not only of telling an untruth but of telling an incomplete truth. But what if Perelman was wrong? What if the part he had explained was correct and represented the complete solution while the rest was superfluous? In math olympiad slang, a solution—or part of a solution—that looked right to its author but was wrong was called a *lipa*, a general Russian slang term for *fake* that literally means "linden" but is probably best translated as *lemon*. Everyone who spoke to me about Perelman specifically mentioned this trait of his: he had no lemons. None. Ever. Such was the precision of his mind: not only was he incapable of telling a lie—he was even incapable of making an honest mistake.

Mathematicians make mistakes. This is part of what they do. Unlike humanities scholars, they cannot allow for the possibility of more than one truth. But unlike natural scientists, they cannot check their hypotheses against empirical truths. So they have only the resources of their own minds—and those of their colleagues —with which to subject their imaginary constructions to sets of imaginary rules, to see if they still hold up. This makes the peer-review process in mathematics even more important than it is in any other academic discipline, and it also explains the importance of having the two-year waiting period imposed by the Clay Institute before it awards one of its Millennium Prizes. Even so, mathematicians make mistakes that sometimes take years to catch. Occasionally they catch them themselves—as Poincaré did when he realized that he had not proved his own conjecture. Sometimes the mistakes are discovered by referees, as when Andrew Wiles released his original attempt to prove Fermat's Last Theorem. The solution turned out to contain a serious flaw, which Wiles fixed himself but not until two years later. Young mathematicians, less adept at subjecting their own solutions to scrutiny, make mistakes more frequently than older ones. It is not surprising that Grisha Perelman could not conceive of himself making mistakes; what is surprising is that he actually did not make them.

So it must have been all the more upsetting to him that when he finally made it to his first national competition that year, he took second place. Both of his coaches—Rukshin and Abramov—claimed that it was after the All-Soviet Olympiad in Saratov that Perelman got mean. He set about ensuring he would never lose to anyone again. "He had now tasted the blood of a freshly killed competitor" was how Rukshin put it. "And his ambitions far exceeded his accomplishments." Here Rukshin's ornate language seemed to get the better of his understanding of Perelman. It seems that what bothered Perelman in Saratov in 1980 was what would always bother him about the world: things had not gone logically. If Perelman was so good that he had never had a lemon, if his mind was so powerful that it had never encountered a problem it could not crack, then why had he not taken first place? The only possible answer lay in unforgivable human failure: Grisha Perelman had not practiced enough. From then on he practiced ceaselessly. While for other kids life was divided into school and leisure, for Perelman it was split into time devoted to solving problems without disruption and the rest of the time.

The 1982 IMO team was to have four members; that meant six would be chosen, so there would be two alternates. In January 1982

Abramov collected a dozen potential members of the team at a school in the science town of Chernogolovka, about fifty miles north of Moscow. The national chemistry and physics coaches were gathering their potential competitors at the same time and in the same place, so about forty of the country's brightest high-school seniors were there, bunking four to a room in the school's dormitory, located in the same building as the school. They were fifteen- to seventeen-year-olds—seventeen being the standard age for a graduating student. But several of these competitors were, like Perelman, precocious; at fifteen and a half, Grisha was not the youngest. So they were not quite grownups, and though several of them lived away from home at specialized schools, they later remembered the odd sensation of being on their own in Chernogolovka. One student recalled waking up in the morning and seeing that water in a jar on the windowsill had frozen because a pane of glass was broken; though the room was nonetheless adequately heated, he felt shocked and depressed by the sight. Another recalled arriving by bus in Chernogolovka in the dark evening—which in January is any time after four in the afternoon—and then, unable to find the school, wandering the empty and poorly lit streets of the town carrying a suitcase with clothes and books and a mesh bag of food supplies that were so heavy they hurt his glove-less hands. Grisha Perelman certainly remembered nothing so traumatic because he traveled to Chernogolovka with his mother. Other trainees thought that was odd and slightly humiliating for a male adolescent, even if he was a math prodigy, but Perelman was apparently oblivious.

As he was oblivious to the grueling physical routine to which the trainees were subjected. In full accordance with Kolmogorov's ideals, the boys were expected to train not only in their chosen sciences but also in athletics—a custom that set the Soviet math-competition training system sharply apart from those of Western countries, which also gathered potential team members for training sessions. "They would collect all the mathematicians, physicists, and chemists—that's more than thirty people right there—in one gym," recalled Alexander Spivak, who eventually made the team. He was a student at the Kolmogorov boarding school in Moscow, where athletics was stressed as an important part of the study program, but as he recalled, he had never been subjected to anything so physically taxing. "To give us all something to do, first they made us run around the perimeter of the gym, and run, and run. And then there were these long benches there, and there was the gym coach and his imagination, which determined what could be done with them. You could do pushups off them. You could lift them over your head. You could jump over them back and forth. And you do all this. And all you see is this bench in front of your eyes. The whole time it's the bench, the bench, the bench."

Spivak recalled that one of the boys fainted, and at one point the others simply stopped and sat down on a bench, all of them in a row. What he remembered about Grisha Perelman was that he was "heroic," which in that case meant that, unlike the other boys, he did not protest, stage a sit-down strike, or generally show any dissatisfaction with the proceedings. He could not have enjoyed the exercise or found it easy: Perelman had a terrible time in gym class at school, and despite everyone's best efforts, he never managed to fulfill the Preparedness for Labor and Defense of the USSR requirements, which called for an upperclassman to run, swim, perform pull-ups, and shoot a small-caliber rifle. Nor did he manage to get above a C-level grade in physical education, which accounted for the only nonperfect grade on his graduating transcript. But rules were rules, and if Grisha was told to hop back and forth over a bench as part of his training for the international mathematics competition, hop he did.

His behavior at the gym may partly explain why some of his fellow trainees remembered Perelman as athletic. "He wasn't formally athletic, as if he had trained in tennis or something like that," recalled Sergei Samborsky, who made the team reserve. "But we all tended to ignore gym class and be shapeless while he was fit, in shape. And if you asked me what kind of sport I would associate with him, I'd say it was boxing." Over the course of a quarter of a century, Samborsky's memory had probably melded the deep impression left by Perelman's competitiveness and confidence with the recollection of Perelman's physical being. Perelman was pale, slightly overweight, and much shorter than his teammates; he was no boxer. But he was a math fighter, certain he would never again be defeated.

He was cocky. "One time one of the coaches reproached him by saying, 'You know, Grisha, everyone else knows derivatives and you don't,'" recalled Samborsky. "That was a part of mathematical analysis, and strictly speaking, as a secondary-school student, he wasn't required to know. But he responded, 'So what, I'll solve the problems without it.' It sounded brazen, but in essence, he was right." And then Samborsky added something that showed he remembered Grisha Perelman perhaps more accurately than he himself realized: "I suspect he knew a lot more than he let on." In fact, he probably knew derivatives. But he left this information out because he was there to solve problems, not to prove anything to the coaches.

Everyone got the point anyway. Coach Abramov remembered Perelman as being the only student who had never seen a competition problem he could not solve. And Samborsky put it simply: "He was better at solving problems—so much better, in fact, that one could say he was better than the rest of us put together. There was Grisha, and then there were the rest of us."

Out of the rest of them, at the end of the winter training camp, five more members of the team were tentatively chosen. The trainees were ranked according to the number of problems solved in the course of the camp. Number six was fifteen-year-old Spivak. An ethnic Russian who came to Moscow from a village in the Urals to study at the Kolmogorov boarding school, he hadn't known he had a Jewish-sounding last name. So he had no way of making sense of things when he was suddenly bumped off the list in favor of an ethnic Ukrainian who ranked seventh.

To the trainees, the winter camp was a succession of problem-solving competitions designed to resemble the actual olympiad; grueling gym sessions; lectures by renowned mathematicians, many of whom were living legends in the boys' world; and a nagging but tolerably quiet buzz produced by various education ministry and Party officials who hovered around the camp and occasionally cornered the trainees to remind them that it was the honor of the great Union they would be defending at the IMO. To the coaches, however, the camp was equal parts training and evaluating the boys and neutralizing the buzzing officials. They chose their battles. Even the obvious, inevitable inclusion of the extraordinary Perelman on the team required that the coaches put up a fight, for a competitor with a surname like that spelled trouble for the ministry minders; the coaches used up all of their fighting points, and the sixth-ranked Spivak, with his suspicious last name, was sacrificed.

When I met Spivak a quarter of a century later, he was an overgrown math boy: huge, with a disheveled head of graying hair, dressed in mismatched multicolored knits, he pleaded with me to relieve him of the social discomfort of a café, and he came to be interviewed at my apartment instead. He was working as a math instructor at one of Moscow's specialized schools, and he had spent much of his life putting together collections of math problems for gifted children. His manner of answering questions was disarmingly direct:

"So do you remember arriving in Chernogolovka?" I asked. "Was it morning, daytime, or evening?"

"I don't see why that's interesting," he responded. "It would be so much more interesting to ask me where everyone was now."

"Indeed it would be," I admitted. "Where is everyone now?"

"I don't know," he answered simply.

I fared barely better with questions regarding the connections that team members had made with one another: Spivak claimed he didn't see what was so special about the experience that it would have made the boys bond. When I argued that stress was a great unifier, he launched into a discussion of the comparative levels of complexity of the problems in different competitions. But he had a striking, emotionally charged memory of his experience of trying to get on the team. He had known that he had to make it in order to gain admission to a university. Even if he was unaware of the suspicious sound of his surname, he had judged—rightly, in all likelihood—that he would be unable to write the essay that was part of the entrance exams. "I just knew that I would be spending two years in the army, and I didn't know what would happen to me there," he told me. He had to claw his way to the IMO. He begged and pleaded, and he caused the coaches and ministry officials to scream at one another, and in the end, while he remained the seventh-ranking competitor, he was allowed to work on the take-home problem set, a small book that filled the potential competitors' time between the January camp and the All-Soviet Olympiad in April.

April saw all the boys in Odessa, a once-grand city on the Black Sea. They spent two days at a seaside resort solving the hardest problems they had ever faced: the consensus was that the All-Soviet problem sets were harder than those at the IMO. Spivak, who felt the rest of his life was at stake, took nothing for granted —he worked frantically, desperately, filling two entire composition books with textbook proofs that formed merely a part of the basis of his solutions and that he should have claimed were well established. Had Perelman perceived the world as the unfair place it was, he also would have had reason to think the rest of his life was at stake. But his confidence in himself and in the order of things was unshakable. He did what he always did: he read the problem, closed his eyes, leaned back, rubbed his pant legs with his palms with growing intensity, then rubbed his hands together, opened his eyes, and wrote down a very precise and very succinct solution to the problem. When solving the more difficult problems, he hummed softly. He filled only a couple of pages with his solutions. Both he and Spivak had perfect scores.

On the final day of the competition, as the jury gathered to grade the results, the top seven contenders—now including Spivak— were chosen to accompany Kolmogorov, who was visiting the national competition for the last time, on a walk through Odessa. Neither Spivak nor Samborsky remembered what Kolmogorov discussed with them—in any case, he was already afflicted with Parkinson's, and making out what he said must have been difficult —but both recalled that at a certain point he commanded the entire group to head for the beach. "The wind from the sea was piercing," recalled Samborsky. "We had to stay by his side because we'd been warned never to leave him alone since he couldn't see well. And Kolmogorov decided to go swimming. He undressed and went into the sea, and I was scared even to look at it; it was so cold it was almost like there were slabs of ice still floating. Waves the color of lead, foaming, wind so strong it could knock you off your feet. None of us followed him." Presently a guard emerged and told the boys to "rescue the grandpa," who surely could not fare well in the sea in this weather. The boys refused—either because none of them could swim well enough, as Spivak remembered, or because none of them dared confront Kolmogorov, as Samborsky recalled.

In either case, the following picture emerges. On a cold gray afternoon in the second half of April 1982, the greatest Russian mathematician of the twentieth century, making his last mathematical journey, went for a swim in the freezing water of the Black Sea while the greatest Russian mathematician of the twenty-first century sat impassively on shore and looked on. He had come because he was instructed to watch over "grandpa"; he had little use for all the walking and small-talking that was tacked onto the body of mathematics, and he had a distinct dislike for the water in which Kolmogorov was now enjoying what was left of his physical strength. The exuberant, expansive era of Russian mathematics was ending; a time of closed, secretive, concentrated individualism was beginning. Of course, no one could know this yet.

While Perelman waited for Kolmogorov on the beach, the All-Soviet Mathematical Olympiad jury worked out the final results of the competition, and Rukshin, Abramov, and several others began the final leg of the long and arduous process of ensuring Perelman would travel to Budapest for the IMO. The previous year, the IMO had been held in Washington, D.C. The Soviet Union's number one that year had been a Kiev high-school senior named Natalia Grinberg, a Jewish girl. This was a year after the United States had boycotted the Olympic Games (not the mathematics variety) held in Moscow. It was a year when Ronald Reagan's Evil Empire rhetoric defined U.S. policy toward Moscow. It was also the year when the Soviet Union de facto ended Jewish emigration. There was no way Soviet officials were going to let a Jewish girl represent the country at an IMO held in Washington: U.S. media coverage of her participation as envisioned by Moscow, as well as the possibility that she would defect—and the publicity surrounding that—added up to unacceptable risks. Grinberg was picked for the team—she had to be—but shortly before the planned trip she was told that her travel documents could not be processed in time. The USSR fielded six competitors instead of the eight required that year—another member of the team also had so-called problems with his documents—

and took ninth place with 230 points; every country that beat the Soviets that year had fielded eight competitors. Abramov was proud of that achievement: he had made sure that the Soviet team was set back no more than the 84 points the two missing members could have brought it.

Natalia Grinberg emigrated to Germany and became a professor of mathematics at Karlsruhe University. Her son, Darij Grinberg, represented Germany at the IMO three times between 2004 and 2006, winning two silver medals and one gold. Upon learning, during the judging of the IMO, that her son had apparently won the gold, Natalia Grinberg congratulated him and the team on a math forum and signed her post, "Natalia Grinberg, former number 1 in the 1981 USSR team, who was not allowed (in the last minute) to quit the beloved motherland to participate at IMO in Washington." For this professor, twenty-five years had clearly not assuaged the pain and insult of having been denied a prize for which she had worked most of her childhood and young adulthood.

As usual, Perelman was lucky and unaware of it. After placing ninth in Washington, the Soviet Union needed to restore its IMO status. The 1982 competition would be held in Budapest, the capital of Hungary, which was a part of the Soviet bloc and so, from a Soviet official's perspective, posed fewer publicity and security concerns than Washington. Nonetheless, competitors would still have contact with students from other parts of the world, including the United States. Further, the IMO was set up in such a way that competitors had next to no adult supervision: since all coaches were engaged in the judging process, teams and their adults had to have separate accommodations and keep contact to a minimum. To ensure that the Soviet competitors performed appropriately in every way, the boys were subjected to regular pep talks by ministry officials reminding them that they were representing the honor of their great land, and the adults were forced to prove to a dozen different officials that their charges were ideologically reliable. And still the risks, in the eyes of the officials, were formidable. Just four years earlier, when the IMO was held in Communist Romania, the Soviet Union had fielded no team at all—because, rumor had it, every single member of the team would have been Jewish.

To be allowed to travel, a Soviet citizen had to be granted a foreign-travel passport—no ordinary person was allowed to hold one as a matter of course—and an exit visa. This required clearance by local officials, travel authorities, and the secret police. To be allowed to travel on official business, representing the country, one also had to be cleared by the Party at every level, working one's way up from the local precinct to the district and, finally, to the federal level. At any of these stages, the documents of someone like Perelman could be stalled indefinitely by an overly cautious bureaucrat. "So Abramov and I made a pact," recalled Rukshin. "He worked on it in Moscow. I worked in St. Petersburg, pushing his documents through. After all, you know, I'd had many students in the club who were the children of someone powerful." Rukshin called in every chip he had; he used his connections to a secret police officer who was the father of one of his students, a local Party boss who was the father of one of his classmates, and another Party boss who was the husband of another classmate. Meanwhile, in Moscow, Abramov made regular visits to the education ministry begging officials there to keep tabs on the bureaucratic progress of the Soviet Union's great mathematical hope.

The six teammates—four members and two alternates—spent the month of June back in Chernogolovka. Incredibly—or, rather, it would have been incredible if they had been six regular teenagers thrown together in close quarters for a month instead of these six boys supremely gifted in mathematics—they did not socialize; they did not bond. They trained for days on end, breaking only for games of volleyball, visits with mathematical luminaries, and the inevitable Party pep talks. By July all four members of the team had their travel documents. They were Spivak; Vladimir Titenko from Belarus; Konstantin Matveev from Novosibirsk; and Perelman, the only Jewish member of the team.

The Soviet team arrived in Budapest on July 7. The competitors were taken to a hotel where each country's team of four had its own room. The students were now on their own; their coach had arrived in Hungary a couple of days earlier to take part in the final preparations—approving the translations of competition problems and assigning points to parts of each solution—and now the ministry handler who had accompanied the boys on the flight was also gone.

The competition lasted two days: July 9 and 10. Each day the 120 participants spent four and a half hours solving a set of three problems. Each problem was worth seven points for a complete solution, and anywhere from one to six points could be awarded for starting off in the right direction without making it to the end. The judging process—a complicated dance of negotiation and sometimes outright haggling involving judges from the host country, adjudicators from the countries where the particular problems originated, and coaches representing the competitors' interests—took three days following the competition.

During that time, the competitors were left to the care of local handlers. They were charged with the task of being good guests and worthy representatives of their countries—social tasks for which they were ill-suited. They submitted to touring around Budapest, taking a boat ride down the Danube, traveling to Balaton Lake for sightseeing and a swim, and visiting Ernő Rubik, inventor of the cube and other torturous mathematical toys that were then enjoying worldwide popularity. For the most part, they traveled speechlessly, though Rubik managed to elicit some questions, mostly concerning the minimum number of moves required to solve his puzzle and the possibility of devising an algorithm for a universal Rubik's Cube solution. Perelman showed no interest in the sights, declined to swim, and had no questions for the great Rubik.

A final social responsibility with which the Soviet team was burdened had to do with a bag of buttons. These had been handed to the team by a ministry official, who had talked of their duty to the motherland, of their responsibility as both competitors and diplomats, and of international friendship. And then she had pulled out the bag of buttons—the tourist variety, with pictures of Moscow and Leningrad on them—and, apparently zooming in on the most vulnerable of the boys, shoved the bag into Spivak's hands. Spivak, who had already done what he could for his country mathematically (he would be awarded a bronze medal), now had to figure out what to do with the souvenirs. He tried to draft his fellow team members into the effort but failed. So he took the bag and headed out into the hotel corridors.

"The order had to be carried out, even if we were not being supervised," Spivak told me. "So I went and tried to hand them out, though I barely spoke English, which made it very difficult, and then I went to the American team's room. And the way they fled the Evil Empire. I mean, they literally climbed under their beds. You would totally get the impression I was about to open fire on them. I tried to say something about friendship and that sort of thing, but I realized it was just too hard." Spivak left the room and disposed of the buttons someplace where he assumed they would not be found.

On July 14, the last day of the 1982 IMO, Perelman collected his trophies: a gold medal, shaped like an elongated hexagon that year; a special award certificate sponsored by Team Kuwait (last place) given to competitors who earned the maximum number of points —forty-two out of forty-two; a giant whip, which the Hungarians gave each medal winner; and a Rubik's Cube, which Grisha gave away when he returned to Leningrad. These were the prizes; Perelman's actual rewards for years of single-minded training were automatic admission to a university and, more central to his needs, the right to be left alone for another five years.

5

Rules for Adulthood

THE UNIVERSITY, FOR PERELMAN, began with long train trips, long lines, and paperwork. Roughly ten members of Rukshin's math club traveled as a pack. As Rukshin saw it, the path to Mathmech had been blazed by Perelman, whose right to be admitted without entrance exams had either forced or allowed the university to exceed its usual two-Jews-per-year quota and accept at least three people who, for the purposes of admissions discrimination policies, were Jewish in every way: their surnames sounded Jewish, and their identity documents stated they were Jewish. One additional Jewish student in an entering class of roughly three hundred and fifty may seem like a drop in the bucket, but for Rukshin, who got to send three rather than two of his Jewish students off to Mathmech, it felt like a victory and even, perhaps—if he was to be believed when he spoke about it a quarter of a century later—a revolution. The other members of the math club who made it to the prestigious mathematics department were either ethnic Russians or, like Golovanov, Jews who through marriage or other circumstances had lucked into Russian surnames and Russian identity documents.

The large entering class was split into groups of about twenty-five people each. Perelman and several others from Rukshin's math club and from Leningrad's other specialized math schools were assigned to the same group, and those who were not arranged to be transferred to it. In the end the group represented a sort of elite learning center within Mathmech, singled out much as its members had been when they were schoolchildren. Most of them traveled daily from the city; in the 1970s Leningrad University had moved its science departments to Petrodvorets, a suburb about twenty miles west of the city. What had been conceived as an ambitious project, a campus that was a city unto itself like a sort of Russian Cambridge University, had fizzled, turning the newly built glass-and-concrete math, physics, and science buildings into a very inconveniently located commuter school (the rest of the university remained in Leningrad). The students took unheated suburban trains with wooden seats, invariably having to run to catch the one that would deliver them to school in time for the day's first lecture and often risking missing the last city-bound train, which left before midnight.

Russian universities offered a highly specialized education. Mathmech was geared toward producing professional mathematicians or, if that failed, mathematics instructors and computer programmers. Detours into what might be considered liberal arts were minimal, while detours into Marxist theory, though not as demanding as they were at the humanities departments, still included required courses in dialectical materialism, historical materialism, scientific communism, scientific atheism, the political economics of capitalism, and an entire course entitled A Critique of Certain Strands of Contemporary Bourgeois Philosophy and

Anti-Communist Ideology, which was taught by a young philosophy professor who managed to sing all the requisite praises of Marxist-Leninist philosophy, brand other contemporary philosophers rotten, and then proceed to tell the students what they had always wanted to know but were afraid to ask about Nietzsche and Kierkegaard. "So this was a class we actually attended," Golovanov told me. Otherwise, most students attempted to devise ways to avoid showing up not only to the ideological classes but also to the large lecture courses and, in most cases, courses that fell outside the area in which they planned to specialize. There was, naturally, one exception: Grisha Perelman attended everything, including the large lectures from which he was exempt because his grades never dipped below a four on a five-point scale.

Golovanov called the Marxism courses "the crazy disciplines." Perelman accepted them as part of the learning package and used the great compacting brain of his to the benefit of all his classmates. "Grisha's clarity of mind was very helpful here," recalled Golovanov. "The thing about all this stream-of-unconsciousness is that you either have to process it all or ignore it completely. The former is impossible for ordinary humans, and the latter is fraught with danger. Grisha somehow managed to find the strands of thought, if you can call it that, in those disciplines. So his notes on all the crazy disciplines were of great value to us all."

What no doubt helped Perelman plow through the dense nonsense of Marxist theory as it was then being taught was his genuine disregard for politics of any sort. "In Grisha's lexicon *politics* was always a swearword," said Golovanov. "Say, if I wanted to organize something to make things better, some campaign aimed at helping our beloved Sergei Rukshin even, he would say, 'That's politics, let's focus on solving problems instead.' And you have to understand that this was a genuine position: he disliked all sorts and directions of politics equally." The traditional Russian intellectual's queasiness at the political process had less to do with Perelman's position than did the fact that he was truly uninterested in anything that was not mathematics. While other students may have felt insulted or excited, Perelman remained dispassionate; none of the issues discussed in these courses had a connection to anything that mattered. His notes on Marxist theory were purely systematizing exercises, performed with his unique efficiency.

The ideology courses notwithstanding—and they were, after all, fewer than at many other departments—Mathmech was what in the Soviet Union passed for a liberal institution of higher learning. Those who wanted to get through its five-year course with minimal effort and minimal knowledge had to suffer through the first year with a heavy learning load and afterward could proceed to coast. Those who wanted to specialize early could tune much of the rest of mathematics out. Perelman represented the rarest breed of Mathmech student: one who sought to be universally educated in mathematics.

Most mathematically ambitious students had for years known their specialization was preordained: they had one sort of brain or the other. The algebraists might then look for the most promising problems of algebra while the geometers might cast about for the most interesting geometer with whom to study, but in general, their directions were set. Perelman's brain was made to embrace all of mathematics. In retrospect, one might suppose that topology ultimately attracted him as the quintessence of mathematics—the province of pure categories and clear systems, with no informational interference—but as a first-year student, he was barely exposed to topology. Most mathematicians remember their one freshman course in topology for teaching them the mental exercise of turning an inner tube inside out using a tiny hole; it is that mind-bending quality of topology that most recall, not its streamlined clarity. Perelman did not have the other usual motivation to specialize early: he had no reason to try to save time by studying only the mathematics in which he planned to work. He was not rushing anywhere. He was living for mathematics and by doing mathematics.

He attended lectures and seminars across mathematical disciplines without much apparent concern for the quality of instruction offered. The effect could be comical. In his fourth year at the university Perelman attended a course in computer science taught by an instructor who had earned the reputation of being one of the department's worst lecturers. "Normal people did not attend this," said Golovanov. Perelman did. And he generally sat at the front of the room, which was probably why he caught the eye of the instructor, who at one particular moment became agitated about the state of mathematical knowledge among Mathmech students in general. "Our fourth-year students can't even solve the simple Cauchy Problem," he declared. He wrote out the classic differential-equation problem on the board and turned to Perelman. "Can you tell me how this problem is solved?"

Perelman approached the board calmly and wrote out the solution.

"Yes," said the instructor. "This student solved the problem correctly."

Where Perelman and his crowd came from, a high-school student who could not produce the solution to the Cauchy Problem on request would be disdained as an imbecile—"and rightly so," commented Golovanov. Still, when the instructor was in a position of authority, Perelman seemed willing to submit to ridiculous exercises without protestation. Later, what he perceived as the need to prove his worthiness to his peers or to academic authorities infuriated him instantly, but within the confines of the university, he apparently gave professors almost unlimited license. This particular computer-science instructor also had the bizarre custom of nailing his students' notes to their desks—to ensure that students actually attended the sessions rather than borrowed one another's notes. Perelman tolerated this indignity too and helped the rest of his group by verbally summarizing the notes.

He was loyal to his group as long as no one broke the rules as he perceived them. A Mathmech custom dictated that students help peers who found themselves stuck during a written test. Outright cheating was impossible, since every student had an individual problem set, drawn at random from a large pool. But if one was stalled desperately, one could generally pass a note to another student that briefly summarized the issue. The response was never a solution but often something along the lines of "Try this tack." Perelman, the universal problem-solver, the fastest thinker in his age group in the Soviet Union and perhaps the world, would have been the best person to answer these sorts of questions. He was, however, unwilling to entertain them, and he let his disapproval of the practice be known: everyone had to solve his own problem for himself.

Somewhere in the transition from adolescence to adulthood, Perelman seemed to have found a way to relieve the tension between prevailing social mores, which he perceived as illogical, internally inconsistent, and perpetually shifting—and they certainly were all of these things—and his idea of how the world should work. He derived a set of his own rules based on the few values he knew to be absolute and proceeded to follow them. As new situations presented themselves, he figured out the rules that applied to them—this too may have seemed inconsistent and shifting to an observer, but only because the observer did not know the algorithm. Naturally, Perelman expected the rest of the world to follow his rules; it would not have occurred to him that other people did not know them. After all, the rules were based on universal values, honesty being primary among them. Honesty meant always telling the whole truth, which is to say, all of the available accurate information—much as Perelman did when he supplied his proofs with information extraneous to the actual solution. Clearly, in the case of a student taking a Mathmech test, supplying *all of the available information* would have included naming the person with whom the idea for the solution had originated, and that would truly have been inconsistent with the rule that every student must do his own work. Later, he would view, say, sloppy footnoting, as practiced by many mathematicians, as plagiarism. It is possible too that a bit of the competitor's habit shaped his perception of the written tests; after all, they did look and, perhaps for Perelman, feel a bit like the olympiad, and it would have been inconceivable for a competitor to ask his fellow problem-solvers for hints.

In the third year, each Mathmech student chose a specialty that would presumably take him through graduate school and into a research career. Golovanov chose number theory. It was a natural choice for a boy who could be knocked out of competitions upon encountering a geometry problem and who seemed to relate to numbers as others did to people. Perelman chose his own destiny. He had picked geometry, he told his group cryptically, because he wanted to go into a field populated by a few remaining dinosaurs so that he might also become one of them. In the 1980s in Leningrad, geometry seemed like an anachronism: it had none of the flair of computer science and none of the romance of numbers, and its practitioners were indeed a few larger-than-life old men. One of his classmates, Mehmet Muslimov, remembered that Perelman's declaration had not sounded pretentious. If anything, it sounded logical: here was a person from another time and place, odd and differently minded even in an environment as full of eccentrics as a university mathematics department; it was only reasonable that he would consciously fashion himself into a dinosaur.

What Perelman may also have been telling his classmates was that he felt quite exasperated with his fellow humans and their ways, and his chosen field seemed to attract the few people whose internal codes of conduct were as strict as his own.

Perelman needed someone to guide him along his path to dinosaurhood—or at least someone who would not get in his way and who would shield him from others if necessary. He was strongly drawn to Viktor Zalgaller, a geometer then in his sixties.

I interviewed Zalgaller in early 2008 in Rehovot, about twenty miles south of Tel Aviv. The town was built around the Weizmann Institute, a mathematics research facility with which Zalgaller was affiliated though he did all his work at his apartment, where his wife lay nearly motionless in the final stages of Alzheimer's disease. "The woman no longer manages the house," Zalgaller said apologetically as he welcomed me in. It was a messy place, lived in awkwardly, with Zalgaller's crumpled bedding on the living room couch, and a clutter of books, papers, and teacups where apparently a homey order had once reigned. Zalgaller himself was similarly unkempt: unshaven, wearing a crewneck sweater over gray pajamas, but entirely coherent and pointedly businesslike in his manner. He spoke of Perelman with awed affection, which was what he had always felt for him: "I had nothing to teach him from the beginning," he claimed.

Zalgaller was a World War II veteran, a charismatic teacher who had almost single-handedly shaped the mathematical curriculum and teaching style of School 239 (in the 1960s he had taken time off from research and university teaching to do this), and he was an incomparable storyteller. All of this had made him popular around the university and at the Leningrad Mathematics Institute, but none of those qualities held any special appeal for Perelman. "He liked me, I have no doubt about it," Zalgaller told me. "It may have had something to do with ethics. What I thought about what people must do." When I asked him to elaborate, Zalgaller claimed, "He liked my style of communicating with students. He must have known that I would not be strict and that studying with me would be interesting." In fact, it seemed Perelman had fairly little concern for the teaching style of his instructors. What must have drawn him to Zalgaller was a more particular aspect of the way he related to the world, exemplified by a story Zalgaller told me but forbade me to tape, apparently because it concerned him, and not Perelman—Zalgaller thought it improper to talk about himself. I wrote it down from memory as soon as I left his apartment.

Like most Soviet men of his generation, Zalgaller joined the Red Army in the early days of World War II, and like a very lucky few he spent the entire four years of the war in the service and survived with nary a scratch. He graduated Leningrad University in the late 1940s, just as Stalin's anti-Semitic Campaign Against Cosmopolitans was getting in full swing and Jews all over the Soviet Union were finding themselves universally turned down by colleges, graduate schools, and employers. Zalgaller was one of five Jews from his graduating class who applied to stay on in graduate school. All were deserving, thought Zalgaller, but when the list of those accepted for graduate study was posted at the university, Zalgaller found his own name on it—and none of the other Jewish students. So he turned the graduate school down.

The old man saw that I now expected him to tell me that he was unwilling to play by rigged rules, that he wanted to stay on in graduate school but could not if he felt he was doing it at another student's expense. "I was no fighter against anti-Semitism," he said, correcting my unspoken misconception with evident irritation. "I just didn't want to be dependent on those people." If he was the only Jew accepted, he would be in receipt of a favor—and that was what he turned down.

Zalgaller proceeded, stubbornly and almost miraculously, to construct a career on his own terms, accepting only those favors he was certain he could repay and conducting himself in accordance with a code that was not only more confining than that of others but also—perhaps equally important to Perelman—often indecipherable to anyone but Zalgaller himself. In the early 1990s, when Soviet researchers started having to write their own funding proposals, Zalgaller devised an ingenious way to solve the perceived dilemma of making the direction of his research contingent on the preferences of funders: he applied for money for projects he had already successfully completed but had not published and then used that money to finance his next project. Surely it was this complicated but internally coherent set of ethical perceptions and behaviors that appealed to Perelman, who asked Zalgaller to be his thesis adviser.

"I had nothing to teach him," Zalgaller repeated. "So what I did was just give him small problems that had evaded solution. Once he solved them, I saw to it that they were published. So by the time Grisha graduated from university, he already had several published papers." In other words, he continued to feed Perelman's brain, continuing what Rukshin had done and ever so gently helping Perelman find his way as a self-declared dinosaur.

Perhaps the single most fateful incident in Perelman's lifetime was the appearance, in Perelman's first year at Leningrad University, of a larger-than-life presence in the form of a small old man with a square gray beard. His name was Alexander Danilovich Alexandrov (his patronymic was generally used, in order to distinguish him from numerous other Alexander Alexandrovs); he was a living legend, and miraculously and almost ridiculously, he was teaching geometry to first-year Mathmech students.

Alexandrov had started out as a physicist but dropped out of graduate school in the 1930s because, he once explained, "I can't promise that I'll always do what I'm expected to do." One of his two advisers, the physicist Vitaly Fok, reportedly said to him, "You are too decent." The other, the mathematician Boris Delone, added, "You are too much not a careerist." He went on to defend two dissertations by the time he was twenty-five, receive a number of prestigious prizes, and in 1952 become president of Leningrad University at age forty.

"Alexandrov had a great influence on Grisha," claimed Golovanov, who had witnessed the beginning of their relationship first-hand: he too attended Alexandrov's freshman geometry course that year. "He was just the type, psychologically, who could exert that kind of influence. To sum up who Alexandrov was, briefly: he was a Young Pioneer of colossal intellectual might. I know quite a lot about him, and I think he is a person who never once in his life wanted to do something bad. Naturally, with this sort of approach to things, he committed bad deeds on an industrial scale—but he never once wanted to." Golovanov was fully aware that his description fit his friend Perelman just as well as it did their teacher. "There is a wonderful [Latin] saying," he continued, "that people consider incorrect, for some reason: *Vos vestros servate, meos mihi linquite mores,* 'I will go my own way and let others stick to theirs.' From a moral standpoint, this position is unassailable. And I think you know at least one other person who acts in accordance with this motto—he just happens not to be a university president," unlike Alexandrov. He happened to be Grisha Perelman.

Alexandrov owed his appointment as president of the university to his background as both a physicist and a mathematician: the two sciences had grown so important during the Soviet nuclear push that physicist-mathematicians had been chosen over Party functionaries to run the Leningrad and Moscow universities in the early 1950s. He was also a member of the Communist Party and remained one, in his true-believer style, until his death in 1999. He was by no means a loyalist, however. His most remarkable accomplishment as president of Leningrad University was preserving the study of genetics—a science banned under Stalin. While geneticists who had worked elsewhere were either jailed or reduced to employment at animal farms at best and menial jobs at worst, he ensured that seminars in genetics continued at his university. After Stalin's death, he even managed to get international geneticists to speak there, long before official Soviet science began its slow reacceptance of genetics. In the 1950s, he played a key role in protecting mathematics from a similar destructive campaign that had seemed to be taking shape. He managed, almost single-handedly, to reframe it as a movement to protect the prestige of Soviet mathematics from imagined Western efforts to denigrate Soviet achievements.

Alexandrov also risked his career—and ultimately lost his post as university president—by supporting mathematicians who came under attack for being either ideologically unreliable or Jewish. In 1951, the year before he became university president, he managed to intervene when the university's department of mathematical analysis was in danger of dissolution because it was staffed primarily by Jews. The department's members had exhausted all their appeals—no one felt powerful or brave enough to help. Then one of the mathematicians dared ask Alexandrov to step in, which was a desperate move on her part, since she had previously made an enemy of Alexandrov by mocking his sideline studies in philosophy. Alexandrov responded and devised a way to stem the attack by replacing the department chair. Almost forty years later, Alexandrov would play a key role in securing Perelman's academic career in the face of anti-Semitic discrimination, and another ten years after that, Olga Ladyzhenskaya, the daring mathematician from that department of mathematical analysis, would become the last person who successfully shielded Perelman from the world of real-life mathematicians.

Alexandrov was a believer—a literal one. He had engineered Leningrad University's move out of the city, and when a former student reproached him for this years later, as he was traveling to the university on one of the overcrowded commuter trains with hard bench seats, Alexandrov shouted for the entire train car to hear: "I believed in the Party program! It said in the appendices that Leningrad would be developing southward and the center would move southward! And then they started building northward." The former student, a very prominent mathematician, commented in a later memoir that by the 1960s everyone knew Party documents were not to be believed. He was probably missing the point: Alexandrov, like Perelman, lacked the disbelieving gene; he had the ability to reject, resist, and even hate, but he could not disbelieve.

Alexandrov was fired as the president in 1964 and proceeded to spend the next two decades in what still amounted to exile of the not-entirely-self-imposed variety in Siberia, helping to create a science town there. In his seventies, he returned to his university with what turned out to be a vain hope of reclaiming a place there: he wanted to fill a vacant chair in geometry. In the run-up to the chair election, he taught a first-year course and charmed students in part because of his openness about the absurdity of his predicament. He was given to quoting, among other things, the numerous poems Mathmech students made up about him. Poems like this one:

> Danilych labored in the math field
> Danilych rose every morning
> Too bad his efforts could but yield
> A course the students found boring

Eventually Alexandrov's hopes of obtaining the chair in geometry were dashed by academic and Party authorities, and he moved to a position at the Leningrad mathematical research institute—

but not before he had chosen Grisha Perelman as his protégé. While other students might have been drawn by Alexandrov's legendary status, his informal approach to teaching, and his intellectual expansiveness, Perelman gravitated not to Alexandrov's style but to his essence, contradictory and rigid as it was.

Indeed, had it not been for Alexandrov's bizarrely fearless management of the university, Perelman's career might have taken an entirely different path. As it happened, the study of topology was barely represented at the university until the early 1960s. When Alexandrov looked for a person who might launch the field in Leningrad, he stumbled upon Vladimir Rokhlin, a student of Kolmogorov's and Pontryagin's who was then eking out an anchorless existence in Moscow. He had served time in the Gulag, was still under surveillance, and was generally considered unhirable. Alexandrov brought Rokhlin to Leningrad and managed to provide him not only with a teaching job at the university but also with an apartment. In Leningrad, Rokhlin would see twelve of his students' dissertations to completion, including that of Mikhail Gromov, one of the world's leading geometers today and the man who would be largely responsible for introducing Perelman to the international mathematics community.

Perelman likely did not know much of this about Alexandrov, and if he had known, he might have disregarded what amounted to Alexandrov's heroism as mere politicking. Nor could he have predicted the role Alexandrov would play in his career. What certainly attracted Perelman to Alexandrov were his approaches to mathematics and to life in general.

On one hand, Alexandrov came from the academic school of unbounded generosity. "He would give topics and promising ideas away to his students," wrote Zalgaller, who was a student of Alexandrov's. On the other hand, he viewed mathematics as one long problem-solving marathon. A student recalled walking into Alexandrov's office.

"'So have you proved it?' Alexandrov asked.

"'What should I have proved?'

"'Anything!'

"It would be difficult to overestimate the influence of such constant expectation of results," wrote the former student. "From that point on I aimed to be prepared for this question."

Alexandrov was the undisputed king of geometry in Leningrad and, possibly, in all of the Soviet Union. Another student recalled Alexandrov's reaction to a request to write a history of Soviet geometry. "That would be immodest," Alexandrov had said. "There was no one there but me." Another student wrote that he had chosen to become a geometer after hearing another professor's words to the effect that "Alexandrov has discovered whole new worlds in mathematics and is now inhabiting them all by his lonesome." Perelman's dinosaur remark referred mostly to Alexandrov.

Around the time Perelman met him, Alexandrov was said to have made the following comment at a geometry seminar: "Everyone is a bastard, everyone is bad, with the possible exception of Jesus Christ. Einstein is bad too, because he did not leave America after the nuclear bomb was detonated over his objections." He once wrote, "In the end, through the general interconnectedness of events, a person becomes, in some way or another, to a greater or lesser extent, party to everything that happens in the world, and if he can exert any influence whatsoever on any event, then he becomes responsible for it." This view of individual responsibility squared perfectly with Perelman's concept of honesty, so he adopted Alexandrov's criteria as his own and would later apply them to everyone he encountered.

When Perelman entered the university, he became, at the advanced age of sixteen, practically an official adult. A more conventional teenager might have celebrated this transition by reassessing the rules, reshuffling authority figures, or claiming more independence. Perelman made the rules stricter, and added Zalgaller and Alexandrov to his pantheon of unassailable authority figures, where they joined his mother and Rukshin. Perelman adopted more-formal signs of his new status as a grownup: he stopped shaving, and in the math-club world, he went from being a student to being a teacher.

Following the established Kolmogorovian tradition, Rukshin sought to turn his first math-club graduates into the first math-club instructors who came from within. He chose Perelman and Golovanov—Perelman being his favorite student and Golovanov showing, even at fourteen, the potential to become a great teacher in Rukshin's mold. Rukshin took both to summer camp as instructors. Neither experiment proved fully successful. Golovanov, it turned out, was just a boy and generally acted like one; this would pass with age, and he would indeed grow into a math coach second in mastery and charisma only to Rukshin. Perelman turned out to be Perelman, which is to say, rigid, demanding, and hypercritical; these qualities would only intensify with age, ultimately making it impossible for him to be any kind of teacher or, indeed, communicator.

Early on in his career as an instructor—either during or right after his first year at the university—Perelman observed, in conversation with Golovanov, that the basic military training that was among Mathmech's required courses had proved useful because the military bylaws he had had to memorize could be applied directly to the running of the math club. "He said this with a smile, of course, because he is very smart," recalled Golovanov. "But one could tell that the share of humor in this supposed joke was no more than ten percent."

At camp following his first year, Perelman served as an instructor to a remarkable group of mathematicians two years younger than he. They included Fedja Nazarov, now a professor at University of Wisconsin; Anna Bogomolnaia, now a professor at Rice University; and Evgeny Abakumov, now a professor at the Université de Marne-la-Vallée in Paris. Every morning Perelman gave them a set of twenty problems—roughly double the club's usual semi-weekly dose. The problems were extremely difficult, and the level of difficulty was increased with little regard for the students' actual abilities and achievements. "The general concept always was that the carrot should be hanging just barely above the level to which the rabbit could jump," Golovanov explained to me. "But Grisha believes that the rabbit should always be jumping higher and higher." A student who failed to solve at least half of the problems by midday was told he or she could not have lunch. "They still got lunch, of course," recalled Golovanov. "But undeservedly."

What was the seventeen-year-old Perelman thinking about his fifteen-year-old charges? Did he suspect that despite all of their considerable accomplishments and their desire to learn, as evidenced by their presence at the math camp, they were secretly intellectually lazy? Possibly. "He certainly thought that they did not take things seriously enough," said Golovanov. "It's also possible that he was so noble that he could not fathom they were just not smart enough—and anyway, considering what they grew into, those kids probably were smart enough." More likely, this was a classic theory-of-mind problem. The seventeen-year-old Perelman —university student, olympiad champion, and universal problem-solving machine—did not and could not imagine that these math-club teenagers, who had two years' fewer problem-solving and competition experience and who simply lacked his problem-crunching skills, could not do what he could if they really, really put their minds to it.

When depriving his hapless students of lunch failed, he started banishing them from the study room. "We tried to explain to Grisha that if a child has been accepted into camp, he cannot be held outside class for days at a time, that this was not punishment but total craziness," recalled Rukshin. "He responded that he would not let the child into class until the child solved such-and-such. It was really hard." Those banished included Bogomolnaia, Nazarov, and Konstantin Kohas; in another dozen years, Kohas would hold the chair in mathematical analysis at Mathmech.

So why did Rukshin keep Perelman, whose lectures could be borderline incomprehensible and whose behavior was clearly abusive? Part of the answer was surely that Rukshin loved Perelman, and having him near—this seems to have been the summer when the two shared a room at the camp—filled his time, and his teaching, with additional meaning. But it also may be that Perelman's limitations as a teacher suited Rukshin's perceptions of how things ought to work. Here is how Rukshin described the situation to me, using terminology from Laurence Peter and Raymond Hull's *The Peter Principle*: "Perelman was a brilliant teacher for super-competent students, a good one for competent students, and a mediocre one for those who were moderately competent. You see, a cobalt-alloy drill bit is a wonderful instrument. But you cannot use it to drill a piece of glass: the glass will crack and crumble. Whereas a bullet will leave a neat little round hole in a piece of glass but absolutely cannot be used to drill metal. A knife and an ax perform similar jobs, but one is far superior for sharpening a pencil while the other is a better tool for felling an oak tree. A teacher is a tool. For a limited group of super-strong students, where discipline is not an issue—I mean, where it came to the organizing duties of a teacher, Perelman did not do as well. But at camp, we have always had this tradition: we do not hire a separate person for making sure the kids are clean and fed and go to bed on time, and a separate teacher who teaches them things. The Holy Trinity is a single being: a teacher, a counselor, and the boss. Because these kids would never have respected some random camp counselor anyway.

They had respect for the kind of teacher who took them hiking, got wet in the rain with them, sweated in the heat, did mathematics, and discussed books—especially since back then I wasn't much older than my students." Rukshin was nine years older than Perelman and ten to twelve years older than most of his students, and, as his diction indicates, he clearly thought he was not just a beloved teacher but God himself. His students turned teachers were therefore angels, and as such, in his mind they had the right to be not only of clearly circumscribed utility but also unreasonable, capricious, and outright childish.

The conflict came, naturally, once the students who had borne the brunt of Perelman's military-style mathematical discipline grew old enough to encounter him as equals. It must have been just before the summer camp season of 1985 when Perelman declared he would not teach summer camp if Nazarov and Bogomolnaia were teaching there too. Twenty-plus years later, Rukshin either could not or would not recall the nature of Perelman's objections to the two younger teachers. It seemed Perelman found Bogomolnaia generally objectionable—because she was a girl who did not wear skirts, for example, and because he had somehow discovered that she did not always tell the truth.

"Did he catch her lying to him?" I asked Rukshin.

"No, he just found out she did not tell the truth at all times," said Rukshin. "I tried to explain to him—I mean, only idiots tell the truth at all times, but I did not tell him that. What I did say was, Grisha, what you are describing is not a part of a human being but a feature of his relationships with others. There are people I would never lie to, and there are people to whom I have no moral obligations. I would prefer not to lie to them, but I cannot exclude the possibility that I would distort the truth or not tell the truth. He would not accept this point of view." In fact, he probably could not; the idea that a behavior—especially a behavior he found unacceptable—was not an inherent quality but a function of something as intangible as a particular human relationship was, in all likelihood, entirely incomprehensible to him. Plus, he knew at least one person who claimed always to tell the truth and to have done so his whole life, thereby giving the lie to Rukshin's basic premise. That person was Alexander Danilovich Alexandrov, whose gravestone in St. Petersburg is inscribed with words that translate to "The truth is the only thing to be worshipped."

Bogomolnaia couldn't recall the incident either, but she remembered the world of math clubs, summer camps, and Rukshin as conflict-ridden. "We were young, we were all difficult to get along with, and it was hard to work alongside one another," she explained, and she continued in a detached tone of voice but using vocabulary that conveyed residual bitterness—mostly, I gathered, toward Rukshin. "In our little snake pit, people would come into conflict with one another for reasons that seem utterly insignificant now that I'm forty."

Generally, Bogomolnaia thought, Perelman was poorly suited for teaching: "He just didn't quite have the temperament—I mean, you have to do something in addition to pure mathematics when you teach." But rather than simply drift away from teaching, he left in a rage—a rage, it seemed, that was fostered in part by Rukshin, who did anything but discourage conflict among his little stable of math angels. "I held discussions with every teacher who had agreed to teach at camp that summer," he told me. "We discussed it and decided that we could not take Grisha with us in light of his ultimatum."

So it was that when Perelman was nineteen, his world began its inexorable narrowing. He lost the social setting that had nurtured him since he was ten years old. At roughly the same time, in the middle of his third year at the university, he picked his specialty, which meant that his path and Golovanov's began to diverge; after almost nine years of traveling to every class and math club together, occasionally stopping to write formulas in chalk on the sidewalk, they now had different schedules. Here began the road that would take Perelman through the next twenty years of his life and to the point where he was speaking regularly to only his mother and Rukshin, who still got to play God in his student's life, now without the diluting and mitigating effects of the angels.

6

Guardian Angels

W HEN HE WAS GRADUATING, his mother came to see me," recalled Zalgaller. "She said it was his dream to stay on at our institute." She meant the Leningrad branch of the Steklov Mathematics Institute of the Russian Academy of Sciences. Apparently Zalgaller did not think there was anything particularly strange about the mother of a grown man going to his adviser to discuss her son's graduate-study prospects. Both Zalgaller and Lubov Perelman probably had good reason to believe that intervention was required, because Grisha himself was unwilling and unable to do what it took to stay on for graduate study.

Little had changed in graduate-school admissions policies since Zalgaller found his name on the roster in the late 1940s: graduate work was still very nearly off-limits to Jews. The Steklov Institute was particularly odious. An open letter circulated by a group of American mathematicians at the world mathematical congress in Helsinki in 1978 stated, "The Steklov Mathematical Institute is a prestigious institution in the field of mathematics. For the last thirty years its director has been academician I. M. Vinogradov, who is proud of the fact that under his leadership the Institute has become 'free of Jews.' . . . The key positions in mathematics nowadays are occupied by people who are not only unwilling to protect the interests of science and scientists in the face of the authorities, but who go even beyond official guidelines in their policies of political and racial discrimination."

Ivan Vinogradov, the number theorist who ran the Steklov for nearly half a century, turned the Soviet policy of anti-Semitic discrimination into a personal crusade. By the time Perelman was nearing university graduation, Vinogradov had been dead four years—not long enough to make a dent in the legacy of fifty years of anti-Semitic policies, which Vinogradov's successors continued with greater or lesser enthusiasm but always in full accordance with basic Soviet policies. Perelman's situation was further complicated by the fact that all Steklov decisions were made in Moscow, with the leadership of the Leningrad branch exercising little influence. In addition, the new director of the Leningrad branch, Ludvig Faddeev, scion of an aristocratic and slightly eccentric (the mathematician was named for Beethoven) St. Petersburg ethnic Russian family, had never indicated whether he personally opposed the anti-Semitic policies of his institution. "I wasn't sure what Faddeev would think of the idea," recalled Zalgaller—"the idea" being to offer a graduate research spot to one of the most gifted and diligent students ever seen at the Mathmech. "So I consulted Burago." Yuri Burago was a former student of Zalgaller's who at that time ran a lab at the Leningrad branch of the Steklov.

Together Zalgaller and Burago concocted a plan. Perelman's application to the Steklov would be preceded by a preventive heavy-artillery strike. Alexander Danilovich Alexandrov would write a letter to the Steklov leadership asking that Perelman be allowed to do his graduate work at the Leningrad Steklov under Alexandrov's supervision. The incongruity of the request—a full member of the Academy of Sciences, the man at the center of all of Soviet geometry, writing a letter on behalf of a lowly university senior—was exactly what would ensure the operation's success. Alexandrov was not a man who either accumulated or tallied favors, but this was a case where his sheer status promised a positive outcome.

"If it had been just Burago wanting to take him on as his student, they wouldn't have let him," Aleksei Verner, a student and coauthor of Alexandrov's, told me. "But they couldn't say no to Alexandrov." Valery Ryzhik, who was sitting next to Verner during this conversation, readily concurred and added that Alexandrov had personally told him what the letter had said, "that this was just the kind of exceptional situation when ethnicity should be ignored." Leaving aside the assumptions behind this recollection— particularly the idea that Alexandrov or Ryzhik or both believed that, ordinarily, ethnicity *should* be taken into account—what was really striking about this story was that it seemed that everyone in the Leningrad mathematics community was in on it. Everyone, that is, except Perelman.

"I was sure Grisha would have problems with admission," recalled Golovanov. "His papers said he was Jewish; mine, as it happened, did not. So the issue was taken up at the highest level, a level that at the time seemed beyond the clouds to me. That was pretty funny in itself. I mean, yes, Grisha is Grisha, but he was still just an aspiring graduate student. And here he had members of the Academy going to do battle for him."

Was Grisha engaged in the effort to get him into graduate school, I asked, or was he oblivious to it? "Being engaged and being oblivious are not the sole possibilities." Golovanov leaned back in his chair and, with a satisfied grin, reiterated a phrase he used continuously throughout our conversations: "Grisha is very smart, I keep repeating this. This is a statement that has no relationship to his mathematical talent, which is recognized by everyone. Grisha is a very smart person. That means I cannot imagine he was oblivious to the process. But I have to admit that we never talked about it at the time."

In other words, Golovanov and Perelman, who had known each other for more than ten years, who had received the bulk of their mathematical education side by side, and who were sitting together for their graduate-school admission exams (there were two: one in their chosen mathematical disciplines and one in the history of the Communist Party), diligently avoided discussing the elephant in the room. Golovanov's motivation was clear: he was an exaggeratedly polite man, almost painfully aware of his friend's potential sensitivities—and in 1987, he was also acutely aware of the unfair advantage he enjoyed simply because his documents did not label him Jewish. Perelman's behavior was also entirely in character. The system of graduate admissions, byzantine and discriminatory as it was, could not possibly have fit Perelman's view of the mathematics world as fair and meritocratic. He might have been not just unwilling but unable to talk about the uncertainty of his future in mathematics and the scheming undertaken to save it.

In effect, Perelman's approach to the graduate-admissions problem was a mirror image of Zalgaller's. The older man so loathed the idea of being indebted to anyone that he had removed himself from the corrupt and corrupting system, literally crossing himself off the list. Perelman, who similarly could not have entertained the idea of being indebted to someone, ignored the behind-the-scenes aspect of his graduate-admissions process, as though crossing out that part of the narrative. In the grand scheme of things as it had been imparted to him by his teachers, Perelman, of course, was right: the indignities to which the Soviet system subjected its scholars, especially the Jews among them, had no relationship to the practice of mathematics and could lay no claim to the mathematician's mind. Traditionally, in the second half of the twentieth century, Soviet mathematicians accepted that those who wished to practice mathematics as it ought to be practiced would be relegated to the world of unofficial mathematics, where they would have the scholarship without the perks. Those who belonged to the world of official mathematics got the office space and the salaries, the apartments apportioned by the Academy of Sciences, and even the occasional trip abroad—but had to abide the ideology, the discrimination, and the corruption. Perelman's totalizing mind could entertain no such dichotomy; he would practice mathematics the way it ought to be practiced in the place where it ought to be practiced—the Leningrad branch of the Steklov Mathematics Institute. The benevolence of colleagues who intervened on his behalf and the kindness of friends who did not push the issue in conversation allowed him to do just that: continue living in the world as he imagined it.

In the fall of 1987 Grigory Perelman became a graduate student at the Leningrad branch of the Steklov. Alexander Danilovich Alexandrov was officially listed as his dissertation adviser—making Perelman the last mathematician who would be so honored—but in fact Perelman took up residence in Burago's lab. No one knew this then, but there had never been a better time and place for a mathematician to start his research career.

Just over a year before Perelman graduated from Leningrad State University, Communist Party general secretary Mikhail Gorbachev announced a sweeping series of reforms, which he dubbed *perestroika*. At the end of 1986, physicist Andrei Sakharov, Nobel Peace Prize recipient and the Soviet Union's leading human rights activist, was allowed to return to Moscow from the city of Gorky, where he had been under house arrest. By early 1987, all Soviet political prisoners had reportedly been released. The year 1988, just after Perelman became a graduate student, saw the dawn of the era of glasnost, the Soviet intellectuals' brief golden age, when the readership of thick intellectual journals shot into the millions and a national public conversation about the future of Russia commenced. In 1989, the year Perelman wrote his dissertation, the entire country was glued to its TV screens watching the first semi-democratic elections and then the first open parliamentary debates that occurred in their lifetimes. So sweeping was the excitement of the time, not even someone as disdainful of politics as Perelman could resist the spirit entirely.

It was an extraordinary stroke of luck that Perelman began his career several years before the economic reforms of the early 1990s impoverished research institutions and condemned Russian academics to either precarious research-grant-to-research-grant existences or moorless lives of shuttling back and forth between teaching gigs abroad and research positions at home. In the late 1980s, in Golovanov's estimation, a graduate student's stipend still placed him "ten rubles a month above the salary level at which one could exist." At the same time, the most important change in how Soviet academic institutions worked was already under way: the Iron Curtain was lifting. Soviet scholars were starting to travel abroad, foreign researchers could come and go unimpeded, censorship of foreign academic journals was lifted (but the economic crisis had not yet caused library subscriptions to lapse), and communication through letters and phone calls became as accessible as it should have been all along. What this meant for institutions such as the Steklov was a daily sense that change and intellectual opportunity were in the air. What it meant for Perelman was that his path to membership in the international mathematical elite would be natural and straightforward—and his view of the world would not be challenged. Plus, he would meet Mikhail Gromov.

After a certain point, Mikhail Gromov's name becomes linked to just about every important thing that Perelman did. Everyone I interviewed to trace Perelman's trajectory past graduate school mentioned Gromov: he recommended Perelman for this or that academic position, he brought him to this conference, he coauthored a paper with him.

Zalgaller called Gromov "the best thing Leningrad University ever produced." Gromov defended his PhD dissertation there in 1968, at the age of twenty-five; his adviser was Vladimir Rokhlin, the topologist whom Alexander Danilovich Alexandrov had saved from persecution. Gromov, whose mother was Jewish, despaired of getting a research position at the Steklov or even a less desirable, to him, professorial appointment at Leningrad State, and in the late 1970s he emigrated to the United States, where he worked at the Courant Institute at New York University. Later, having established himself as one of the world's leading geometers, he started dividing his time between the Courant and the extraordinarily prestigious Institut des Hautes Études Scientifiques, outside of Paris.

I interviewed Gromov in Paris at the Institut Henri Poincaré, the part of the Université Pierre et Marie Curie reserved for conferences and seminars in mathematics and theoretical physics. So said the university's website and so said laminated signs placed on the large round wooden tables in the institute's cafeteria: RE-SERVED FOR THE USE OF MATHEMATICIANS AND THEORETI-CAL PHYSICISTS. As I arrived in the cafeteria, I saw Gromov engaged in an animated discussion with the American topologist Bruce Kleiner, whom I had interviewed in New York a couple of months earlier. Kleiner rose to leave when I approached the table but seemed too agitated by the discussion to say hello to me. Instead, he turned back to face Gromov and said that a science in which nothing had to be proved was no science at all. Gromov responded that an alternative system could still be consistent. "Have you ever talked to a street person?" Kleiner demanded, apparently infuriated. "They have some great ideas." I think he meant to say something about every crazy person having an internally consistent system to offer, but Kleiner had become too upset to articulate the idea. Gromov too became enraged, waving his arms and saying, "No, no!" He looked very much like a street person himself: his clothes hung loosely and awkwardly on his very thin frame; his black belted jeans were stained; his light green button-down shirt had thinned on the chest and frayed at the cuffs; and both his gray beard and his gray hair stuck out haphazardly in every direction.

Kleiner stomped off, and Gromov turned to me, apparently still irritated. First, he bristled at my questions about his reasons for leaving the Soviet Union. "Why not?" he asked, speaking Russian that was distinctly affected by the three decades he had spent away from the mother country. "Everyone was leaving, and I left too. I was offered a job in America and went there, and then I was offered a job here and came here." I already had enough information to know he was not exactly telling me the truth, but I also knew not to push: he was obviously in no mood to talk about the long-ago hardships of Jewish emigration from the Soviet Union.

"I understand you are the person who brought Perelman to the West," I attempted.

"I took part in it," Gromov responded, still annoyed. "But it was Burago's initiative."

"A lot of people have told me that you were the one who came and said there was this great new mathematician."

"Burago told me that. I may have mentioned it to other people."

"And what had Burago told you?"

"He said he had this good young mathematician."

"Who needed to be brought here?"

"Yes, it had to be arranged for him to come here."

Gromov arranged for Perelman to spend a few months at IHES as soon as he defended his dissertation at the Steklov in 1990. At IHES Perelman began working on Alexandrov spaces, a topological phenomenon named for Alexander Danilovich Alexandrov. The old man had abandoned this topic in the 1950s, but now three of his mathematical descendants—Burago, Gromov, and Perelman—had come together to work on it.

In 1991, Gromov helped bring Perelman to the Geometry Festival, an annual event held on the East Coast of the United States at a different location each year. That year it was at Duke University. Perelman gave a talk on Alexandrov spaces that the following year became his first major published work, coauthored with Gromov and Burago. Gromov mentioned Perelman to all the right people to ensure that he would be invited to do postdoctoral research in the United States.

As Gromov and I talked, I began to understand Gromov's motivation—or, rather, the depth of his commitment to the Perelman project. "When he entered geometry," Gromov said, "he was, at the time, the strongest geometer. Before he went underground, he was certainly the best in the world."

"What does that mean?"

"He did the best work," Gromov responded with perfect precision. I immediately remembered a joke told to me by a mathematician: A group of people taking a ride in a hot-air balloon get carried away by the wind. After drifting some distance, they spot a man below and shout to him, "Where are we?" The man, who happens to be a mathematician, responds, "You are in a hot-air balloon."

But as we talked more, I realized Gromov thought Perelman was actually the best *man* in the world—not just the best geometer, but the best human being involved in mathematics. Gromov compared Perelman to Isaac Newton, then immediately amended the comparison to say, "Newton was a rather bad person. Perelman is much better. He has some faults, but very few." His faults, Gromov explained, sometimes led him to attack his friends, but these conflicts were minor compared to Perelman's overwhelming natural goodness. "He has moral principles to which he holds. And this surprises people. They often say that he acts strange because he acts honest, in a nonconformist manner, which is unpopular in this community—even though it should be the norm. His main peculiarity is that he acts decently. He follows ideals that are tacitly accepted in science."

In other words, Perelman was what a mathematician—and a man—ought to be. Later that day I walked around Paris with a French mathematician and historian of science who bemoaned the state of French mathematics, the commercialization of science, and the unprincipled participation of people like Gromov who, this man claimed, stood by while IHES printed up vapid fundraising brochures. I realized that Gromov probably wished he could be as principled as Perelman, as resolutely removed from the institutionalization of mathematics, and as sincerely disdainful of empty recognition. Which was clearly why Gromov had adopted Perelman as a cause—and also why he resisted taking credit for having helped him.

So continued the line of Perelman's guardian angels: Rukshin shepherded him into competitive mathematics, Ryzhik coddled him through high school, Zalgaller nurtured his problem-solving skills at the university and handed him off to Alexandrov and Burago to ensure that he practiced mathematics uninterrupted and unimpeded. Burago passed him on to Gromov, who led him out into the world.

7

Round Trip

HAD GRIGORY PERELMAN been born ten or even five years earlier than he was, his career may well have ground to a halt around the time he finished writing his dissertation: it would have been difficult, if not outright impossible, for a Jew to defend his dissertation at the Steklov and stay on in a research position there; even the intervention of someone as influential as Alexander Danilovich Alexandrov might not have guaranteed success. Had Perelman been born ten or even five years later than he was, he might never have entered graduate school at all: State anti-Semitism would no longer have been an issue, but his family would likely have been unable to afford to keep him in school at a time when a graduate student's stipend barely bought three loaves of black bread. But Grisha Perelman was born at just the right time, and when he completed his dissertation, he was in exactly the right place: a country that was collapsing, which freed its citizens to travel abroad for the first time in seven decades. He belonged to the luckiest generation of Russian mathematicians. Like millions of other Soviet citizens, Perelman began a new life sometime around 1990, a life out in the world. So fortuitous was the timing of this change that Perelman might be forgiven for believing the world worked exactly as it should. Just when Perelman needed to broaden his circle of mathematical communication, the opportunities to do so presented themselves.

In this new part of Perelman's life, a new cast of characters appeared. Whether they knew it or not—and most likely they did not, for Perelman was as reserved with them as he was with most people—and whether he cared or not, they would play important roles in the development of his career. In addition to Gromov, these included Jeff Cheeger, Michael Anderson, Gang Tian, John Morgan, and Bruce Kleiner.

Cheeger is an important American mathematician, a generation older than Perelman. He works at the Courant, in a large sparse office in a high-rise building on the NYU campus. Like other American acquaintances of Perelman, Cheeger seemed to find him both sympathetic and inscrutable, if occasionally slightly infuriating, and he spoke carefully, hoping to avoid offending him. Cheeger recalled that he first heard about Perelman from Gromov: "He came back and mentioned that he had met this young fellow who was extraordinarily impressive." In 1991, Cheeger saw Perelman at the Geometry Festival at Duke. And then Perelman came to the Courant as a postdoctoral fellow in the fall of 1992. He was still working on Alexandrov spaces.

By the time Perelman arrived in the United States, he was twenty-six, no longer pudgy but tall and apparently fit. His beard had passed out of its extended awkward-tuft stage and was thick, black, and bushy. His hair was long. He did not believe in cutting hair or fingernails—some people thought they remembered his saying something about the unnaturalness of such trimming, but no one can vouch for this recollection and chances are at least as good that Perelman found the conventions of personal hygiene and appearance both taxing and unreasonable. "He was very, you know, known as eccentric," said Cheeger, citing the nails, the hair, the habit of wearing the same clothes every day—most notably a brown corduroy jacket—and his holding forth on the virtues of a particular kind of black bread that could be procured only from a Russian store in Brooklyn Beach, where Perelman walked from Manhattan.

Structurally, the life of a postdoc in the United States differed little from the life of a graduate student in Russia. Perelman was left largely to his own devices, but he apparently saw no reason not to spend most of his time at the Courant. The institute was conveniently located in a concrete-block tower as square and impersonal as anything that had been built in Russia in the previous thirty years. It looked out on Washington Square Park, a place as flat, geometrical, and ceremoniously architectural as any park in St. Petersburg or Paris, where Perelman had just spent several months. To complete his sense of familiarity, Perelman had to travel to the outer reaches of Brooklyn to get his bread and fermented milk—and by making the journey on foot, he ensured that he had both solitude and the usual measure of physical hardship. After a while, he had his mother waiting for him at the other end of the journey to Brooklyn; she had followed him to the United States and was staying with relatives in Brighton Beach. Within Courant Institute itself, Perelman did not find the social demands taxing; the typical regimen of mathematics seminars was accompanied by a familiar array of faces, since Gromov, Burago, and other St. Petersburg mathematicians were occasional residents there.

Perelman made a friend at Courant. I am not sure Gang Tian knew he was Perelman's friend, but Viktor Zalgaller, Perelman's old teacher in Israel, was certain he was. "He made a friend there, a young Chinese mathematician," he told me. "They suited each other." This they certainly did. I went to see Tian at the Institute for Advanced Study at Princeton, one of the world's most prestigious mathematical institutions, where Tian now occupied another cold concrete box. He spoke very softly and sadly, if not as reluctantly as Cheeger. He had already made the mistake of speaking to the media, and he believed this was why Grisha had not responded to his letters in several years. Tian did not think he and Perelman had been friends. "We talked quite often," he acknowledged, but it was all about math. "I don't think we talked much other than that. There are probably other people with whom he was friendly and talked more about other things. He did talk about bread. He somehow cared a lot about bread. He found a place to buy good bread in Brooklyn and near the Brooklyn Bridge." What kind of bread was it? I asked. "I'm not so sure," responded Tian, "because I'm not that fond of bread. I eat bread but I don't really care which one." Aside from the bread issue, Tian and Perelman really were perfect for each other: both were interested in little outside of mathematics, and their mathematical interests were shared.

It was with Tian that Perelman started going to lectures at the Institute for Advanced Study at Princeton. Cheeger came along too. During one of these visits Perelman surprised Cheeger by joining a game of volleyball after a lecture. "You look at him and think this is something he'd have no interest in or couldn't do," recalled Cheeger. "But I remember one time watching it, the game, and he said, you know, 'Well, I think I could do that.' And you know, he was pretty good." I nodded. My lack of surprise surprised Cheeger. I explained that Perelman had had to take part in numerous games of volleyball while he was training for the International Mathematical Olympiad as well as when he was at the math camps. Then Cheeger looked slightly annoyed. Even on this small score, he had been misled by Perelman's habit of underplaying both his abilities and his interest. This was, of course, the same man who later told no one he was working on the Poincaré Conjecture and who posted his solution on the Internet without claiming it was in fact the solution. It was only after someone asked him if he had proved the conjecture that he said he had. Most likely, if Cheeger had asked him directly whether he had had much volleyball practice, Perelman would have said yes. He still believed in telling the entire truth—but only when asked. He just didn't see the utility of volunteering information, especially information about himself. I suspect he also took some pleasure in demonstrating that he could solve any problem he picked—even a game of volleyball.

Another Perelman incident that surprised Cheeger during the New York period was harder to explain. In 1993 Cheeger and Gromov went to a conference in Israel that had been convened in part to celebrate their fiftieth birthdays. Perelman came, as did his mother—but that was not what surprised Cheeger. What he found startling was that he saw Perelman renting a car at the airport, using a credit card. I have talked to no one else who ever witnessed Perelman drive a car—indeed, some people claimed he rejected cars as "unnatural"—but it is conceivable he could have obtained a driver's license and a credit card during his first semester in New York. The reason he might have done this was that, for a fleeting moment, Perelman seems to have planned to move permanently to the United States.

"You see, it often happens that when someone crosses the border with Russia in any direction, he has a very strong reaction," Golovanov explained to me. "In Grisha's case, it was the only time he experienced something resembling political enthusiasm. As soon as he ended up there, he started sending letters decreeing that the entire family had to move." The entirety of the family remaining in St. Petersburg at this time was Grisha's younger sister,

Lena, who had just graduated from high school. Their father had emigrated to Israel, and their mother was in New York hovering over Grisha, so in essence, he was campaigning for his sister to go to college in the United States. Lena decided to move to Israel, where she obtained her PhD in mathematics from the Weizmann Institute in 2004.

To the best of Golovanov's recollection, Perelman did not try to make a case for the move: he "decreed" it, as Golovanov put it, in accordance with his understanding of his role in the family, which was to "know what is right." Making an argument to his little sister may also have seemed to him to be beneath his dignity or, in any case, a waste of time. When he talked to colleagues, however, he made the argument that Western mathematicians, while suffering from too narrow a focus compared with their Russian counter-parts, organized their research more effectively and accomplished more. This may have been a classic solipsism, for in 1993 Perelman did exactly what postdoctoral researchers who are unencumbered by formal academic obligations and are at the height of their cre-ative and mental abilities are supposed to do at that stage in their lives: he solved an important long-standing problem, and he did it in a way that, to mathematicians, possessed breathtaking beauty.

Twenty years before Perelman arrived at Courant, Cheeger and his coauthor Detlef Gromoll had published a paper outlining a way of deducing the properties of certain mathematical objects from small regions of these objects, which they called the *soul* of the ob-jects, for, like the imaginary human soul, the imaginary soul of the imaginary mathematical object also possessed all the qualities that made the whole what it was. Cheeger and Gromoll proved part of what they set out to show, and this became known as the Soul Theorem, but they could only suppose the rest, and this became known as the Soul Conjecture. It remained a conjecture—that is, a mathematical supposition without proof—until Perelman showed that it was true. His paper was four pages long.

"It seemed to be extraordinarily hard," Cheeger told me. "At least a couple of people had written very long and technical papers on it. And they only proved part of it. And he realized that everyone had been missing the point, you could say. And he made a very short proof of it. He used something—something nontrivial, but something that had been in the public domain since the late seventies."

This was the trick Perelman's friends at the math club had called his "stick": absorbing the problem in its entirety and then boiling it down to an essence that proved simpler than everyone had assumed. "Part of it was that the problem was not as difficult as people had thought it was," Cheeger continued. "Part of it was, you could say, the force of his personality. I mean when you talked to him it was clear you were dealing with an unusually penetrating and powerful mind. A personality that's very forceful in a certain direction, very believing in his own insights. You could say almost stubborn in a way, not aggressive, but you could almost say a little arrogant."

You could certainly say that. Cheeger encountered this aspect of Perelman's personality when he tried to convince the younger mathematician to expand one of his papers to allow more exposition of his ideas. "One of the papers he wrote while he was here was very short; it was a mixture of power and arrogance. It was very striking. I read it and admired it a lot. But I felt it was a little bit too terse, a little bit not making the insights as manifest as they could be. So I said this to him and he said he would consider it. But I couldn't really get him to change. I don't know. Have you seen the film *Amadeus*?" The scene Cheeger was recalling was the one in which Mozart presents an opera he has written and the emperor suggests the piece is wonderful but not perfect: it has too many notes. "Just cut a few and it will be perfect," he says. "Which few did you have in mind, Majesty?" responds Mozart. By 1992, Perelman was apparently quite certain he was the Mozart of contemporary mathematics. No one, not even an outstanding mathematician twenty-three years his senior, was going to tell him what to do or how to present his ideas to the world.

For the spring semester of 1993, Perelman went to the State University of New York's Stony Brook campus—one of the best American graduate programs in mathematics. Located just sixty-five miles from New York City, Stony Brook was probably as different from St. Petersburg and New York as any place Perelman had ever visited. Its architecture was square, and its landscape consisted of parking lots, low buildings, and large fields. Its railroad station was a tiny two-room structure across the tracks from campus. To an outsider—and Perelman would always be an outsider, wherever he went—it must have felt utterly desolate.

Mike Anderson, a geometer Perelman had met earlier—currently the director of SUNY Stony Brook's graduate math program —helped Perelman find an apartment. Perelman's criteria were "quiet and small," and he found a studio apartment that cost roughly three hundred dollars a month. He slept on a futon he borrowed from the Andersons. The pay for a postdoc at the time was about thirty-five to forty thousand dollars a year, and Perelman, who lived on bread and yogurt, put most of that money away in his bank account. His mother stayed in Brooklyn but came to visit frequently.

Perelman continued to wear the same brown corduroy jacket. People continued to notice his long hair and fingernails. His personal hygiene may have deteriorated slightly; he gave the impression of someone who bathed regularly, but the futon on which he slept took on a smell so strong that the Andersons had to throw it out when he returned it. His extraordinary long nails, however, remained clean.

Perelman taught a course on Alexandrov geometry. The following summer, he traveled to Zurich to speak on Alexandrov spaces at the International Congress of Mathematicians. It was a prestigious opportunity; the congress took place just once every four years, and that year only fifty-five of the world's top mathematicians, most of them significantly older than Perelman, had been invited to speak—four Fields Medalists, past and future, among them. With his proof of the Soul Conjecture, Perelman had become an undisputed young star. In Zurich, he spoke on the paper he had coauthored with Gromov and Burago. His first talk at the congress probably attracted people who wanted to see the twenty-eight-year-old who, if Gromov was to be believed, was doing the best work in the world in his field. But Perelman apparently exhibited the worst of his public-speaking habits during the talk. He started by sketching something on the board and then began pacing back and forth as he talked. His speech seemed vague and disconnected and essentially incomprehensible.

If Perelman was true to his habit of describing his personal relationship with the problem rather than the problem itself, it might explain why his Zurich talk was a disaster. He had lectured on this paper before—at the Geometry Festival at Duke in 1991, and at a couple of American universities immediately following the festival. He had been clear at the time—as the geometer Bruce Kleiner, who heard him speak at both Duke and the University of Pennsylvania that year, recalled, it was obvious that "the mathematics was very, very good." But by 1994, his relationship with Alexandrov spaces had grown complicated.

After a semester at Stony Brook, in the fall of 1993, Perelman moved to the West Coast to take up a two-year Miller Fellowship—an enviable position at the University of California at Berkeley that offered generous funding for research in one of the basic sciences without any teaching responsibilities. In fact, the conditions of the fellowship stated explicitly that fellows were "granted more independence than other postdocs on campus" and could participate in the lives of their host departments as much or as little as they desired. This was the kind of setting for which Perelman had been raised by his early mathematical mentors—the kind of setting he had praised in his conversations with Russian colleagues—but it did not work. Or something didn't work. Perelman had been trying to press on with Alexandrov spaces, and he had gotten stuck.

"That's normal," Gromov told me. "Out of everything you try, most things don't work out. That's just the way life is." Gromov might have been talking about life in mathematics or life in general, but in either case, he was speaking from experience, which Perelman, even in his late twenties, simply did not have. Improbably, with the possible exception of his second-place showing at the All-Soviet Math Olympiad at the age of fourteen, he had never failed to accomplish what he had set out to accomplish, or to receive what he was due, or to solve a problem he had taken on. Moreover, all the hours of practice and all the behind-the-scenes anxiety and intrigue notwithstanding, in the eyes of observers, he had accomplished everything with ease. At this point, following the Soul Conjecture proof and the international congress, he had more mathematical eyes trained on him than ever before—and he was facing the unfamiliar experience of failure.

Kleiner spent the 1993–1994 academic year at Berkeley too, and he and Perelman "had several math conversations during that year," he recalled. Perelman occasionally ventured into areas adjacent to Alexandrov spaces. He talked about the Geometrization Conjecture, a long-unsolved problem that included the Poincaré Conjecture; that is, if someone proved Geometrization, Poincaré would also be proved along the way. He talked about the possibility

of applying Alexandrov spaces to Geometrization, and "there was
no obvious way or scheme," said Kleiner. Perelman also considered
dipping into Ricci flow, an approach invented by another mathematician to prove the Poincaré Conjecture—but that mathematician had himself gotten stuck years before. Perelman wondered
out loud whether Ricci flow might be applied usefully to Alexandrov spaces. Had there been any indication that Perelman might
actually take up the Poincaré and Geometrization conjectures? No
—but, recalled Kleiner, "he was not very open about what exactly
he was working on or thinking about. He was no more reticent
than many people would be in a similar situation. It's not necessarily a good idea to share your ideas openly because, unless you really
know the person and trust them, they could start working on it
themselves or they could pass information on to a third party who
might start working on it. You'll find someone competing against
you using your same ideas, which is not a very comfortable situation." Kleiner's own area of research lay quite near Perelman's, so
Perelman's reticence seemed reasonable to him.

But there was probably another reason for the reticence, one
that Perelman articulated in a conversation with Cheeger in 1995.
As Cheeger recalled, Perelman stopped by his office while he was
briefly in New York City and they discussed some issues related to
Alexandrov spaces but not to the specific aspects Perelman had
studied in the past. This time, however, Perelman was very interested and even referred to one of the questions as the "holy grail"
of the subject. "And I ask him, 'Didn't you say you had no interest
in it?'" Cheeger recalled. "And he said, 'Well, whether a problem is
interesting depends on whether there's any chance of solving it.'"
As pompous as that statement sounds, Perelman was probably telling an important emotional truth about himself: he could become
engaged with a problem only if he could fully grasp it—and if he
grasped a problem fully, down to the nature of every minute tech-

nical complication, he could certainly solve it. What had happened between Perelman and Alexandrov spaces was that he had come up against technical difficulties he could not penetrate, and so he had grown emotionally disengaged. Hence the nebulous, rambling talk at the congress.

Perelman's term as a Miller Fellow ended in the spring of 1995. His paper on the Soul Conjecture had come out the previous year, and he had spoken at the International Congress of Mathematicians, so it is not surprising that even though he put no effort into securing an academic position after Berkeley, he was courted by several leading institutions. He turned all of them down, and the way he did it—specifically, the way he rejected Princeton—has become part of American and Russian mathematical lore. I had heard about it on both sides of the Atlantic before I asked one of the immediate participants what had happened, and his account differed little from what I had been told.

Peter Sarnak, a Princeton professor who became chair of the mathematics department in 1996, first heard of Perelman from Gromov, who, Sarnak recalled in an e-mail message, had said Perelman was "exceptionally good." In the winter of 1994–1995, Perelman came to Princeton to give a talk on his proof of the Soul Conjecture. Few people showed up, but the math department's brass was there: distinguished professor John Mather, then–department chair Simon Kochen, and Sarnak all attended. Perelman gave a great lecture: clear, precise, and engaging—probably because his personal relationship with the Soul Conjecture had been brief and satisfying and was resolved. "After the lecture the three of us approached Perelman saying we would like to arrange for him to come to Princeton as an assistant professor," recalled Sarnak. Legend has it—though Sarnak did not remember it—that at this point Perelman asked why they would want to bring him to Princeton when no one there was interested in his areas of research—an impression perhaps intensified by the nearly empty auditorium and which, Sarnak acknowledged, was an accurate reflection of the situation, "which we were eager to change." Sarnak remembered Perelman making clear "that he wanted a tenured position, to which we responded that we would have to look into that and in any case we need some information from him such as a CV. He was surprised by the latter, saying something like 'you have heard my lecture, why would you need any more information?' Given that he wasn't interested in a tenure track position we didn't pursue this any further. History has proven that we made a mistake in not being more aggressive in recruiting him."

Perelman told several people at the time that he would settle for nothing less than immediate tenure—an audacious position for a twenty-nine-year-old mathematician with few publications and only a semester's worth of teaching experience. But Perelman's own logic was impeccable. He was not out looking for work, so the job offers were coming from institutions—or, rather, people—who, as Cheeger put it, "knew how terrific he was." In other words, they knew what Perelman and Gromov knew: that he was the best in the world. Why, then, would they want to put him through the conventional paces of earning his full professorship? Why even make him submit his CV before they offered him his well-deserved job? It would not have occurred to Perelman that his well-intentioned interlocutors did not perceive his place in the mathematical hierarchy quite the same way he did and simply did not realize that his would be a star presence in any university mathematics department. Or his insistence on immediate tenure might merely have been a way of setting the bar so high as to cut off any further discussion of his staying in the United States. The University of Tel Aviv, where Perelman's sister was by then a student, actually offered him a full professorship, and Perelman, as Cheeger recalled, "ended up turning them down or not responding at all." So Sarnak might take some consolation in the knowledge that even if Princeton had been more aggressive, it probably would not have succeeded in drawing Perelman.

Getting ready to return to Russia, Perelman told his American colleagues he could work better back home—the exact opposite of what he had told his family in Russia three years earlier but in all likelihood the exact same sort of solipsism. Back when breakthroughs came easily to him, his American environment had seemed to be on his side; now that he was stuck, a return to Russia held the promise of rejuvenation, a renewed ability to work. What it was he was working on, no one knew. The questions he asked Cheeger when he was passing through New York on his way to St. Petersburg in 1995 seemed to indicate he was broadening his focus on Alexandrov spaces—in a way that, in retrospect, may have meant he was edging closer to tackling the Poincaré Conjecture.

Back in St. Petersburg, Perelman took up residence in Kupchino with his mother and reclaimed his spot in Burago's laboratory at the Steklov Institute. He would not have any teaching responsibilities—or, for that matter, any obligations at all. By the mid-1990s, institutions of the Russian Academy of Sciences had fallen into physical disrepair and organizational chaos. Researchers no longer had to submit regular reports on their work or account for their time in any way; institute rolls gradually filled up with dead souls —or, in any case, long-absent émigré souls. Buildings, which had been maintained at architectural subsistence levels in the Soviet era, literally began to crumble after about five years of neglect. The Steklov building in St. Petersburg, a once-lovely low-rise structure on the Fontanka River in the very center of town, grew increasingly cold and drafty. Researchers' salaries were so far out of sync with inflation as to be laughable; many people did not even bother showing up at their institutes to pick up the wads of worthless cash that was their pay. They sought sources of income elsewhere —mostly in the West, where many stayed all the time while others created complicated schedules of semester-on/semester-off teaching. But none of this bothered Perelman. At the institute, there was heat, and there was electricity, and the phone lines worked—most days, anyway. At home, his mother catered to his ascetic needs. The subway continued to run from the center of town to Kupchino. And Perelman had saved tens of thousands of dollars while he was in the United States; in 1995, a family of two in St. Petersburg could live well enough on less than a hundred dollars a month. It seemed he would never again have to worry about anything but mathematics. With the distraction of exams, competitions, dissertation, and teaching behind him, he would lead the life he had been raised to live: the life of the pure mathematician.

Whatever patience he had once had for distractions was now gone. In 1996, the European Mathematical Society held its second quadrennial congress in Budapest and awarded prizes to mathematicians under the age of thirty-two. Gromov, Burago, and St. Petersburg Mathematical Society president Anatoly Vershik submitted Perelman's name for his work on Alexandrov spaces. "I was always interested in making sure that our young mathematicians looked good," Vershik explained to me. "They decided to award it to him, but as soon as he learned about it—I don't remember whether I was the one who told him or if it was someone else—he said he did not want it and would not accept it. And he said that he would create a scandal if it was announced that he was a recipient of this prize. I was very surprised and very upset. He had in fact known that he was up for the award and had said nothing about this. I had to have some emergency communication with the chairman of the prize committee, who was an acquaintance of mine, to make sure they did not announce the prize."

A dozen years after the incident, Vershik, a soft-spoken, bearded

man in his early seventies, still seemed to feel betrayed by Perelman's behavior. He told me he would rather refrain from trying to
find the reason for Perelman's rejection of the prize. If Perelman
was opposed to prizes on principle, this was news to Vershik: in
the very early 1990s the Mathematical Society had awarded Perelman a prize, which Perelman had accepted; he even gave a talk on
the occasion. Later Perelman apparently told someone that the
European Mathematical Society had no one who was qualified to
judge his work, but Vershik did not recall hearing anything of the
sort then—and with Gromov and Burago on board, that would
have seemed an odd argument. "He did say one thing to me at the
time, and it actually sounded convincing. He said the work was not
complete. But I said there were reviewers and the jury had decided
he deserved the prize." Still, the idea that anyone might be better
suited than he was to judge whether a paper of his deserved a prize
could only have infuriated Perelman.

Unlike Vershik, Gromov thought Perelman's behavior entirely
acceptable, even though Gromov had been one of the three mathematicians who had submitted Perelman's name for the prize. "He
believes he is the one who decides when he should be getting a
prize and when he should not be," Gromov told me quite simply.
"So he decided that he had not fulfilled his program and they can
just take their prize and stuff it. And, of course, he also wanted to
show off." Or at least show that he wanted to be left alone.

He continued to accept invitations to take part in mathematical
community events, especially ones involving children. Apparently
this was not so much because he had any affection for children as
it was that he had respect for the tradition of the clubs and competitions in which he had been reared. But Perelman grew increasingly resistant to entertaining any questions concerning his projects. His American colleagues soon discovered he did not answer
e-mail messages. In 1996, Kleiner went to St. Petersburg for a con-

ference on Alexandrov spaces that Perelman also attended. Even though the two men had had a few mathematical conversations at Berkeley a couple of years earlier, Kleiner could not find a way to approach Perelman with questions about his current research. A friend of Kleiner's, a German mathematician named Bernhard Leeb, who had met Perelman at the International Mathematical Olympiad, did manage to ask a question—but not to get an answer. As Kleiner recalled twelve years later, Perelman said to him, "I don't want to tell you." Leeb's own recollection differed in tone if not substance. "I did ask him what he was working on," he wrote to me. "He told me that he would be working on some topic in geometry but he did not want to become specific. I find this attitude very reasonable. If one is working on a big problem like the Poincaré Conjecture, one is well advised to be extremely reluctant to talk about it."

No one knew what was occupying Perelman's mind. Even Gromov heard nothing from him and assumed he was still stuck on Alexandrov spaces—in other words, that he had joined the sizable ranks of talented mathematicians who did brilliant early work and then disappeared into the black hole of some impossible problem.

In February 2000, Mike Anderson at Stony Brook suddenly received an e-mail message from Perelman. "Dear Mike," it began. "I've just read your paper on generalised Lichnerovicz thm, and there is one point in your paper that disturbs me." Perelman went on to describe the nature of his doubts in one long, perfectly constructed sentence and finished with: "Am I missing something? Best regards, Grisha." There were no unnecessary niceties one might expect in a letter like this—nothing along the lines of "I hope this finds you well" or "It has been a long time." But the letter was perfectly polite, and Perelman's English—presumably disused for more than five years—all but impeccable.

Anderson responded the next day with a letter that by the standards of the mathematical world was downright effusive:

Dear Grisha,

It was a surprise to hear from you again—a pleasant surprise. I often ask people who I see from St. Petersburg if they know how you are and what you are thinking about these days.

I just returned from a short trip, and so haven't been able to think yet in detail about your remarks on my stationary paper. But I see your points, and agree I have made an error here. I don't think these two errors effect [sic] the results, and that the proofs require only minor modifications. I will think this through in the next couple of days and report back to you.

I'd also like to hear how you are, and what kind of mathematical or other issues you are concerned about these days.

Best regards to you,

Mike

Three days later, Anderson sent Perelman a more detailed e-mail message, outlining a fix for the mistakes Perelman had found. Again, he inserted a note of personal and professional interest: "I thank you very much for spotting these errors. Are you becoming interesting [sic] in these areas yourself?" Anderson also complained that so few people were working in his area—geometrization—that he had no one to double-check his ideas. He asked if Perelman had looked at his other two papers on related topics.

Perelman replied the next day. He thanked Anderson for his prompt response but ignored every single one of his questions. He wrote only that Anderson's paper had drawn his attention because it was "tangentially related" to Perelman's own current interests —and also, he noted, because it was short. He did not invite further communication. Nor did he promise he would look at Anderson's other papers—he wrote that he had them but had not read them. In fact, it seems likely that he subsequently read the papers but, finding no errors, saw no reason to write to Anderson again.

Anderson still tried to pursue the dialogue. He sent Perelman a file containing a more detailed fix for his paper. Perelman responded by saying he could not open the file without somebody's help ("I do not know computers at all," he claimed) and explained that his sister had helped print out the original Anderson papers when he visited her in Rehovot, where she was a graduate student. He proceeded to write that sending the file to a Steklov computer to open there might make it accessible to other people, so in the end he would rather wait until Anderson published the paper. In other words, he had gotten all he needed from this exchange with his colleague.

The message was a curious document in other respects. It seems that in the five years since leaving the United States, Perelman had drifted far from the practical aspects even of mathematics: he didn't seem to know how to use his office computer to log onto the SUNY e-mail account he used to correspond with Anderson or how to forward the file to a Web-based address no one else could access. At the same time, Perelman was using his lack of technical expertise to close the conversation, which had evidently outworn its usefulness to him. After all, when he actually needed Anderson's preprints, he had been resourceful enough to ask his sister for help. It is remarkable too how casually Perelman shared the details of his life and his sister's. It was never his intention to hide his family life or refuse to discuss himself or his relatives; it was just very rarely relevant to any conversation he found worth having.

It would be two and a half years before Mike Anderson heard from Perelman again.

8

The Problem

THE VERY POSSIBILITY of mathematical science seems an insoluble contradiction." So, more than a century ago, wrote Henri Poincaré, known among mathematicians as the last universalist, for he excelled in all areas of mathematics. If the objects of study are confined to the imagination, "from whence is derived that perfect rigor which is challenged by none?" And when rules of formal logic have replaced the experiment, "how is it that mathematics is not reduced to a gigantic tautology?" Finally, "are we then to admit that . . . all the theorems with which so many volumes are filled are only indirect ways of saying that A is A?"

Poincaré went on to explain that mathematics was a science because its reasoning traveled from the particular to the general. A mathematician who conducted his mental experiments with sufficient rigor could derive the rules that governed the rest of the imaginary terrain he shared with other mathematicians. In other words, he not only proved that A was A but also explained what made A quintessentially an A and where other A's might be found or how they might be constructed. "We know what it is to be in love or to feel pain, and we don't need precise definitions to communicate," wrote an American mathematics professor who, after authoring many academic books, undertook to explain topology to a general audience. "The objects of mathematics lie outside common experience, however. If one doesn't define these objects carefully, one cannot manipulate them meaningfully or talk to others about them." This may or may not be so. Most of us are, in fact, perfectly satisfied with our casual understandings of distances long and short, of slopes smooth and steep, and of lines and circles and spheres. We're satisfied with a gut feeling that puncturing a hole can sometimes but not always change the nature of an object— that is, a punctured balloon is entirely different from an intact one, while, say, a jelly-filled doughnut without a hole is, to us, essentially similar to a doughnut with a hole in the middle, with or without jelly. All of these things are in their simplest forms parts of our common experience. But in the disjointed world of the mathematician, shifting understandings and imprecise coordinates muddle the picture intolerably. In his world, nothing is like anything else unless proven similar; nothing is familiar until thoroughly defined; nothing—or very nearly nothing—is self-evident.

At the dawn of mathematics, Euclid attempted to start with things that were self-evident. He began his *Elements* with thirty-five definitions, five postulates, and five common notions, or axioms. Definitions ranged from that of a point ("that which has no parts, or which has no magnitude") to that of parallel straight lines ("such as are in the same plane, and which being produced ever so far do not meet"). Then he made a series of statements such as "things that are equal to the same thing are equal to one another." And the five postulates were:

1. "A straight line may be drawn from any one point to any other point" (interpreted to mean that only one straight line may be drawn from any point to any other).
2. "A terminated straight line may be produced at any length in a straight line" (in other words, a segment may be extended indefinitely into a straight line).
3. "A circle may be described at any center, at any distance from that center."
4. "All right angles equal one another."
5. "If a straight line falling on two straight lines makes the interior angles on the same side less than two right angles, the two straight lines, if produced indefinitely, meet on that side on which are the angles less than the two right angles."

To a true classifier, even these five statements take too much for granted. "I had been told that Euclid proved things, and was much disappointed that he started with axioms," wrote Bertrand Russell of his first childhood encounter with the *Elements*. "At first, I refused to accept them unless my brother could offer me some reason for doing so, but he said, 'If you don't accept them, we cannot go on,' and so, as I wished to go on, I reluctantly admitted them."

As a place to start, the first four postulates struck Euclid, his contemporaries, and the generations of mathematicians to follow as indeed self-evident. Since they are confined to a space we can not only visualize but actually *see*, the postulates could be checked empirically by drawing with a straightedge or a compass or by stretching a piece of string. As a segment grew in length or a circle in radius, even past the point where a human eye might be able to grasp it, it would not change essentially, and this was as close as anything could get to being obvious and not requiring further proof. But the fifth postulate made claims on the imagination. It said that if two lines were not parallel, they had to cross eventually.

Conversely, it said that two parallel lines would never cross, no matter how far they traveled. It was also interpreted to mean that for any straight line, only one parallel could be drawn through any given point not on the original line. This was not obvious; it could not be verified. And because it could not be verified, it had to be proved. For centuries mathematicians struggled to find proof of this claim, and found none.

The eighteenth century saw two mathematicians' attempts to prove the fifth postulate by first assuming that it was not correct. The objective of such an exercise is to build on an assumption until it grows evidently absurd, thereby debunking the original premise. But the examples failed to show themselves wrong; the exercises produced internally consistent pictures that settled in the imagination quite comfortably and quite separately from Euclid's fifth. Both mathematicians deemed this ridiculous and abandoned their efforts. After another century, three different mathematicians—the Russian Nikolai Lobachevski, the Hungarian János Bolyai, and his teacher the German Johann Karl Friedrich Gauss—decided that other, non-Euclidean geometries could exist where four of the postulates obtained but the fifth did not. But what does it mean that they *could* exist? Do they exist? They do, as long as mathematicians can find no holes or, rather, internal contradictions in them. Can we see them the same way we can see a line segment and a circle? Sure, no less and no more than we can see a strictly Euclidean geometry. So how do we know which is right? The great American mathematician Richard Courant (for whom the Courant Institute of Mathematical Sciences at New York University is named) and his coauthor Herbert Robbins, then a professor at Rutgers University, wrote that for our purposes it did not matter and we might as well choose Euclid: "Since the Euclidean system is rather simpler to deal with, we are justified in using it exclusively as long as fairly small distances (of a few million miles!) are under consideration. But we should not necessarily expect it to be suitable for describing the universe as a whole."

But how about describing a small piece of the universe? Say, the planet Earth. Or an apple. Remember this for future reference: the Earth and an apple are essentially the same. Let us think about the surface of the Earth, or of an apple, as the plane we are studying. Take an apple and draw a triangle on it. Now, if Euclidean geometry obtained for the surface of the apple, the sum of the angles of this triangle would equal 180 degrees. But because the surface of the apple is curved, the sum of the angles of the triangle is greater. This would mean that the fifth postulate is not true for this surface. Indeed, it is easy to see that on this surface, any two straight lines—a straight line being the extension of a segment that connects two points in the shortest possible way—will cross. All straight lines on the apple, or on the Earth, are "great circles" with their centers at the center of the sphere.

It was the nineteenth-century German mathematician Bernhard Riemann who developed a geometry of curved spaces, where straight lines are called geodesics and any two of them will cross. The geometry is called elliptic, or simply Riemannian, geometry, and it is the geometry used in Einstein's general theory of relativity.

Euclid's world, limited to his immediate surroundings, was, for all intents and purposes, flat. Our world is curved. Humans now routinely travel distances great enough to make the curvature of the Earth part of our lived experience. Not all of us travel so far all the time, but in the imagination—the very place where mathematics resides—the shortest distance between two points is the trajectory described by an airplane, which generally lies along a geodesic, even if we have never heard the word. These straight lines do not go on forever but, being circles, inevitably close in on themselves. And, of course, they cross, any two of them. What seemed absurd in the eighteenth century is now an accurate reflection of the way we experience the world.

In other words, our world has grown bigger. But that raises two questions: How much bigger can it get? and What does *bigger* mean? Here, allow me formally to introduce topology, an area of mathematics born in St. Petersburg in 1736, when the Swiss mathematician Leonhard Euler, who was teaching there, freed geometry of the burden of measuring distances. He published a paper on the solution to the Königsberg bridge problem, which had been posed by the mayor of the eponymous city, who had wanted Euler to devise a walking tour that would have an individual pass through each of Königsberg's seven bridges exactly once. Euler concluded that this could not be done. He also showed, first, that in any city with bridges, such a walking tour could be designed if and only if an odd number of bridges led to two areas of the town or to no areas, and, second, that it could not be designed if an odd number of bridges led to one area or to more than two. The third thing that Euler did while solving a problem where locations, not distances, were important was herald a new area of mathematics, which he termed "geometry of position."

In this new discipline, size—distance—in the familiar sense of the word did not matter. The number of steps that made up the walking tour made no difference; it was the way these steps were taken. What made an object lesser or greater in this new field was the amount of information required to locate it; to be precise, it was the number of coordinates needed to describe it. A single point has dimension zero; a line segment has one dimension; the surface of something such as a triangle or a square or a sphere has two dimensions. That is correct: the surface of something that we envision as flat and the surface of something that we envision as solid are, for the purposes of topology, the same. This is because when topologists talk about the surface of a sphere, or, say, an apple, they mean *just* the surface, with no regard for the solid internal space of the apple. Put another way, a topologist is like a tiny bug crawling on the apple, or like Euclid walking on the Earth: neither the bug nor Euclid has much reason to suspect that a triangle he describes will have angles amounting in sum to more than 180 degrees or that the straight line he is walking will not go on forever but will eventually close in on itself, describing a great circle. The curved nature of the surface is a function of the third dimension, of which neither of them has any experience.

We modern humans, who know firsthand that the Earth is a sphere and that its surface is therefore curved, live in three dimensions. But there is a fourth dimension—we know there is—and it is called time. We cannot move ourselves back and forth in time, so we cannot observe our three-dimensional habitat the way we can observe, by being lifted up into the air, the two-dimensional habitat of lesser animals. We are reduced to exploring the space that surrounds us and making guesses as to what it would look like from a vantage point we can suggest but cannot experience or, really, imagine. This is the nature of the Poincaré Conjecture: the last universalist supposed that the universe was shaped like a sphere—a three-dimensional sphere.

The young mathematician who gave me topology lessons for this book—who watched as I painfully tried to wrap my mind, like so many tight rubber bands, around the basic concepts of topology —cringed whenever he encountered references to the Poincaré Conjecture describing the shape of the universe. It would be more accurate to state that the proof of the Poincaré Conjecture will probably aid science greatly in learning the shape and properties of the universe, but this was not the issue Grigory Perelman tackled: he attacked a simply stated, much discussed mathematical problem that had gone unsolved for more than a century. Just like my young tutor and many other mathematicians I met along the way, he emphatically did not care about the physical shape of the universe or the experience of people who inhabited it; mathematics had given him the liberty to live among abstract objects in his own imagination, which was exactly where this problem had to be solved.

In 1904 Henri Poincaré published a paper on three-dimensional manifolds. What is a manifold? It is an object, or a space, existing in the mathematician's imagination—whether or not something like it can actually be observed in reality—that can be divided into many neighborhoods. Each neighborhood, taken separately, has a basic Euclidean geometry or can be explained through it, but all the neighborhoods together may add up to something much more complicated. The best example of a manifold is the Earth as portrayed through a series of maps, each showing only a small part of its surface. Imagine a map of Manhattan, for example: its Euclidean nature is obvious. When maps are put together in an atlas, their parallel lines continue not to cross and their triangles maintain their 180-degree nature. But if we used the maps to try to replicate the actual surface of the Earth, we would start with something that looked like a many-many-faceted disco ball, and then we would smooth out the edges and ultimately get a globe that reflected the Earth's curved complexity—and if we extended Manhattan's First Avenue and Second Avenue, they would cross. These concepts—*maps, atlases,* and *manifolds*—are basic to topology.

What makes one manifold different from another is its having a hole, or more than one hole. To a topologist, a ball, a box, a bun, and a blob are essentially the same. But a bagel is different. The key to this is the rubber band, an instrument as important to the topological imagination as the atlas. The imaginary rubber band is placed around the imaginary object and allowed to do its rubber-band thing, which is contract. If a rubber band—a very tight rubber band—is placed around a ball, it will find a way to contract and slip off the ball. It is significant that this will happen no matter where on the ball the band is placed. A bagel, however, is different: if one end of your imaginary rubber band has been threaded through the hole in the bagel and then reconnected to itself, it will stay around the bagel, never slipping off no matter how tight it is. A rubber band can be slipped off any place on a ball, a box, a bun, or a blob without a hole, which makes them all essentially similar or, in the language of topology, diffeomorphic to one another. This means you can reshape any one of them into any other and then back again.

This more or less brings us to the point where we can understand the Poincaré Conjecture. A bit more than a hundred years ago, Poincaré posed an innocent-sounding question: if a three-dimensional manifold is smooth and simply connected, then is it diffeomorphic to a three-dimensional sphere? *Smooth* means that the manifold is not twisted (you can imagine that twisting something would cause some problems with the papering-over map project). *Simply connected* means that it has no holes. And we know what *diffeomorphic* means. We also know what *three-dimensional* means: a three-dimensional manifold is the surface of a four-dimensional object. Let us also pause to consider what a *sphere* is. A sphere is a collection of points that are all equally far from a given point—the center. A one-dimensional sphere (a circumference in regular school geometry) is all of these points in a two-dimensional space (a plane). A two-dimensional sphere (the surface of a ball) is all of these points in a three-dimensional space. What makes spheres particularly interesting to topologists is that they belong to a category called hypersurfaces—objects that have as many dimensions as is possible in a given space (one dimension in a two-dimensional space, two dimensions in a three-dimensional space, and so on). The three-dimensional sphere that so interested Poincaré was the surface of a four-dimensional ball. We cannot imagine this thing, but we just might inhabit it.

Topologists often tackle problems by trying to solve them for a different number of dimensions. The equivalent of the Poincaré Conjecture for two dimensions—the understanding that the surfaces of a ball, a box, a bun, and a blob without a hole are essentially the same—is basic to topology. But in three dimensions—when we actually get to the conjecture itself—it gets tricky. Mathematicians struggled with the Poincaré Conjecture in its original three dimensions for the better part of a century, but the first breakthroughs came from a different place—or, rather, in higher dimensions.

At the dawn of the 1960s, several mathematicians—exactly how many and under what circumstances is still a matter of some dispute—proved the Poincaré Conjecture for dimensions five and higher. One was the American John Stallings, who in 1960 published a proof of the conjecture for seven dimensions or more just a year after he received his PhD from Princeton. Next was the American Stephen Smale, who probably completed his proof earlier than Stallings but published it several months later; he, however, proved the conjecture for dimensions five and higher. Then the British mathematician Christopher Zeeman extended Stallings's proof to dimensions five and six. A fourth man in the mix was Andrew Wallace, an American mathematician who in 1961 published a proof essentially similar to Smale's. There was also a Japanese mathematician named Hiroshi Yamasuge who published his own proof for dimensions five and higher in 1961.

So, more than fifty years after it was originally posed, the Poincaré Conjecture started to give—ever so slightly. All of these mathematicians, like countless others who were far less successful, had hoped to prove the conjecture itself—for the three dimensions for which it was stated. And while they will probably be remembered for their groundbreaking contributions to the cause of cracking the conjecture, at least one of them seemed to think himself most remarkable for the contribution he did not make. John Stallings, a professor emeritus at Berkeley, listed only a few of his papers on his personal website. The first published paper he mentioned dated back to 1966, and it was called "How Not to Solve the Poincaré Conjecture."

"I have committed—the sin of falsely proving Poincaré's Conjecture," Stallings began. "Now, in hope of deterring others from making similar mistakes, I shall describe my mistaken proof. Who knows but that somehow a small change, a new interpretation, and this line of proof may be rectified!" That is the spirit of hope against hope, at once conscious of the futility of efforts and obsessively incapable of giving up, that characterized the nearly hundred-year battle against the conjecture.

It was twenty years before the conjecture yielded slightly once again. In 1982 the young—he was thirty-one at the time—American mathematician Michael Freedman published a proof of the conjecture for dimension four. The accomplishment was hailed as a breakthrough; Freedman received the Fields Medal. But the conjecture for dimension three remained unproven. None of the methods used in the higher dimensions worked for dimension three; there was not enough room in this dimension to allow topologists to wield the tools they used in higher dimensions. It seemed to call for a revolutionary approach, something Poincaré himself could not have envisioned or even suspected.

Perhaps one of the problems with four-dimensional spaces is that, unlike higher-dimensional ones, they are not quite abstractions; it seems that we humans may very well inhabit a three-dimensional space embedded in four dimensions, even if most of us cannot wrap our minds around it. But experts say there is one living man, the American geometer William Thurston, who can imagine four dimensions. Thurston, they say, is possessed of a geometric intuition unlike that of any other human. "When you see him or talk to him, he is often staring out into space and you can see that he sees these pictures," said John Morgan, a professor at Columbia University, a friend of Thurston's, and a coauthor of one of several books written about Perelman's proof of the Poincaré Conjecture. "His geometric insight is unlike anyone I've ever met. So can there be a type of mathematician like Bill Thurston? How can someone have that kind of geometric insight? You know, I've got a fair amount of mathematical talent myself but I don't approach the human conclusions he does."

Thurston talked of three-dimensional manifolds in four-dimensional spaces as though he could see and manipulate them. He described the ways they could be cut up, and what would happen if they were. To a topologist, this was a very important exercise; complex objects are usually studied through their simpler composite parts, and understanding the nature of these parts and their relationships is essential to understanding the larger object. Thurston suggested that all three-dimensional manifolds could be carved up in particular ways that yielded objects that belonged to one of eight specific varieties of three-dimensional manifolds. It would not be quite right to call Thurston's conjecture a step toward proving Poincaré's. Indeed, it was even more ambitious, if a bit less famous. If Thurston had proved his conjecture, Poincaré's would automatically have followed. But he could not prove it.

"I watched Bill make progress," Morgan recalled. "And when he didn't get it, I thought, 'I'm not going to get it, nobody is going to get it.' Just as Jeff [Cheeger] said one time, 'It just gets too complicated to keep practicing the Poincaré Conjecture.'"

While other mathematicians wisely chose to direct their energies elsewhere, a Berkeley professor named Richard Hamilton persisted in tackling the Poincaré and then the Thurston conjectures. The standard journalistic description of Hamilton usually contains the word *flamboyant*, which seems to mean, basically, that he is interested not only in mathematics but also in surfing and in women. He is sociable, charming, and absolutely brilliant—for it was he who devised the way to prove both of the conjectures.

In the early 1980s Hamilton proposed something that can sound deceptively obvious. The surface of a sphere in any dimension has a constant positive curvature; this is a basic quality of the object. So if one could find a way to measure the curvature of an unidentifiable, unimaginable three-dimensional blob and then start reshaping the blob, all the while measuring its curvature, then one might eventually get to the point where the curvature was both positive and constant, whereby the blob would definitively be proven to be a three-dimensional sphere. That would mean that the blob had been a sphere all along, since reshaping does not actually change the topological qualities of objects—it just makes them more recognizable.

Hamilton devised a way of placing a metric on the blob to measure the curvature, and he wrote an equation that showed the way the blob, and the metric, would change over time. He proved that as the blob was molded, its curvature would not decrease but would necessarily grow—and this helped him demonstrate that the curvature would indeed be positive. But how to ensure that it would be constant? Hamilton got stuck.

Think about a simple function of the sort you studied in high school. Say, $1/x$. A graph of this function would look like a smooth line until it got to the point where $x = 0$. Then things would get crazy, because you cannot divide by zero. The line of your graph would suddenly soar toward eternity. This is called a singularity.

The process of transforming the metric described by the equation devised by Hamilton is called the Ricci flow. As the flow worked its theoretical magic on the imaginary metric on the unimaginable blob, every so often, a singularity would develop. Hamilton suggested that the singularities could be predicted and disarmed by stopping the function—the Ricci flow—fixing the problem by hand, and resuming the flow. When a mathematician says that he has fixed something "by hand," he actually means that he has devised a different function for the problem piece. An example is something that often happens in computer programming, where different functions are used depending on the conditions. When, say, your function is equal to x for all cases where x is equal to or greater than 0, and equal to $-x$ for all cases where x is less than 0. In topology, where imaginary hands intervene in the imaginary transformation of an object, this intervention is called *surgery*. So the process that Hamilton envisioned was Ricci flow with surgery.

Hamilton was not the first mathematician who thought he knew how to prove the Poincaré Conjecture. He was also not the first to encounter insurmountable obstacles on his way to a proof. In order for his program—as mathematicians call it—to work, several things had to be true. First, the curvature he was attempting to measure had to have a constant limit, a sort of uniform boundary; if he assumed this was true, the proof would probably work—but how could he know that his assumption was correct? Second, while Hamilton devised Ricci flow with surgery and could show that it would be effective in some cases, he could not prove that it could be used effectively no matter what kind of singularity developed. He could theorize about the sorts of singularities that would appear, but he could not find a way to tame all of them or even claim to have identified all of them. Here was another man who "made progress and then didn't get it." Here was another man for whom, as Morgan quoted Jeff Cheeger as saying, it got "too complicated to keep practicing the Poincaré Conjecture."

Twenty-five years later, two things are perfectly clear. First, Hamilton did indeed create the blueprint for proving both the Poincaré and the Geometrization conjectures. Second, his personal tragedy was as great as his professional achievement: at the age of forty, Hamilton became stuck and, apparently, remained stuck.

The point at which Hamilton got stuck is roughly the point at which Perelman began to engage the Poincaré Conjecture. It was also the point at which Perelman began to disappear; he went to fewer seminars, gradually reduced his hours at the Steklov so that he really only appeared when it was time to pick up his monthly pay. He slowed his e-mail correspondence to such a degree that most acquaintances assumed he had become yet another mathematician who had once shown promise but then met a problem and was crushed by it, reduced to mathematical nonexistence.

We know now that this was not the case. Rather, Perelman had completed his mathematical education and began to apply it. As it happened, the process of being educated—or, perhaps more precisely, the desire he had for mathematical knowledge that could be imparted by others—was what had kept him connected to the outside world. Now that world was more or less used up; its utility was negligible, and its demands therefore incomprehensible and even more irritating than before. Perelman, naturally, turned his back on the world and faced the problem.

What the world had given Perelman was the habit of honing the power of his incomparable mind on a single problem. What Hamilton had essentially done was turn the Poincaré Conjecture into a super mathematical-olympiad problem. He had, in a sense, taken it down a notch. In the world of top mathematicians, the intellectual elite are people who open new horizons by posing questions no one else has thought to ask. A step down are the people who devise ways to answer those questions; often these are members of the elite at earlier stages in their career—a few years after obtaining their PhDs, for example, when they are proving other people's theorems before they start formulating their own. And finally, there are the rare birds, those who take the last steps in completing proofs. These are the persistent, exacting, patient mathematicians who finally lay down the paths others have dreamed up and marked out. In our story, Poincaré and Thurston represent the first group, Hamilton the second group, and Perelman the one who finished the job.

So who was he? He was the man who had never met a problem he could not solve. Whatever he had been trying to do with Alexandrov spaces at Berkeley might have been an exception—he might indeed have gotten stuck—but then it might also have been the only time he tried to do something that fell into the second or even the first category of mathematical work rather than the third. The third category is essentially similar to solving a mathematical-olympiad problem: it has been clearly stated, and restrictions have been placed on its solution—the path to proof had been marked out by Hamilton. This was a very, very complicated olympiad problem; it could not be solved in hours, or weeks, or even months. Indeed, it was a problem that perhaps could not be solved in any amount of time by anyone—except Perelman. And Perelman was a man in search of just such a problem, one that would finally utilize the full capacity of the supercompactor that was his mind.

Perelman managed to prove two main things. First, he showed that Hamilton did not need to assume that the curvature would always be uniformly bound; in the imaginary space in which the proof unfolded, this simply would always be the case. Second, he showed that all the singularities that could develop stemmed from the same root; they would appear when the curvature began to "blow up," to grow unmanageable. Since all the singularities had the same nature, a single tool would be effective against all of them—and the surgery originally envisioned by Hamilton would do the job. Moreover, Perelman proved that some of the singularities Hamilton had hypothesized would never occur at all.

There is something peculiar and slightly ironic in the logic of Perelman's proof. He succeeded because he used the unfathomable power of his mind to grasp the entire scope of possibilities: he was ultimately able to claim that he knew all that could happen as the matrix grew and the object reshaped itself. Knowing it all, he was able to exclude some of the topological developments as impossible. Speaking of the imaginary four-dimensional space, he referred to things that could and could not occur "in nature." In essence, he was able to do in mathematics what he had tried to do in life: grasp at once all the possibilities of nature and annihilate everything that fell outside that realm—castrati voices, cars, anti-Semitism, and any other uncomfortable singularity.

9

The Proof Emerges

Date: Tue, 12 Nov 2002 05:09:02 -0500 (EST)
From: Grigori Perelman
To: [multiple recipients]
Subject: new preprint

Dear [Name],

may I bring to your attention my paper in arXiv math.DG 0211159.

Abstract:

We present a monotonic expression for the Ricci flow, valid in all dimensions and without curvature assumptions. It is interpreted as an entropy for a certain canonical ensemble. Several geometric applications are given. In particular, (1) Ricci flow, considered on the space of riemannian metrics modulo diffeomorphism and scaling, has no nontrivial periodic orbits (that is, other than fixed points); (2) In a region, where singularity is forming in finite time, the injectivity radius is controlled by the curvature; (3) Ricci flow can not quickly turn an almost euclidean region into a very curved one, no matter what happens far away. We also verify several assertions related to Richard Hamilton's program for the proof of Thurston geometrization conjecture for closed three-manifolds, and give a sketch of an eclectic proof of this conjecture, making use of earlier results on collapsing with local lower curvature bound.

Best regards,

Grisha

About a dozen U.S. mathematicians received this message. It said that the day before, Perelman had posted a paper on arXiv.org, a website hosted by the Cornell University Library and created for the express purpose of facilitating electronic communication among mathematicians and scientists. The preprint was the first of three papers that contained the results of Perelman's seven-year attack on the Poincaré and Geometrization conjectures.

"So I start looking at the paper," Michael Anderson told me. "I'm not an expert on Ricci flow—nevertheless, looking through it, it became clear that he had made huge advances, that the solution to the Geometrization Conjecture and therefore the Poincaré Conjecture was within sight." Every recipient of the e-mail had been on his own crusade against one of the problems for many years. Every one of them had a conflicted reaction to the news: if Perelman had indeed proved the conjectures, this was a mathematical accomplishment of monumental proportions, and it had to inspire a sense of triumph—but it was someone else's triumph, and it dashed many mathematicians' hopes for their own breakthroughs. Anderson had been working on Geometrization for almost ten years and was, as he told me, "getting bogged down in technical issues. I was still hoping that I'd have some insight or some breakthrough but really came to the conclusion that it wouldn't happen.

But if anybody was going to do it, good that it was Grisha. I liked him. So the next day I invited him to come here, and a day later I was really surprised that he said yes."

Meanwhile, a flurry of e-mails began to travel among American and European topologists. Mike Anderson sent out a few that read as follows:

Hi [Name],

Hope all is well with you. I don't know if you've noticed yet but Grisha Perelman has put up a paper on the Ricci flow at mathDG/0211159 that you and your friends working in the area may want to look at. Grisha is a very unusual and also very bright guy—I first met him about 9 years ago, and we used to talk about Ricci flow and geometrization of 3-manifolds a fair amount in the early 90's. Out of the blue he sent me an e-mail yesterday informing me of his paper.

Basically, I know very little about the Ricci flow, but it seems to me he has answered, in this paper, many of the fundamental problems that people have been trying to solve. It may be that he is even very close to the solution of Hamilton's goal, i.e. proving Thurston's conjecture. The ideas in the paper appear to me to be completely new and original—typical Grisha. (He solved a number of other outstanding problems in other areas in the early 90's and then "disappeared" from the scene. It seems he has now resurfaced.)

Anyway, I wanted to inform you of this, and also ask if you could keep me "in the loop" on discussions/rumors regarding this work . . . Of course, what I'd really like to know is how close one now is to solving Thurston's conjecture—since this affects some of my work a lot. I'm assuming here that his paper is correct—which to me is a reasonable bet, knowing Grisha.

I'm sending a similar message to a few other friends I know
working on Ricci flow.
Best regards, Mike

Someone who had never heard of Perelman might be forgiven
for not taking the paper seriously: work claiming to prove the Poincaré Conjecture appeared regularly, yet in almost a hundred years,
no one had solved the problem. Everyone, including mathematicians of great repute—indeed, including Poincaré himself—had
made mistakes. Purported proofs appeared every few years, and all
of them had been debunked—some sooner, some later. One had to
know Perelman—be aware that he never produced lemons, as his
math-club mates used to say, and have a sense of his propensity for
the well-prepared gesture—to know just how seriously this particular attempt at the Poincaré should be taken.

But how was one to determine whether it was in fact correct?
The paper pulled together techniques and even problems from several distinct specialties inside mathematics; they were not even all
limited to topology. In addition, Perelman's presentation was so
condensed that a judgment on his proof would first require, in essence, deciphering his paper. Nor did he help by stating up front
what he proposed to do and how. He did not even claim he had
proved the Poincaré and Geometrization conjectures until he was
asked the question directly. Anderson's e-mails were some of the
first steps in starting this process of verification. *This guy should be
taken seriously,* he was saying, *and please let me know whether he has
done what I think he has done.* Anderson wrote this e-mail message
at 5:38 in the morning the day after he'd received Perelman's
e-mail alerting him to the preprint.

Within a few hours, Anderson started getting responses from
geometers who apparently had also stayed up all night reading the
paper. They reported that what the mathematicians called "the

Ricci flow community" was in a frenzy—and noted that none of them had heard of Perelman before.

None of the topologists with whom Perelman had been acquainted in the United States belonged to the Ricci flow community, which centered around Richard Hamilton—the most important addressee of Perelman's e-mail announcement and, in a sense, of his entire paper. As the e-mails flew back and forth among geometers, Hamilton remained conspicuously silent. "Has there emerged yet any impressions of Perelman's work?" Anderson wrote to another Ricci flow-er a few days later. "Are some of you in Hamilton's group going over the paper? Does Hamilton know about it? Any ideas how close [Perelman] may be to finishing the program?"

Hamilton knew about the paper, the correspondents reported. The paper appeared very important indeed.

In fact, it took Perelman less than half of his first paper to get past the point at which Hamilton had been stuck for two decades. No wonder Hamilton was silent. One can only imagine what it must have felt like to see one's life's ambition hijacked and then fulfilled by some upstart with unkempt hair and long fingernails. One can imagine, that is, if one understands that ambition, competitiveness, and a sense of professional self-worth are what likely motivates human behavior—not, say, the best interests of mathematics. Grisha Perelman did not have that understanding.

Indeed, one of the most remarkable aspects of the story of Perelman's proof is the number of mathematicians who temporarily set aside their own professional ambitions to devote themselves to the deciphering and interpretation of his preprints. In November 2002, Bruce Kleiner was traveling in Europe. Just as he was about to begin a lecture at the University of Bonn, Ursula Hamenstaedt, a local professor who was in the audience, asked him: "Oh, by the way, did you see the preprint that Perelman just posted with proof of the geometrization of the Poincaré Conjecture?" At least, this was what he remembered her saying. She might in fact have been more cautious in her assessment—but Kleiner knew just how seriously Perelman was to be taken.

"Nobody who knew his papers or had listened to his lectures had ever suggested he made claims that would later collapse, or would say things that he hadn't thought through carefully," Kleiner told me. "And here he was posting something on the arXiv, which is a very public forum. So, unless there was some personality change that had taken place since the early nineties, I thought there was a very good chance there was something there or maybe he had solved it completely." And this meant that Kleiner's professional life was taking a sudden turn. Like Anderson, Kleiner had for years been working on an aspect of the Geometrization Conjecture, though using an entirely different approach. Unlike Anderson, he did not yet suspect that his pursuit would prove fruitless. He did know that, as he put it, "it was a high-risk project," a famous conjecture with which someone else might succeed sooner, but he was hardly prepared to hear, just before his own lecture, that his project was effectively over. For the next year and a half, Kleiner would be working on Project Perelman.

Perelman, meanwhile, was preparing for his trip to the United States. He had received invitations from Anderson at Stony Brook and Tian, now at MIT, and he decided to spend two weeks at each place. He had told Anderson at the outset that he would be in the United States no more than a month because he could not leave his mother alone for longer. The plan later changed to include his mother on the journey, but Perelman stuck to the original length of the trip.

Perelman now seemed fully re-engaged with the world. He handled the U.S. visa formalities—burdensome even for people seasoned in dealing with bureaucracies—on his own, securing visas for himself and his mother. He bought his tickets himself, apparently using money still left in his American bank account. He had been living frugally the past seven years, using his postdoc savings—he even added a footnote to that effect to his first preprint, obsessively true to his ideal of giving credit where credit was due, however irrelevant it was to the matter at hand. He corresponded with Anderson and Tian regarding the scheduling and logistics of his travels, including medical insurance, an issue that apparently concerned him a great deal.

Perelman's re-emergence from his near hermithood did not seem to impair his ability to continue writing up his proof. He submitted the second of his three preprints to the arXiv on March 10, 2003, while he was in the process of obtaining his U.S. visa. At twenty-two pages, this one was eight pages shorter than the first installment. He had apparently formulated the proof so clearly in his mind that distractions, minor and major, did not take away from his ability to devote a couple of weeks at a time to these concentrated write-ups (that spring he would tell Jeff Cheeger that it had taken him three weeks to write the first paper—less time than it had taken Cheeger to read and understand it).

Perelman arrived at MIT at the beginning of April 2003. To Gang Tian, he looked more or less as Tian had remembered him: lean, long-haired, and with long fingernails, although without the brown corduroy jacket. To those who were seeing him for the first time, Perelman looked striking but entirely within the weirdness bounds of mathematicians. At his lecture, the hall was packed. A number of people in the audience had been reading Perelman's first paper and writing their own notes on it; several of them were doing this in a seminar started by Tian. But a majority were curious mathematicians who had come to look at the man who might have made the biggest mathematical breakthrough in a century. These mathematicians were qualified to follow the narrative line of his lecture but would certainly have been unable to ask meaningful questions after the lecture—which made them, to Perelman, uninteresting at best and annoying at worst. He had banned videotaping of the lecture and had made it clear he did not want any media publicity, but a couple of journalists made it into the audience that day anyway.

Almost incredibly, those who had come hoping for a mathematical spectacle got one. In sharp contrast to his speech at the 1994 international congress, Perelman presented an organized, lucid, and at times even playful narrative. He was at the peak of his relationship with the Poincaré Conjecture. If the Poincaré Conjecture were a person, this might have been the moment when Perelman would have chosen to marry it: a time when he could see their entire history together clearly, and when he was most free of doubt and most certain of the future.

Almost daily for two weeks after his first presentation, Perelman gave talks on his work to smaller audiences. He spent several hours a day answering questions, mostly about the Geometrization Conjecture. In the mornings before his lectures, Perelman made a habit of stopping by Tian's office to talk, mostly about mathematics. He may have been looking for new problems to tackle; he asked Tian about his own research and even floated some ideas related to Tian's specialization at the time rather than to geometrization. Tian, unlike Anderson and Morgan—who regularly attempted to draw out Perelman—rarely ventured outside the narrow discussions of mathematical problems. "He was focused and very single-minded," Tian told me. "I respect that he can ignore many things other people pay attention to and focus on doing mathematics."

Perelman seemed so relaxed and friendly during this visit that in one of their morning talks Tian broached the subject of Perelman's staying at MIT. The university was interested in making an offer, and some colleagues of Tian's had approached Perelman the previous evening and attempted to convince him that the resources of MIT would allow him to work more productively. Tian asked Perelman for his reaction. Whatever Perelman said to him in response, the polite, exceedingly soft-spoken Tian would not repeat to me. "He made some comments," Tian allowed. "I don't want to say them." The problem was not just that this time Perelman had no interest in staying on in the United States. It was that the idea of being rewarded now with a comfortable university position insulted him. He had expected a full professorship eight years earlier. His brain had been the same then as it was now; he had been just as deserving; and yet they had wanted him to prove that he was good enough to teach mathematics. Now they acted as though he had finally proved it, when in fact he had proved the Poincaré Conjecture, which was its own reward.

The two returned to their civilized discussions of manifolds, metrics, and estimates. Perelman's irritation surfaced just once more in their discussions. The first of what Tian called "incidents" must have occurred April 15, toward the end of Perelman's stay at MIT, when the *New York Times* published an article titled "Russian Reports He Has Solved a Celebrated Math Problem." Just about every word in the title was an insult to Perelman. He had "reported" nothing; he had been careful to make his claims only in response to direct queries. To call the Poincaré Conjecture "celebrated," and to do so in a mass-circulation newspaper, was, from Perelman's standpoint, unconscionably vulgar. And the story itself heaped on the insults. The fourth paragraph of the article began, "If his proof is accepted for publication in a refereed research journal and survives two years of scrutiny, Dr. Perelman could be eligible for a $1 million prize." This seemed to imply that Perelman had taken on the problem in order to win the million dollars—that he had any interest in the money at all—and that he would actually submit his work for publication in a refereed journal. All of this was demonstrably untrue. Perelman had started working on the conjecture years before the Clay prize was created. While he used money and had some appreciation for it, he felt little need and, certainly, no desire for it. Finally, his decision to post his proof on the arXiv had been an intentional revolt against the very idea of scientific journals distributed by paid subscription. And now that he had solved one of the hardest problems in mathematics, Perelman would not be asking anyone to vet his proof for publication.

Before coming to the United States, Perelman had made it clear to those who asked—and Mike Anderson, for one, was very careful to ask—that at that point he did not want any publicity outside the mathematics community. Perelman did not say he never wanted publicity; he made it clear he did not think the time was right for it. And as strict as he was on the issue of speaking to journalists, he took a relaxed attitude toward publicizing his lectures and his work among colleagues: he was happy to let the organizers of his lectures use their professional mailing lists, or not, as they saw fit. He had an implicit trust in mathematicians of many stripes, and he had just as instinctive a mistrust of journalists. The *New York Times* article not only reinforced his suspicions of journalists—the author misinterpreted events and motivations in all the ways Perelman had probably feared—but also undermined his trust in his colleagues; one of the reporter's two quoted sources was a mathematician who had attended Tian's seminar and Perelman's talks. Thomas Mrowka was no idle observer, yet he had offered an appraisal that served as the perfect kicker for the article and likely made Perelman cringe: "Either he's done it or he's made some really significant progress, and we're going to learn from it."

On the day Perelman left MIT, he and Tian went across the river to Boston's historic Back Bay to have lunch, which Perelman seemed to enjoy. Perelman even talked of the possibility of returning to the United States; he said he had offers from Stanford, Berkeley, MIT—in fact, by that point he could have had any terms he desired at any mathematics department in the country. In a perfectly Bostonian flourish, the two mathematicians followed the lunch with a walk along the Charles River. Perelman's relaxed state must have given way to anxiety, for he confided to Tian that things had gone sour between him and Burago—and, more generally, between him and the Russian mathematical establishment. Tian, again, would not reveal the details to me—saying only that he doubted that his friend was right this time—but the rupture was so much discussed in St. Petersburg that the details were easy to obtain. The conflict involved another researcher at Burago's laboratory, one whose footnoting practices, Perelman believed, were so sloppy as to border on plagiarism. The man followed a generally accepted footnoting practice of referencing the latest appearance of an item rather than providing all the available truth on its origins. Perelman had demanded that the notoriously tolerant Burago subject his researcher to all but a public scientific whipping. In Perelman's estimation, Burago's refusal made him an accomplice to what amounted very nearly to a crime; Perelman's screaming at his mentor had been heard in the halls of the Steklov. Perelman left Burago's laboratory and found refuge in the lab of Olga Ladyzhenskaya, a remarkable mathematician who was old enough, wise enough, and woman enough to accept Perelman just as he was. Everyone else—including Burago and Gromov, who generally saw Perelman as nearly faultless—seemed willing to forgive him, but they were incapable of seeing his approach to footnoting as anything but capricious at best and meanly ridiculous at worst.

Following his lectures at MIT, Perelman went to New York City, where his mother was once again staying with relatives. He stayed the weekend and traveled to Stony Brook by train on Sunday evening. Mike Anderson picked him up at the station and delivered him to the dormitory where he was staying; Perelman had explicitly requested that his accommodations be "as modest as possible." He started lecturing the following day, establishing a consistent schedule for the next two weeks: morning lectures followed by afternoon discussion sessions. To those attending, these sessions seemed nothing short of a miracle. Here was a man some of them had never heard of and others had believed had vanished who had slain the Poincaré and now exhibited fantastic clarity in his lectures and unparalleled patience during the discussions.

This was how Perelman had been taught mathematics should be practiced. He went to the lecture hall every day to fulfill his destiny, and this explained both his clarity and his patience. But in the world outside the Stony Brook classrooms, things increasingly diverged from his expectations. On the day he arrived at Stony Brook, the *New York Times* published another article. This one too started out by stating, inaccurately, that Perelman claimed to have proved the Poincaré Conjecture and linked that solution to the million-dollar prize, and it then went on to quote a single source: Michael Freedman, who had received the Fields Medal after solving the Poincaré for dimension four, and who was now working at Microsoft. Freedman, incredibly, called Perelman's achievement "a small sorrow" for topology: Perelman had solved the biggest problems in the field, which made it less attractive, he reasoned, and so "you won't have the brilliant young people you have now."

This was probably a fairly serious insult. After Perelman's falling-out with Burago, his reference group, which was small to begin with, had shrunk to include just a few people who were in a position to understand his proof. Back at MIT, he had told Tian he thought it would take a year and a half or two years for his proof to be understood. But someone like Freedman might have been expected to have an immediate overall grasp of the elegance—and the correctness—of Perelman's solution. For Freedman to frame Perelman's proof as a setback for their once-shared area, and do so in an interview with a newspaper whose readership would never understand the problem or the solution, had to be hurtful—all the more so because Freedman's reaction seemed so illogical.

If anyone could speak authoritatively on what Perelman had done—particularly on what he had laid out in his first paper—it was Richard Hamilton. After all, Perelman had followed Hamilton's program. One of the oddest and most tragic aspects of this story is the extent to which Perelman's and Hamilton's orbits missed each other. Perelman did not belong to what Anderson and others called the "Ricci flow community," which had grown up around Hamilton in the two decades he had been trying to force the matrix to conform to the conjecture. Perelman had apparently approached Hamilton twice—once following a lecture of his, and once in writing, after Perelman had returned to St. Petersburg. Both times, Perelman was asking for a clarification of something Hamilton had said or written. On the second occasion, Hamilton failed to respond—something Perelman might have understood perfectly if he held others to the same standards of behavior to which he held himself. Indeed, for reasons that were probably entirely different from Perelman's—Hamilton, by all accounts, was an atypically sociable mathematician—Hamilton tended to be elusive, occasionally reclusive, and usually very slow to respond to letters and calls. But rather than recognize familiar patterns, Perelman probably felt significantly frustrated by Hamilton's silence; he generally expected his own needs, few as they were, to be met.

Now, too, Hamilton was keeping his silence. That he had not attended Perelman's lectures at MIT might have been disappointing but was understandable. But when Perelman began his stint at Stony Brook, just an hour and a half from New York City, where Hamilton was teaching at Columbia University, Hamilton's absence became conspicuous. Other mathematicians from New York attended. One of them, John Morgan, asked Perelman to lecture at Columbia over the weekend. Perelman agreed, and then agreed to give another lecture that weekend at Princeton.

On Friday, April 25, Perelman lectured at Princeton. The university again made him an offer. Perelman turned it down. On Saturday, he lectured at Columbia. Hamilton came and stayed for the discussion after the lunch break—until the only people in the room were he, Perelman, Morgan, and Gromov, who was then at Courant. "Everybody was waiting for Richard to say either he got it or he doesn't get it," Morgan told me. "It's his theory, his idea. This is the way to do it. He's the obvious person to pass judgment."

And did he? This is where it gets tricky. "Richard from the beginning was willing to and did acknowledge that what was in the first paper was correct and it was a huge advance," said Morgan, now trying to tread carefully so as not to offend a colleague. The first paper dealt solely with Ricci flow, which was Hamilton's invention and his area of total confidence. The second paper dealt with Ricci flow with surgery, which was also Hamilton's invention but which in Perelman's treatment intermingled with Alexandrov spaces and the work Perelman had done with Gromov and Burago. Hamilton was less of an expert here, and that may have made him both less confident and, perhaps, more hopeful that Perelman had failed. "I think maybe he thought, *Well, this is a mistake*," said Morgan, "*and if it's a mistake, that would leave room for me to produce something more that I wanted to contribute.* So I think he was sort of withholding judgment, waiting to see." If there was a chance that Perelman had taken things in the wrong direction with his second paper, then someone else—most logically, Hamilton himself—could build on the breakthroughs of Perelman's first paper. All of this, however, is conjecture: when Hamilton spoke of Perelman's work publicly, he always did so graciously; he just did it far less frequently than many—including Perelman—might have expected.

That day at Columbia, as Morgan remembered it, "It was proper but distant. There didn't seem to be any overt tension. Grisha was not going to aggressively approach anybody. If you looked at it from the outside, it looked like any other math conversation: ideas coming in and going out. In other words, whatever Richard's private feelings were about his distance, in this conversation at least, he was sort of normal about it."

Morgan invited Perelman to come to his house for brunch the following morning. "And he said, 'Well, who would be there?' I said, 'Oh, my wife, my daughter, I may invite a couple other people.' He said, 'Oh, no. I don't think so.' So my take on that is, had it been a mathematical gathering, maybe he would have come. But a social gathering he was not at all interested." That day, Perelman walked around New York with Gromov and talked to him about the Poincaré Conjecture and about his conflict with Burago. Then he went back to Brighton Beach, where his mother was staying, planning to return to Stony Brook the following night for another week of lectures and discussions.

Perelman went back to Stony Brook discouraged. He told Anderson he was disappointed at the level of questions Hamilton had asked him: it seemed the inventor of Ricci flow had not taken the time to delve deeply into Perelman's proof. In all likelihood, the reasons for this were complex: Hamilton was conflicted about engaging Perelman's work, and, in addition, it may have been both psychologically and mathematically difficult to absorb a sudden break in the wall against which he had been beating his head for twenty years. But, just like twenty years earlier, while Perelman could be endlessly patient in reiterating his explanations to interested listeners, he could not imagine that anyone might have a difficult time with something that seemed, to Perelman, transparent and nearly self-evident.

Perelman was annoyed too with Princeton's insistent courtship attempts. Someone from that university called Anderson following Perelman's lecture to ask for help in recruiting Perelman. At Perelman's request, Anderson declined to help, but Princeton got a formal offer in the mail to Perelman anyway—and this he found upsetting. "They are being pushy," he told Anderson. Among Perelman's many rules of behavior, articulated and perhaps even formulated a couple of years after the Princeton offer, was the rule that "one should never force oneself on anyone." Princeton, which had offended Perelman by asking him to apply for a job, now offended him by being too persistent in its affections.

Anderson, who in addition to his genuine admiration for Perelman also seemed to have a keen sense of Perelman's boundaries, apparently managed not to offend Perelman while pursuing the same agenda as all of Perelman's other American hosts: to convince him to stay at his university and to draw him out socially. Anderson daily took great pains to convince Perelman to go out to dinner, and occasionally he succeeded. He also held a party for Perelman at his house, which, in retrospect, seemed a bit of a disaster: Anderson and his friend Cheeger got into a loud argument over the U.S. invasion of Iraq, which Cheeger supported and Anderson did not. Anderson remembered getting very angry. "Grisha just listened," he recalled. "He didn't seem to have an opinion." Except, of course, for the firmly held opinion that the discussion of politics was beneath the dignity of a mathematician.

Anderson took Perelman to meet Jim Simons, the extraordinary man who had transformed the Stony Brook math department into one of the top such departments in the country and then become a hedge-fund manager and amassed impressive wealth, which he shared with many charities as well as with the university at Stony Brook. "So Simons made it clear that he'd like Grisha to come here—any terms he wants, any salary, or even one month a year," said Anderson, "because Simons has the influence and money to make this possible. Grisha says, 'Thank you, that's very nice, but I don't want to talk about this now. I have to go back to St. Petersburg to teach high-school students.' He had a commitment in fall 2003."

Perelman's answer might have been fully understood only by Perelman himself. A popular Russian joke tells of an actor courted by a major Hollywood studio. The actor is going to star in a film, and he is very excited, until he finds out that the filming is scheduled for December. "I can't do it," he says. "I have New Year's parties," meaning that he is scheduled to play Grandfather Frost (Santa's Russian cousin) at children's parties—and since he values this gig, he will have to pass up the opportunity of a lifetime. Perelman's excuse sounded equally absurd and touching—but apparently it was just an excuse. From what I could tell, his sole commitment in the fall of 2003 was to attend a daylong math competition at a physics-and-math school in St. Petersburg, which he did, but which in no way would have precluded his accepting any of the many offers American institutions were making. The real reason he didn't was simple: he abhorred the idea of being some department's prized possession.

Perelman went back to Russia at the end of April. He submitted the third and last in his Poincaré series of preprints on July 17; this time, it was just seven pages. The discussions went on without him. In June, Kleiner and his University of Michigan colleague John Lott started a Web page where they posted their notes on Perelman's first paper. Toward the end of the year, the American Institute of Mathematics in Palo Alto and the Mathematical Sciences Research Institute in Berkeley held a joint workshop on the first preprint; Kleiner, Lott, Tian, and Morgan were its most active participants. In the summer of 2004, all four attended a workshop at Princeton sponsored by the Clay Institute, which, as the administrator of the million-dollar prize, had a stake in encouraging the appraisal of Perelman's proof. Around the time of the Clay workshop, the four mathematicians most involved in closely reading the papers seemed to dispense with any residual doubts that the proof was correct. There were some mistakes, it seemed, and there were many gaps in the narrative Perelman presented, but none of this any longer seemed to challenge the assertion that Perelman had proved the Poincaré Conjecture and, probably, the Geometrization Conjecture (consensus on geometrization would come a bit later). Just as Perelman had predicted, this understanding came about a year and a half after his colleagues started studying his proof.

Following the summer 2004 workshop, Tian and Morgan decided to collaborate on a book about Perelman's proof; it was eventually published by the Clay Institute, which also funded Kleiner and Lott's work. In the summer of 2005, the institute sponsored a month-long workshop on the proof. The study of Perelman's preprints was turning into a mathematical cottage industry, which was just as it should be; many of the mathematicians involved had spent significant portions of their professional lives attacking these conjectures, and now each sacrificed the hope of a starring role for the opportunity to play a supporting part in the greatest mathematical production of the age.

Had Perelman followed the more traditional route—had he written a conventional paper or papers and submitted them to a mathematical journal—his work could hardly have been subjected to any more scrutiny. A journal would have sent his papers to be reviewed by his peers—who, the world of topology being so small, would have been some of the same people who pored over his preprints now. The difference is that, as reviewers, they would have read the papers in private, not in a seminar, workshop, or summer-school setting, and they would have revealed the results of their examination in a letter to the journal rather than in notes posted on the Web for all interested parties to see. The process Perelman set in motion by posting his proof, in highly concentrated form, on the Web probably involved as many people as journal publication would have, but it turned out to be far more collaborative and public than the traditional procedure. It was also faster: before going public, Perelman did not take the typical months or years to frame his results in a traditional mathematical narrative. Perelman's revolt against the conventions of scientific publishing was not based on an ideology; he simply had no use and therefore no regard for them.

But outside of a traditional publishing framework, what were the roles of people like Kleiner, Lott, Tian, and Morgan, who had set out not only to understand but also to explain Perelman's proof? In a sense, they became his coauthors. Perelman had coauthored one of his most important early papers in a similar manner. When I asked Gromov what it had been like to write an article with Perelman, he said, "It wasn't like anything. I didn't actually interact with him. Burago came here and we talked, and then Burago went back and they talked, and I guess Perelman wrote it up."

"So you didn't look at the manuscript?" I asked, incredulous.

"No."

"But wasn't there the risk that someone would have gotten something wrong along the way?"

"There is, there always is. It often happens that somebody writes part of the work and someone else writes another and it actually doesn't come together. Some very well-known mathematicians have had bad articles like that."

"But that's not a reason to read the manuscript?"

"The manuscript? Of course not. It's not interesting to read about work that you've already done. You do it—and you forget about it."

This was Perelman's school. While Perelman was lecturing at

Stony Brook, Kleiner and Lott found him as approachable and willing to engage in conversation about his proof as any mathematician could be. But when, toward the end of Perelman's stay, Kleiner and Lott asked him whether he would look over their notes once they were done, Perelman said he would not. "He could have spent a half-hour sort of looking through and making some comment," said Kleiner, who five years later still seemed perplexed by Perelman's reaction. "That would be sort of the typical thing one might expect at the minimum. But, you know, he's not a typical guy." As Kleiner recalled, Perelman had explained that looking at their notes would make him in some way responsible for the work Kleiner and Lott had done. This was a perfect combination of Perelman's exaggerated sense of personal responsibility and his equally solipsistic perception of the importance of any given mathematical problem. At the center of the universe in which Perelman stood, the Poincaré Conjecture was fading into the past. As Gromov said, "You do it—and you forget about it." Perelman knew that months later, once Kleiner and Lott had finished their notes, he would no longer be interested in discussing the Poincaré.

Kleiner and Lott went on to work on Perelman's papers without Perelman. They found some problems along the way—at one point, in fact, Kleiner was convinced that they had found a serious, possibly fatal flaw, but Lott disabused him of this idea—and they found that even in the highly condensed preprints, Perelman had stayed true to his manner of relaying not so much the solution to the problem as the history of his own relationship with the problem. As Kleiner and Lott's exploration moved toward the end of the first preprint, they realized that some of the earlier sections of the paper were self-contained pieces that had no bearing on the eventual trajectory of the proof.

In September 2004, following the Clay workshop, Tian sent Perelman an e-mail note "saying that we now understood the proof." He pointed out that a year and a half had passed since their walk along the Charles River. Tian asked him if he would be publishing his preprints, for he and Morgan were now thinking of a book. Perelman did not respond. "He may think that he had done enough for publication by posting his preprints on the arXiv," Tian suggested when he talked to me. "Or he could be already uncomfortable with me by that time. I tried to avoid talking to reporters, because first, I didn't really enjoy talking to reporters; secondly, it takes time." But in the spring of 2004 Tian had, at a friend's request, broken his silence and talked to a freelance reporter for *Science* magazine—and now he suspected that Perelman was aware of this breach and had not written back for this reason. Most likely, though, Perelman simply had nothing to say. His prediction about the proof had come true, and he had never planned to publish his preprints—why would any further comment be necessary?

Morgan had better luck with Perelman. In the Tian-Morgan tandem, it was Morgan who wrote to Perelman to ask mathematical questions. He was consistently amazed with the precision of the responses he received. "I would ask him a mathematical question and I would almost immediately get back the answer I was looking for," Morgan told me. "Now a much more typical mathematical interchange is: You ask a question, the person you ask it to either doesn't quite understand what you're asking or because he's coming at it from inside a different point of view answers it slightly obliquely from what you're looking for. So then you ask it again. You reformulate it; refine it. And then maybe you get back an answer that is really what you're looking for. That never happened with Perelman, I'd ask him a question and it was like he knew exactly what point I was confused about or didn't understand, and exactly what I needed in order to clarify the situation."

So Morgan tried his luck with other questions. He had several sets of pressing ones. First, he wanted to see Perelman's preprints in published form—for the historical record if for no other reason. He suggested he would edit them himself and place them in a journal he coedited. He also invited Perelman to Columbia University: "Would you like to come for a week, a month, a semester, a year, for the rest of your life?" Morgan inserted these sorts of questions carefully between his mathematical requests. "And I would get back responses like: 'The answer to question one is that; here's the answer to question two. I have no answers to your other questions.' So he did acknowledge them, which is more than he did with most people." But he certainly did not answer them. After a while, Morgan ran out of mathematical questions.

When Morgan and Tian completed their manuscript in 2006, they mailed it to Perelman. The package came back stamped SERVICE REFUSED.

10

The Madness

PERELMAN RETURNED TO St. Petersburg in May of 2004. Late spring is the only time Petersburg becomes not just livable but attractive; its usual grayness gives way to a soft, cool light that refuses to dim well into the night. The city's residents pour out onto its sidewalks and embankments and start taking all the strolls they did not take in the cold, wet winter months. Perelman, who always walked, and Rukshin, who made a point of doing all things beautiful in St. Petersburg, went for a walk. The weather must have been much the same as it had been in Boston weeks earlier, when Perelman had walked along the Charles with Tian. He said many of the same things too, but more emphatically this time—or Rukshin heard them more clearly and louder than Tian had heard them. Perelman said he was disappointed in the world of mathematics.

"It took him eight or nine years to solve the Poincaré," Rukshin told me, recalling that conversation. "Now imagine that for eight years you did not know whether your child, who was born ill, would survive. You have spent eight years caring for him day and night. And now he has grown strong. From an ugly duckling, he has turned to a fine swan. And now someone says to you, 'Why don't you sell your baby to me? Here is some grant money, for half a year, or perhaps a year, we could publish the work together, we'd make this a joint result.'"

Normally, when you're having a conversation with a mathematician, pointing out logical errors will enrich the exchange. This was clearly not the case here. First, no one sends a child into the world at the tender age of eight, nor would one perceive it as offensive if, say, one's eighteen-year-old child were offered a spot at university. The thing was, even if Rukshin twisted the logic of what Perelman had said to him, he was likely still conveying the emotions correctly. In a sense, the point was precisely that this was a bad comparison: Perelman's proof of the Poincaré Conjecture was not as vulnerable or as valuable as a human child, but Perelman's experience of the incongruity of his accomplishment and the rewards he had been offered was like that of a doting parent who had been offered money for his baby. Rukshin, who was highly suspicious of the world in general and given to feeling slighted, surely added his own interpretations to Perelman's emotional charge. This was how, in the retelling, offers of professorial appointments turned into not-so-veiled attempts to buy the right of coauthorship of the proof; and how in Rukshin's and perhaps Perelman's imaginations, Kleiner and Lott's, and later Tian and Morgan's, work on interpreting the proof turned into attempts to usurp credit for it.

Concluded Rukshin: "The world of science—the science that Perelman had considered the most honest of the sciences—had turned its other side to him. It had been soiled and turned into market goods."

Perelman presented similarly charged recollections of his lecture tour to several other St. Petersburg colleagues. They too embellished his narrative with details that served to justify his anger and pain. For example, one person told me that Perelman had been hurt when Hamilton "walked out of the lecture, stomping his feet." When I asked for clarification, my interlocutor conceded, "I added the part about his stomping his feet. But from what I have been told, he did leave demonstratively."

When Perelman spoke to two *New Yorker* writers in the summer of 2006, he told them that Hamilton had shown up late for his lecture and asked no questions during the discussion session or the lunch—a recollection that is at odds with Morgan's. In all likelihood, Hamilton had asked no questions that indicated to Perelman that the older mathematician had made a serious effort to understand his work. "I'm a disciple of Hamilton's, though I haven't received his authorization," Perelman told the *New Yorker* and added, "I had the impression he had read only the first part of my paper."

The more Perelman talked about his disappointment with the mathematical establishment, and the more his acquaintances decorated his stories with demonizing details, the more Perelman's sense of betrayal deepened. His world, which had begun narrowing in his first university year and then broadened slightly both times he had traveled to the United States, was now headed for its final, disastrous narrowing. Like a rubber band slipping inexorably off a sphere, his world was about to shrink to a point.

From the moment Perelman entered Rukshin's math club at the age of ten—or perhaps from a much earlier point, when his mother told her professor she was leaving mathematics to have a baby —Perelman had been a human math project. He was raised by his mother, reared by Rukshin, coddled by Ryzhik, coached by Abramov, directed by Zalgaller, protected by Alexandrov, tended by Burago, and promoted by Gromov so that he could do pure mathematics in a world of pure mathematics. Perelman repaid his teachers and benefactors by doing just that: solving the hardest problem he could find—and by devoting himself to this process fully. And when he was done, he expected certain things. Just as he had been convinced that he should not untie his hat and had always, against all evidence, believed in meritocracy, so now he had in his head a perfect picture of how things should go. He had, in essence, a script. This script apparently indicated that Hamilton would attend all of Perelman's lectures at Stony Brook, possibly even his first lecture at MIT, and Hamilton and the whole Ricci flow community would delve deeply into Perelman's proof, making every effort to understand it. Other mathematicians would do this too; this would be their natural way of responding to his contribution and of showing mathematical appreciation.

Perelman's disappointment in Hamilton was all the more painful because he had apparently perceived Hamilton as a member of the pure-mathematician caste. In his conversation with the *New Yorker* journalists, Perelman recalled his first encounter with Hamilton, at Princeton, in a way that made this clear: "'I really wanted to ask him something,' Perelman recalled. 'He was smiling, and he was quite patient. He actually told me a couple of things that he published a few years later. He did not hesitate to tell me. Hamilton's openness and generosity—it really attracted me. I can't say that most mathematicians act like that.'" So striking and stable was this image of Hamilton in Perelman's memory that he seemed to have ignored Hamilton's nonresponse to his initial letter regarding Ricci flow and Hamilton's nonreaction to the first preprint—and so he kept expecting that Hamilton would stick to the script during the lecture tour.

The script also contained rules, obvious ones. People should not talk about things they do not understand; if it was going to take a year and a half for anyone to understand the proof, no one should talk about the proof until then. Great mathematical achievement should be rewarded with professional recognition, which can take only one form: the form of studying and understanding the work that the person has done. Money is no substitute for work. In fact, money is insulting. If you think it is natural for a university to offer money to someone who has solved a huge problem even though no one at this university understands the solution, imagine the following parallel: a publisher approaches a writer, saying, "I have not read any of your books; in fact, no one has gotten to the end of one, but they say you are a genius, so we want to sign you to a contract." This is a caricature. There was no place for caricatures in Perelman's script.

Back in the summer of 1981, the first year Sergei Rukshin managed to organize a summer mathematics training camp, Grisha Perelman lived away from home for the first time. Rukshin transported a score of his club members, age thirteen to sixteen, to a pioneer camp outside of Leningrad, a grouping of low stone buildings situated scenically in a mixed wood with easy access to a cold lake. Rukshin's agenda called for roughly four hours of problem-crunching per day, diluted with some swimming, hiking, walking through the woods listening to Rukshin recite poetry, and resting indoors listening to classical music. The arrangement with camp officials stipulated that the mathematicians would be a unit within the camp; they would have their own sleeping quarters and their own schedule, but they would have to wear Young Pioneer uniforms—white or blue button-down shirts and red neckerchiefs—and participate in some campwide activities, like politics lessons.

So it was at the beginning of the camp season that Rukshin's boys attended a lecture on foreign affairs. "The international situation," said the speaker, a young Komsomol worker, "is particularly tense today." The entire mathematics contingent broke out laughing. It is particularly tense today! Get it? It is like it was not at all tense yesterday but is *particularly* tense *today.*

If you do not find that especially funny, then chances are you do not have Asperger's syndrome. The condition got its name from the Austrian pediatrician Hans Asperger, who was long believed to have been the first to define it, in the 1940s. In fact, it seems it was the Soviet child psychiatrist Grunya Sukhareva who first grouped the symptoms, in the 1920s; she, however, called the syndrome a schizoid personality disorder, which may partly account for why it has not become a popular diagnosis in Russia. Asperger's is a disorder that's part of the autism spectrum. Unlike most autistics, Aspergians tend to have normal or high IQs, but their mental development still proceeds in ways that are markedly different from neuronormals', as people in Aspergian circles call them. Hans Asperger observed that these children's social maturity and social reasoning were delayed, and some of their social abilities remained, as he kindly put it, "quite unusual" for life. They had difficulty making friends; they had trouble communicating—the tone, rhythm, and pitch of their speech were often odd and off-putting to others; they had trouble understanding and controlling their emotions; and many of them needed profound assistance in organizing their lives, so they were often dependent on their mothers for their day-to-day functioning.

More than forty years after Hans Asperger, a British psychologist named Simon Baron-Cohen came to study autism and Asperger's syndrome and figured out several things that seem to me to be very useful in understanding Grigory Perelman. First, Baron-Cohen suggested that the autistic brain was lopsided in a particular way. Where a neuronormal brain has the ability to both systemize and empathize, the autistic brain might be excellent at the former but is always lousy at the latter—causing Baron-Cohen to dub the autistic brain "the extreme male brain." Baron-Cohen defined systemizing as "the drive to analyze and/or build a system (of any kind) based on identifying input-operation-output rules" and theorized that great systemizers might be at increased risk for autism. When he tested this theory on a population of Cambridge University undergraduates, it turned out that the mathematicians among them were three to seven times more likely than other students to have a diagnosis of an autistic condition. Baron-Cohen also developed the AQ, or the autism-spectrum quotient, test, which he administered to adults with Asperger's or high-functioning autism as well as to randomly selected controls and Cambridge students and winners of the British Mathematical Olympiad. The correlation between math and autism and/or Asperger's was proved again: mathematicians scored higher than other scientists, who scored higher than students in the humanities, who scored roughly the same as the random controls. I took the AQ test too when Baron-Cohen e-mailed it to me, and scored as high as Baron-Cohen would probably expect a former math-school student to score, which is very high. Grigory Perelman, as far as I know, never took the AQ test and certainly cannot be diagnosed by someone who has not talked to him, though after I spent an hour on the phone describing Perelman to Baron-Cohen, the famous psychologist volunteered to fly to St. Petersburg to evaluate the famous mathematician—who sounded so very much like many of his clients—thus joining the long list of people who had volunteered help that Perelman did not welcome.

Had Baron-Cohen chosen Russian rather than British mathematicians as his subjects, the results would probably have been either the same or even more clearly pronounced. After all, Russian mathematical prodigies are often grouped with others of their kind in environments that are especially tolerant of their particular brand of weirdness. The tradition of forgiving mathematicians their autistic rudenesses dates back as far as anyone can remember. Many memoirs of Kolmogorov cite his peculiar manner of walking away in midconversation, demonstrating both his utter disregard for social convention and his pragmatic approach to socializing, which is typical of Aspergians: once he had received the information he sought, he had no further use for communication. In one instance, Kolmogorov, then a dean at Moscow University, was accosted in a hallway by a man who said repeatedly, "Hello, I am Professor Such-and-Such." Kolmogorov did not answer. Finally, the professor said, "You do not recognize me, do you?" Responded Kolmogorov: "I do, and I realize that you are Professor Such-and-Such." In the Aspergian world, conversations are exchanges of information, not exchanges of pleasantries. Most of Kolmogorov's students cited another of their teacher's typically Aspergian traits: what they called his "temper" and what were actually frightening episodes of apparently uncontrollable rage. That Kolmogorov's marked social problems did not impair his career is a measure of the degree to which a sort of Aspergian culture was built into the larger Russian culture of mathematics.

Baron-Cohen's other key insight is the concept that people with autism do not have a "theory of mind"—that is, the ability to imagine that other people have ideas, perceptions, and experiences that are different from one's own. In a striking experiment, Baron-Cohen tested normally developing children, children with autism, and children with Down syndrome. All children watched a brief play involving two dolls and a marble. One of the dolls placed the marble in a basket and left the room. While she was gone, the other doll moved the marble. When the first doll returned, the experimenter asked the children where she would look for the marble. The mentally retarded Down syndrome children and the normal children did equally well on the test: they realized that the doll would look for the marble in the basket, where she had left it. But sixteen out of twenty autistic children were certain she would look for the marble where it really was, not where the doll would have believed it to be. These children were believers in a single truth, utterly incapable of adjusting for human limitations.

Another world authority on Asperger's syndrome, an Australian psychologist named Tony Attwood, believes it is the theory-of-mind impairment that causes Aspergians to interpret everything they hear literally. In one of his books he described a child who sketched a picture at the end of an essay because the teacher had told students to "draw their own conclusions." The belief that people mean exactly what they say is what can lead Aspergians to laugh at a political lecture that to them sounds like a weather forecast ("the political situation is tense *today*"). It also leads them to believe that things work exactly as they are said to work. "I suspect that many 'whistle-blowers' have Asperger syndrome," wrote Attwood. "I have certainly met several who have applied a company's or government department's code of conduct to their work and reported wrongdoing and corruption. They have subsequently been astounded that the organization culture, line managers and colleagues have been less than supportive."

So it is perhaps no accident that the founders of the dissident movement in the Soviet Union were mathematicians and physicists. The Soviet Union was not a good place for people who took things literally and expected the world to function in predictable, logical, and fair ways. But the math clubs, such as the one run by Rukshin, provided a refuge. Rukshin saw it as his mission to shelter the black sheep of Soviet schoolchildren, and he saw a certain posture of social withdrawal as the mark of a gifted mathematician. The first time I interviewed Rukshin, he had a later appointment with an eleven-year-old boy; the child's mother was bringing him "to be looked at," which meant that Rukshin would spend an hour or two or three giving the boy math problems in order to decide whether to accept him to the club. At the appointed time,

Rukshin opened his office door to see if the boy had shown up yet. He had, and was sitting quietly in the lone armchair in the hallway. "I can tell he is gifted," Rukshin said, closing the door. "I can spot them." I knew exactly what he meant: the boy was pale and awkward, and he looked absent. If Attwood and Baron-Cohen had looked at him, they probably would have seen familiar signs as well: physical awkwardness and inappropriate facial expressions are among the outward signs of Asperger's syndrome.

Virtually everything people have recounted to me about Perelman's behavior, starting from the time when he joined the math club, fits the typical picture of a person with Asperger's syndrome. His apparent disregard for the conventions of personal hygiene is common to Aspergians, who perceive it as a nuisance forced upon them by the incomprehensible world of social mores. The trouble he had with articulating his solutions to problems is also classic. "People with Asperger often put in far too much detail," said Baron-Cohen. "They don't know what to leave out. They are not taking into account what the listener needs to know." That is the theory-of-mind problem: the point of telling is not to get a point across but solely to tell. Schoolmates told me Grisha was always willing to answer questions about mathematics; the problems arose if the questioner did not understand the explanation. "He was very patient," a former classmate recalled. "He would just repeat the exact same explanation, again and again. It was as though he could not imagine that somebody found it hard to understand." She was probably exactly right: he really could not imagine it.

His trouble with relating his solutions may also be interpreted in this light. If Perelman has Asperger's, the lack of an ability to see the big picture may be one of his curious shortcomings. British psychologists Uta Frith and Francesca Happé have written on what they call "weak central coherence," a quality that characterizes the thinking of people with autism-spectrum disorders, who focus on detail to the detriment of the big picture. When they are able to arrive at a big picture, it is usually because they have arranged elements—say, the elements in the periodic table—in a pattern, which systemizers find extremely satisfying. "The most interesting facts are those which can be used several times, those which have a chance of recurring," Henri Poincaré, one of the great systemizers of all time, wrote more than a hundred years ago. "We have been fortunate enough to be born in a world where there are such facts. Suppose that instead of eighty chemical elements we had eighty millions, and that they were not some common and others rare, but uniformly distributed. Then each time we picked up a new pebble there would be a strong probability that it was composed of some unknown substance . . . In such a world there would be no science . . . Providentially it is not so."

Aspergians learn the world pebble by pebble, ever grateful for the periodic table that allows them to recognize patterns of pebbles. Discussing the existence of Aspergians in the social world, Attwood used the metaphor of a "jigsaw puzzle of 5000 pieces," where "typical people have the picture on the box of the completed puzzle," which accounts for their social intuition. Aspergians do not have that picture and have to painfully assemble the puzzle by trying to fit the pieces together. Perhaps rules such as "never untie your fur hat" and "read the books on the school's reading list" were Grisha Perelman's attempts to envision the missing picture on the box, elements of his periodic table of the world. Only by sticking to them could he live his life.

The amount of human interaction in which Perelman engaged had been dwindling for eight years. Whatever social skills he had once had—he had exercised them in graduate school and as a postdoc, and they had been adequate, though minimally nuanced—had grown rusty with disuse. So had his tolerance for the behavior of others. Aspergians, it appears, are by and large capable of adjusting to social relationships, though this does not come naturally to them, as it does to neuronormals. John Elder Robison, the author of a memoir of life with Asperger's, described the process as a tradeoff: socialization seemed to rob the person of some of his extraordinary powers of systemizing concentration. Conversely, intense concentration over the course of several years seemed to have robbed Perelman of any social skills he had had. One can imagine how grating he had found the heated political argument between Cheeger and Anderson at Anderson's party, how disinclined he was to engage in anything superfluous and how completely unwilling to entertain any ironies, real or imagined, connected with his work—such as the idea that his proof might drive people away from topology. And he had had such high expectations. He had given mathematics something great, something truly valuable. Mathematics had responded feebly, trying to convince him to accept substitutes for true recognition. No wonder he was disappointed in mathematics.

For the moment, though, Perelman's disappointment was limited to the international mathematics establishment. The Steklov Institute was exempt, or rather his laboratory, his safe harbor after the falling-out with Burago, was exempt. Perelman resumed his activities, such as they were, at the institute: he attended seminars, sometimes several times a week, and he occasionally went by to check his e-mail. In the months before he had left for his lecture tour, he had maintained an even relationship with Ladyzhenskaya, the head of his new lab. She had died in January 2004, at the age of eighty-two, and after that Perelman rarely talked to anyone. As soon as Perelman returned, he wrote up the final installment of his proof, which he posted on the arXiv in June, and then he seemed to be exploring other problems. He was reticent, as usual, to talk about them, but he had apparently moved closer to Ladyzhenskaya's research interests.

Perelman got a promotion at the Steklov: he now held the title of lead researcher. Russian academic institutions assign their researchers to one of four levels, lead researcher being the top. Simple PhDs rarely hold this title; Russia maintains a two-tier dissertation system, in which the first dissertation—the one Perelman had written at the end of his graduate studies and that qualified him as a doctor of philosophy in the United States—ranks one as a candidate, while a second dissertation entitles one to be called Doctor. Steklov well-wishers kept telling Perelman to write his second, doctoral dissertation. The process required a traditional publication, and a defense. Perelman, naturally, scoffed at the idea. "He didn't think he needed it," Steklov director Sergei Kislyakov told me in a slightly puzzled tone of voice. Kislyakov seemed to personify the attitude that grated on Perelman the most: he liked Perelman and wished him well, but Kislyakov sincerely thought rules were the same for everyone, and this meant that a lead researcher should really get his act together and write and defend a second dissertation. Perelman, of course, also thought that rules were rules—but by now this applied only to rules of his choosing and, increasingly, of his own invention. He considered other rules to be sorts of impostors, all the more offensive for pretending to be real rules.

Meanwhile, the Russian Academy of Sciences was putting its house in order, trying to restore itself, after the chaos of the 1990s, to its former buttoned-down glory. On the one hand, Academy property was gradually being repaired—the Steklov got a decent paint job and new plumbing—and salaries were going up; a lead researcher's pay had gone from what literally amounted to pennies in the early 1990s to about four hundred dollars a month in 2004 (though Perelman would have made more had he secured his doctorate). On the other hand, the Academy was now demanding paperwork, reports on research and publishing activity. Perelman, predictably, bristled at the very idea of filling out paperwork to justify his mathematical existence. Ladyzhenskaya's successor, Grigori Seregin, shielded Perelman, ensuring his continued peaceful existence at the Steklov.

In late 2004 Perelman even traveled to Moscow to represent the St. Petersburg branch of the Steklov at a year-end Academy meeting. He gave a talk on the Poincaré. When he returned to St. Petersburg, he was unable to file his expense report. Russian law required that a person dispatched by an institution on official business have his documents stamped at his final destination in order to qualify for reimbursement. Surely someone who just a few months earlier had navigated the U.S. visa maze could easily have managed the Russian business-trip maze. In fact, Perelman had not had his documents stamped on principle: "I cannot go robbing the institute," he told the staff at the accounting office back in St. Petersburg. The accountant had to mail Perelman's documents to the Academy in Moscow so they could be stamped and returned. Still, Perelman would not accept the reimbursement money until the accountant had shown him the books proving that the reimbursement would come out of a special travel fund that was entirely separate from the Steklov's salary budget. Clearly, Perelman's rules on handling money had grown as exacting and as convoluted as his rules on footnoting. And as with footnotes, while the standards were known only to Perelman himself, he believed they were universal—and if he caught anyone violating them, he was merciless.

Merciless he was in the summer of 2005, when he showed up at the Steklov accounting office to ask why he had been paid more than his usual monthly salary. By this time the Steklov was depositing its researchers' pay directly into their accounts, so Perelman had made his discovery at a bank machine. The accountant, a short, overweight woman in her fifties who had seen a lot of mathematician weirdness in her nearly thirty years at the Steklov, confirmed that Perelman had been paid eight thousand rubles—a bit less than three hundred dollars—over his usual monthly amount, thereby receiving almost double his normal monthly pay. The reason was no mystery: his lab had completed a project and had some grant money left over. In keeping with the usual practice, Seregin, the head of the lab, had instructed the accounting office to divide the leftover funds among the staff of his lab. He had made one mistake. Perelman's previous bosses had known he did not approve of the practice—much as he had not approved of exam-time cooperation at the Mathmech, another generally accepted activity that could probably be seen as violating the letter of the law—and so they had always left him off the list of beneficiaries. Seregin did not know of Perelman's position and so placed him on the list.

Perelman asked the accountant to name the exact amount he had been overpaid. He then left the institute and returned a short time later with eight thousand rubles in cash. He wanted to give the money back to the accounting office. The accountant suggested he take it to the lab, where Seregin could decide how to dispose of it. Perelman insisted on returning the money directly to the institute. This is probably the point in the conversation where, as some Steklov staff members later reported, Perelman's shouting could be heard in the hallways. The accountant, however, denies that there was yelling—though over her years at the Steklov she may have grown accustomed to extreme and unexpected expressions of human emotion. Perelman finally prevailed: he convinced the accountant to write a receipt saying she had accepted the money.

The grant story, absurd and telling as it is, is famous in St. Petersburg and among mathematicians elsewhere. In fact, I heard it for the first time in the United States. But the first three or four times I heard it, it was purported to be the story of how Perelman left the Steklov. He refused to take the money and walked out, slamming the door behind him, the story went. That would be a very neat narrative, but it was not what happened. Perelman quit his job at the Steklov half a year later, in early December 2005, for no apparent reason. He came to the Steklov and tendered his resignation letter to the secretary. She ran to the director to alert him. Kislyakov asked Perelman to come in. Perelman went into the director's long rectangular office, with its endless polished-wood conference table, and said calmly, "I have nothing against the people here, but I have no friends, and anyway, I have been disappointed in mathematics and I want to try something else. I quit."

Kislyakov suggested it might be a good idea for him to stay until the end of the month, so he would be able to draw the traditional December bonus—four hundred dollars or so. Perelman declined. He canceled his e-mail account at the Steklov and left mathematics by walking out through the heavy oak double doors that led onto the embankment of the Fontanka River and into the oppressing grayness that masqueraded as daylight in St. Petersburg in winter.

"Something just snapped," Kislyakov told me, shrugging. He had no idea what had snapped. There was a chance that Perelman encountered a difficulty with a problem he was tackling—but then, he had encountered difficulties before and they had not caused him to reject mathematics. Anyway, he was certainly a marathoner. There was a possibility that his final disappointment had to do with the second anniversary of his posting the first Poincaré preprint. Perhaps he had given the mathematical establishment a grace period. After all, the Clay Institute's rules said the million-dollar prize could be awarded two years after publication. (In fact, the rules said a committee to administer the prize could be appointed two years following a *refereed* publication, but Rukshin, for one, willfully ignored the subtleties when he spoke to me about the Clay prize, claiming to represent Perelman's position.) November 2005 may have been the mathematical establishment's last chance to redeem itself in Perelman's eyes. By ignoring the superfluous parts of the rules that made no sense to Perelman and observing only the rules that did make sense, the Clay Institute could have declared Perelman the winner of its million-dollar prize. The money was, as ever, not the issue; the recognition was—and the recognition had to be as singular as Perelman's achievement. He would have been the first person ever to receive the Clay prize. He would have received it alone. And he would have received it on his own terms.

This did not happen.

What happened next was very strange. The June 2006 issue of the *Asian Journal of Mathematics* came out. The journal's entire three hundred pages were devoted to an article by two Chinese mathematicians, Huai-Dong Cao and Xi-Ping Zhu, titled "A Complete Proof of the Poincaré and Geometrization Conjectures—Application of the Hamilton-Perelman Theory of the Ricci Flow." At first glance, this might have appeared to be another explication of Perelman's proof, along the lines of what Kleiner and Lott and Morgan and Tian had been doing—with the important distinction that Cao and Zhu had not been public about their work and had not participated in any of the seminars and workshops sponsored by Clay. They had worked under the tutelage of Shing-Tung Yau, a Harvard professor, Fields Medalist, close friend of Hamilton's, one of the most powerful mathematicians in both the United States and China, and the editor of the *Asian Journal of Mathematics*. Yau had been among the recipients of Perelman's e-mail message drawing attention to his first preprint. He had not responded in any way save for telling *Science* magazine that he thought Perelman's proof might contain a fatal flaw connected with the number of surgeries required to complete the flow.

The abstract of the Cao and Zhu paper read more like a marketing pitch than perhaps any mathematical abstract ever written. In fact, there was nothing obviously mathematical about it. It said, in its entirety: "In this paper, we give a complete proof of the Poincaré and the geometrization conjectures. This work depends on the accumulative works of many geometric analysts in the past thirty years. This proof should be considered as the crowning achievement of the Hamilton-Perelman theory of Ricci flow." The authors appeared to be claiming that Hamilton and Perelman had laid the groundwork for the proofs of the Poincaré and Geometrization conjectures but the last mile had been covered by the Chinese mathematicians, hence the breakthrough—and, it would seem to follow, the fame, glory, and the million dollars—rightfully belonged to them. Such is the law of mathematics: the person who takes the final step gets all the credit for the proof. The difference between taking the final step and providing the explication of the proof is substance, and substance can be a difficult thing to measure. Yau held a press conference at his mathematics institute in Beijing on June 3, and the acting director of the institute declared, "Hamilton contributed over fifty percent; the Russian, Perelman, about twenty-five percent; and the Chinese, Yau, Zhu, and Cao et al., about thirty percent" (there had apparently been a miracle of arithmetic, among other things, and Yau has disputed this account, which was originally printed in a Chinese paper and later reproduced in the West).

A week later, Yau held a conference in Beijing that was headlined by Stephen Hawking. Though most of the several hundred people in attendance were physicists, Yau used the occasion to announce Cao and Zhu's putative breakthrough, saying, "Chinese mathematicians should have every reason to be proud of such a big success in completely solving the puzzle."

Yau was frantically creating a chronology to support his narrative, in which Cao and Zhu were the mathematical heroes. In an article he published in June 2006, Yau painted the following picture: "In the last three years, many mathematicians have attempted to see whether the ideas of Hamilton and Perelman can hold to-gether. Kleiner and Lott (in 2004) posted on their web page some notes on several parts of Perelman's work. However, these notes were far from complete. After the work of Cao-Zhu was accepted and announced by the journal in April, 2006 (it was distributed on June 1, 2006) [sic]. On May 24, 2006, Kleiner and Lott put up an-other, more complete, version of their notes. Their approach is dif-ferent from Cao-Zhu's. It will take some time to understand their notes which seem to be sketchy at several important points." In fact, it appears Yau rushed the Cao-Zhu paper through to publica-tion, effectively forgoing the review process and preempting previ-ously scheduled content, specifically so the authors could claim not to have read Kleiner and Lott's notes—which stated clearly, at the outset, that the proof explicated was Perelman's.

The race was on, because the end of the summer would see the International Congress of Mathematicians—the first such gather-ing since Perelman started posting his preprints. The Poincaré proof—and the million-dollar prize that went with it—would cer-tainly be the main topics of the congress.

The ICM in Madrid began on August 22. On the morning of the opening, publications all over the world received a press release —embargoed until noon that day, when the information would be made public—announcing that Perelman would be awarded the Fields Medal "for his contributions to geometry and his revolution-ary insights into the analytical and geometric structure of the Ricci flow." The document went on to explain, "As of the summer of 2006, the mathematical community is still in the process of check-ing his work to ensure that it is entirely correct and that the con-jectures have been proved. After more than three years of intense scrutiny, top experts have encountered no serious problems in the work." In other words, the official press release stopped short of giving Perelman credit for proving the Poincaré. On the same day, the new edition of the *New Yorker* went on sale; it included an article called "Manifold Destiny," written by *A Beautiful Mind* author Sylvia Nasar and science journalist David Gruber. The article traced the story of Perelman's proof, Cao and Zhu's paper, and Yau's promotion of the Chinese scientists' authorship of the proof, and it even contained excerpts from a conversation with Perelman, whom the authors had convinced to speak with them in St. Petersburg. The article quoted Anderson, who said, "Yau wants to be the king of geometry. He believes that everything should issue from him, that he should have oversight. He doesn't like people encroaching on his territory." It also quoted Morgan, who contradicted Cao and Zhu's claim that Perelman's proof had contained catastrophic gaps that they had filled in. "Perelman already did it and what he did was complete and correct," Morgan told the *New Yorker* writers. "I don't see that they did anything different."

"It was so much fun," one mathematician told me. "It came out right during the congress, and the copy machines immediately started working at full capacity. I might have been bored there otherwise, but as it was, it was really fun."

On August 29, the day after the *New Yorker*'s cover date, the daily ICM newsletter published back-to-back interviews with Cao and Jim Carlson, head of the Clay Institute. Cao extolled Hamilton and Perelman, saying that they "have done the most important fundamental works," and adding, "They are the giants and our heroes!" But he stopped conspicuously short of saying that it was Perelman who had proved the Poincaré and Geometrization—indeed, he made both Hamilton and Perelman sound like giants from the past on whose shoulders modern-day mathematicians had stood to construct the ultimate proof. Carlson, on the other hand, was decisive: "Perelman fulfills all the requirements of the Millennium Prize," he said, naming the work of Kleiner and Lott, Morgan and Tian, and Cao and Zhu as the papers that completed the Clay Institute's refereed-publication requirement.

Mathematicians are not accustomed to controversies this heated and publicity this broad. There had been arguments over author-ship and credit before—including one involving a Russian topolo-gist, Alexander Givental, and Yau and one of his students, who claimed to have completed a proof Givental had begun—but they had never spilled over into the mainstream media. Unlike social scientists or even doctors, mathematicians whom Nasar and Gru-ber interviewed had no experience talking to the press. When they saw their words in print—and copiously reproduced for their col-leagues' entertainment—they were aghast. Yau engaged a lawyer, who wrote a letter to the *New Yorker* demanding a correction and an apology, because, Yau now claimed, he had never tried to wrest credit away from Perelman. Three mathematicians quoted in the article wrote what amounted to letters of apology to Yau and al-lowed them to be posted on various websites. Anderson was among those who claimed to have been quoted out of context. And when I spoke to him a year later, he was extremely reluctant to go on the record. He also tried to convince me that the Yau controversy had been unnecessarily exaggerated by nonmathematicians.

Perelman likely did not follow this story. He had positioned himself outside the mathematics community, and he had never been much of a Web surfer. But Rukshin, who was expert at scour-ing blogs and tracing links, was in his element following this un-precedented mathematical scandal. It would have given him satis-faction to report back to Perelman what both had long suspected: the mathematics community did not stand up for its own, not even for one who had given mathematics its biggest gift in a hundred years.

The mathematics community in the United States, and even in the world, is very small and very peaceful. "And that's one of the great joys of being a mathematician," John Morgan told me about a year after the controversy. "It's not like sociology or history, where it does become quite political. And maybe that's another reason why people shy away from these controversies, hoping they'll go away. You know, you start having war in camps and then suddenly the department explodes. The X supporters are separated from the Y supporters and the anti-Y supporters and, you know, that doesn't do anybody any good. Keep it a pleasant place to do the work. So few people understand what we do, appreciate what we do, it's nice. This community is actually a community of people who respect each other and treat each other decently." Most of the people, most of the time, that is. In a community this small, one cannot afford to burn bridges. Yau, with his academic positions and his army of professor-students on two continents, is not only extremely powerful institutionally but also central to a large and vibrant intellectual community, being shut out of which would amount to a tragic loss for most mathematicians.

The contemporary Western mathematics community acts like a corporation, albeit a very small one: it protects its own from the outside world, and it depends on peace, cooperation, and communication to function. But being a very small corporation, it also sometimes acts like a family, sacrificing ideals and principles for shared history and interdependence. Perelman had almost as little use for family, outside of his mother, as he did for corporations. He simply did not understand either. And he did not like to deal with things he did not understand. In fact, he refused to deal with them.

About a year before all hell broke loose in the summer of 2006, the ICM program committee sent Perelman a letter inviting him to give a lecture at the Madrid congress. The program committee and the medal committee worked independently; the members of both were kept secret until the congress, and only the names of the chairs were released. Perelman did not respond to this letter or to subsequent others. A committee representative then called

Kislyakov—Perelman was still on staff at the Steklov then—and Kislyakov called Perelman at home. Perelman explained to Kislyakov that he had not responded to the letters precisely because the names of committee members were kept secret. He would not, he said, deal with conspiracies.

Kislyakov conveyed Perelman's reasoning back to the committee, which followed with another letter, this time disclosing the names of its members. Perelman again did not respond; the committee again requested Kislyakov's intervention; and the Steklov director again called Perelman at home. Perelman explained that the committee's disclosure was too little, too late—and he would not entertain further discussion.

Perelman's refusal to deal with the program committee, which amounted to his refusal to speak at the congress, was an almost debilitating blow to the ICM organizers. It was obvious that the topic of the Poincaré Conjecture would dominate the congress. At the same time, the Fields Medal committee had decided that Perelman should be one of the recipients. The Fields Medal, often called the Nobel Prize of mathematics (there is, in fact, no Nobel Prize for mathematics), is awarded every four years to two to four mathematicians age forty or younger. Perelman would turn forty just before the congress, making it the last year he would be eligible. And although by the summer of 2005 a consensus had formed among topologists that Perelman had indeed proved the Poincaré—and the committee was aware of this consensus, because Jeff Cheeger was one of its members—final certainty was lacking. Kleiner and Lott and Morgan and Tian were not yet done with their explorations of the proof, so no one could guarantee that a major flaw—or even a fatal one, as Yau had implied—would not emerge. The committee drafted a carefully worded invitation to Perelman to accept the Fields Medal—an invitation that, much like the press release a year later, did not state that he had proved the Poincaré Conjecture.

Normally the names of Fields Medalists are not released to anyone, including the laureates themselves, until they are announced at the ICM. Naturally, though, the medal recipients are usually present at the congress and already scheduled to give speeches. But Perelman had refused to speak, and this was what necessitated the special invitation. Imagine Perelman's reaction. Was this all the mathematics community had to offer him, after all he had contributed? Recognition along with three other mathematicians, none of whom had accomplished anything as momentous as the proof of the Poincaré? And recognition that was carefully worded so as to avoid giving Perelman true credit for what he had done! If ever Perelman had seen mathematics taking on the worst traits of politics, it was then.

To ensure that Perelman would agree to attend the congress and accept the medal, the Fields Medal committee dispatched its chairman—president of the International Mathematical Union, Oxford professor Sir John Ball—to St. Petersburg. This was an unprecedented mission, but then, there had never been as difficult a problem as the Poincaré Conjecture or as difficult a medal recipient as Grisha Perelman. The week before Perelman was due to be awarded the medal, he and Ball spent hours speaking at a conference center in St. Petersburg. Perelman would not accept the medal. Ball offered him a number of alternatives, including the delivery of the medal to St. Petersburg—as had been done decades before when Soviet mathematicians were not allowed to travel to the ICM and the medal had been awarded whenever it could physically meet its recipient—but Perelman refused.

On August 22 in Madrid, during the ICM opening ceremony, John Ball announced the names of the four Fields Medal recipients. They were Andrei Okounkov, a Russian mathematician working at Princeton; Perelman; Terence Tao, a onetime Australian wunderkind now at the University of California at Los Angeles; and the French mathematician Wendelin Werner. Perelman came second on Ball's list, as the list was arranged alphabetically. "A Fields Medal is awarded to Grigory Perelman, of St. Petersburg, for his contributions to geometry and his revolutionary insights into the analytical and geometric structure of the Ricci flow," said Ball. "I regret that Dr. Perelman has declined to accept the medal."

When the *New Yorker* writers visited Perelman earlier that summer, he told them it was the prospect of being awarded the Fields Medal that had forced him to make a complete break with the mathematics community: he was becoming too conspicuous, getting roped into the limelight. He might have been engaging in a bit of justification postdating: when he had quit the Steklov in early December 2005, declaring on his way out that he was abandoning mathematics altogether, the Fields Medal, while certainly a predictable possibility, was not yet a subject of discussion. "At a certain level you could say he lives absolutely by his principles," Jeff Cheeger said to me almost two years later. "But he is certainly not entirely open about his motivations, and in particular I believe he's quite an emotional person. And he uses his powerful mind to sort of explain his emotions after the fact."

The Fields Medal debacle seems to have tried Cheeger's patience with his brilliant younger colleague. "It's sort of like he is above it and maybe there is something wrong with practitioners in general," Cheeger told me, trying as hard as he could to choose words that would not offend Perelman, on the infinitesimal chance that he ever reads this book. "His behavior was supposed to be purer than pure, but it wound up having the effect of essentially focusing all the attention on him—not just because of the extraordinary importance of what he had done, but seemingly paradoxically. To the relative exclusion of all the other Fields Medalists."

If part of what insulted Perelman about the Fields Medal was the suggestion of his sharing with three other mathematicians what he felt should have been a singular honor, then by rejecting the medal, he set himself firmly apart. The same way that Perelman's refusal to accept the European honor in 1996 had hurt Vershik, now a number of his colleagues felt slighted, insulted, or at least misunderstood and puzzled by Perelman's behavior. Only Gromov claimed to understand Perelman's reasoning perfectly and to support it fully.

"When he got the letter from the committee inviting him to give a talk, he said he wouldn't talk to committees," Gromov recounted for me. "And that is absolutely the right thing to do! There are all sorts of things that we accept that we shouldn't accept. And he looks extreme only against the backdrop of conformism that is characteristic of mathematicians in general."

"But why shouldn't one talk to a committee?" I asked.

"One doesn't talk to committees!" Gromov exclaimed, exasperated. "One talks to people! How is it possible to talk to a committee? Who is on that committee? It might be Yasir Arafat is on it."

"But they sent him the list of committee members and he still refused to talk," I objected.

"After the way it started, he was right not to talk to them," Gromov persisted. "The moment the community begins to act like a machine, you have to stop dealing with it—that is all! The only strange thing is that more mathematicians don't act that way. That is the strange thing! Most people are perfectly content to talk to committees. They are satisfied to travel to Beijing and accept a prize from the hands of Chairman Mao. Or the king of Spain, which is the same thing."

Why, I pleaded, was the king of Spain undeserving of the honor of hanging a medal around Perelman's neck?

"Who the hell are kings?" Gromov was really cranked up now. "Kings are the same kind of crap as communists. Why should a king give a mathematician his prize? Who is he? He is nothing. From a mathematician's point of view, he is nothing. Same as

Chairman Mao. So one of them seized power like a robber while the other got it from his father. That's no difference." In contrast to these people, Gromov explained, Perelman had actually made a real contribution.

Following my interview with Gromov, I walked around Paris with a French mathematician who had refashioned himself as a historian of science. I had met Jean-Michel Kantor at a conference on mathematics and philosophy. Here was a classic French intellectual, a short, disheveled man who had to rush off to an editorial meeting of a highbrow book-review journal following our walk. As we walked, he criticized Gromov. The geometer, he said, had stood idly by as French mathematics sank into the abyss: mathematical institutions now issued fundraising brochures, blatant appeals for money that contributed nothing to the mathematical discourse. And professors shamelessly entered into salary negotiations, sometimes even making their plans contingent on the remuneration. Where was their love of the science and their will to sacrifice material comforts for the common cause of mathematics?

What this man was describing was the Americanization of French mathematics. And what I found invaluable about his perspective was that he still managed to see the money-centric, marketing-driven messages of the mathematical establishment as outrageous rather than obvious and expected, as they are in the United States. To someone like this—and to someone like Gromov, who seemed sensitive to criticism that he was becoming a capitalist conformist—Perelman, with his disregard for money and aversion to institutions, appeared very much like the Platonic ideal of a mathematician.

In 2006, the ICM went forward without Perelman. John Lott gave what would ordinarily have been the laudation but was instead a presentation devoted to Perelman's mathematical career trajectory and the trajectory of his proof. Two hours later, Richard Hamilton led a discussion of the Poincaré Conjecture. The announcement of this session in the program, presumably submitted by Hamilton, adopted a virtuoso approach to apportioning credit: the program for the solution, it said, had been invented by Hamilton and Yau, followed by Perelman, who supplied an important part of the solution and "announced the completion of the program," crowned by Cao and Zhu's paper, which Hamilton called "a full exposition." Such wording did not suggest that Cao and Zhu deserved credit for the proof, but it also did not state that Perelman did—only that Perelman himself believed so. During the actual discussion in Madrid, however, Hamilton was as gracious when speaking of Perelman as he had ever been. One participant recalled that Hamilton said he had not originally believed Perelman's claims that he had resolved the problems with his Ricci flow program and taken it to its completion but on closer inspection had seen that Perelman was right. "It was an expression of real admiration," recalled Jeff Cheeger. "Even more so because his initial reaction was 'this guy has got to be crazy!'"

By the end of the congress, the international mathematics community had fully accepted the majority topologists' position: Perelman had completed the proof of the Poincaré Conjecture. The Clay Institute would now use the ICM as the starting point for its countdown to the prize.

Any lingering idea that Cao and Zhu deserved ultimate credit was quietly put to rest the following fall, when a pdf file started circulating among mathematicians. Its left column contained excerpts from Kleiner and Lott's notes on the first Perelman preprint, which had been posted on the Web in 2003; the right column contained excerpts from Cao and Zhu's later paper. Sizable passages appeared to match verbatim. In an erratum note they submitted to the *Asian Journal of Mathematics*, Cao and Zhu claimed they had forgotten they had copied the material into their notes three years earlier. In early December, Cao and Zhu posted a revised version of their article to the arXiv. Now it was called "Hamilton-Perelman's Proof of the Poincaré Conjecture and the Geometrization Conjecture," and the abstract no longer claimed to give the complete proof or be the "crowning achievement." It now read almost contrite: "In this paper, we provide an essentially self-contained and detailed account of the fundamental works of Hamilton and the recent breakthrough of Perelman on the Ricci flow and their application to the geometrization of three-manifolds. In particular, we give a detailed exposition of a complete proof of the Poincaré conjecture due to Hamilton and Perelman."

Following the ICM and the *New Yorker* article, a frenzy broke out where it could hurt Perelman most: the Russian media. Journalists from all sorts of newspapers, including tabloids with press runs of more than a million copies, began calling constantly. Some days, School 239 seemed engaged in a nonstop press conference. Perelman's old teachers weighed in on the subjects of his sanity and his relationship with the mathematics community. Channel 1, which reached more than 98 percent of Russian households, reported that Perelman had turned down the million-dollar prize. Tamara Yefimova, the director of School 239, told a tabloid newspaper that Perelman had not attended the ICM in Spain because he did not have the money to buy a ticket. Alexander Abramov, his old coach, contributed an article to a highbrow Moscow weekly, arguing that there was "no Perelman mystery," just the failure of Russian academic institutions to recognize his achievements. Channel 1 called Perelman at home and broadcast the conversation, in which he said he was no longer doing mathematics and had not been since he left the Steklov Institute. "You could say I'm engaged in self-education," he said. "I cannot predict what I am going to be doing." A camera crew from a Channel 1 tabloid-style talk show burst into his apartment, pushing his mother out of the way on camera in order to film an unmade bed. People began recognizing him in the street and at the opera. He took to saying he was not Grigory Perelman. Strangers snapped pictures of him with their mobile phones and posted them on the Internet.

Politicians joined in the madness too. The St. Petersburg city council considered stationing guards outside the apartment he shared with his mother. It seemed that everyone wanted to give him money. A cabinet member asked to talk to him. Perelman wanted no part of this. Elderly teachers of his, approached by powerful, respected men, agreed to act as intermediaries and called him. He shouted profanities, which the teachers would not repeat. They told me only that he had been rude, very rude. On one occasion, a private Moscow foundation in cooperation with Rukshin cooked up a scheme to give money to his mother, a sort of reward for nurturing a genius son. Perelman overheard her speaking on the phone and ripped the receiver out of her hands, shouting. The once meek, conspicuously well-behaved Jewish boy had, cornered, turned into a domestic tyrant. If the world was not going to respect his seclusion, he would consider the world—the whole world—his enemy.

A year later, when I asked Rukshin to get a copy of Morgan and Tian's new book to Perelman, Rukshin demurred; the last time he had tried to pass on a gift from a foreign admirer, he said, Perelman had lobbed the gift—a classical-music CD—at Rukshin's head.

11

The Million-Dollar Question

W HEN JIM CARLSON was in elementary school, he found arithmetic tedious; his mind wandered. His mother had to tutor him with flash cards to prevent a failing grade. When Carlson was in his senior year of high school, his mathematics teacher handed him a typewritten sheet of paper and sent him to the back of the room. The sheet contained the names of a dozen books on mathematics that the teacher thought Carlson would find interesting—and he could study them on his own time in the back of the room so long as he got his other work done. The list included Courant and Robbins's classic *What Is Mathematics?*, where Carlson read about irrational numbers, among other things, for the first time. When Carlson started college at the University of Idaho in 1963, he planned to major in either physics or psychology. He never took a course in psychology; physics fared a little better, but by the time Carlson was a sophomore, he was doing graduate-level work in mathematics.

He received his PhD from Princeton in 1971, taught at Stanford and Brandeis, and finally settled at the University of Utah, where he spent a quarter of a century, eventually becoming chair of the mathematics department. Then he left for Cambridge, Massachusetts, to run the Clay Mathematics Institute. He had taken the job for a variety of reasons, including the fact that the schedule suited his personal circumstances, but the mission suited him as well. His job was to promote mathematics. Part of that job was to ensure that children and young people would enter mathematics in more elegant ways than he had—that is, through the back of the mathematics classroom. In a sense, he had to give American mathematics some of the luster and streamlined institutionalization that distinguished Russian mathematics. And one of the tools he was handed for popularizing mathematics was the ambitious and extremely well-funded Millennium Prize project. Though truth be told, Jim Carlson did not expect to be wielding that sort of money; he did not think any of the Millennium Problems would actually be solved in his lifetime.

Carlson assumed his position as president of the Clay Institute in the summer of 2004, just as the controversy that would eventually surround Perelman's proof and his prize started to brew. I always had the impression that to be who he was and do what he did, Carlson had to constantly keep at bay great, potentially overwhelming shyness. He was soft-spoken, retiring, exceedingly polite, and the last person one could imagine at the center of a controversy. Fortuitously, when he began his tenure as president of the Clay Institute, he did not know enough to expect the kind of media storm that ultimately surrounded the award. "I heard reports [about Perelman's preprints]," Carlson recalled when he talked to me. "I actually remember thinking, 'My goodness, isn't this fantastic that perhaps there will be a solution to the Poincaré Conjecture?' And of course I started thinking about the Millennium Prizes. And of course, isn't this remarkable, it will certainly be the only one in my lifetime that anyone will receive. But you know, one really doesn't know. I liken it to an earthquake: You know it when it happens. And maybe you could say that tension is building up in the rocks, but no one has successfully been able to predict earthquakes. And nobody knows when somebody will find that breakthrough idea that leads to a solution."

That was what Carlson thought a couple of months before he took the reins at the Clay Institute. He knew that Perelman had posted his preprints on the arXiv—not an unusual circumstance these days; many mathematicians post their articles as soon as they submit them to journals, to spur mathematical discussion before the peer-review process is over. But it was becoming apparent that Perelman had not submitted his papers to any journals and had no intention of doing so. What had seemed a perfectly innocuous and self-evident condition of the Millennium Prizes was emerging as a potential sticking point.

Carlson steered the Millennium boat gracefully and skillfully, funding workshops on Perelman's proof and on Kleiner and Lott's and Morgan and Tian's work explicating it. When he talked to me, he likened Perelman's work to a "flash of light that allows you to get through the forest." Sure, "there is a lot of work to be done, you have to cut down a lot of trees and climb over some boulders and stuff, but it's finding that new way that is so difficult. And if you can't find that, it doesn't matter how much work you do, it will be in vain. And this is what Perelman did." The projects undertaken by those who wrote the explications were clearly much less re-warding than the original solution, and this too filled Carlson with admiration—both for the mathematicians and for the mathematical system, which somehow bent itself to the unusual conditions set by Perelman to deliver the kind of examination and explanation his proof required.

Carlson opened his MacBook Air to read aloud a passage he had found particularly striking, from Kleiner and Lott's published notes on Perelman's proof: "Here it is. 'We did not find any serious problems, meaning problems that cannot be corrected using the methods introduced by Perelman.' I think that is a very accurate statement of what happened. You know, there was a very substantial amount of work to be done to ensure this was correct and complete. But the key thing is that there were no 'serious problems, meaning problems that cannot be corrected using the methods introduced by Perelman.' And there were many methods and ideas. It's always hard to communicate these to a general audience, but I hope you can do that when you write your book." What he wanted me to say, in other words, was that Perelman was the indisputable author of the proof, and that Kleiner and Lott had affirmed this in a way that Carlson greatly admired.

The months leading up to the ICM in Madrid, with the Cao and Zhu paper and the unfamiliar media attention, had been nerve-racking. But the ICM seemed to settle the score, and the evidence of plagiarism that emerged in the fall of 2006 rendered the issue of authorship entirely moot. The publication of Morgan and Tian's book on the proof followed; the Clay Institute commenced the two-year waiting period required by the rules of the Millennium Prizes. At the end of that time it will appoint a committee, which could make its recommendations by fall 2009. Barring the emergence of an error in the proof or some other unforeseen and highly improbable disaster, the committee will recommend that the million-dollar prize be given to Grigory Perelman. Which leaves only one question: Then what?

If Perelman's reasoning on prizes, awards, and honors were consistent, he might accept the Clay million if it was offered to him. After all, his stated objection to the European prize had been that it would have been given for work he did not consider complete. Nothing of the sort could be said of the Poincaré proof. Not only did other mathematicians consider it complete but Perelman himself clearly believed he had completed his project this time. His objection to the Fields Medal, though never stated as clearly, seemed to have been twofold: first, he no longer considered himself a mathematician and hence could not accept a prize intended for the encouragement of midcareer researchers; and second, he wanted no part of the ICM, with all the attendant publicity, speeches, ceremony, and king of Spain.

The Clay prize, however, was designed to be awarded for a particular achievement; there was no stipulation that the recipient had to continue practicing mathematics. Nor did it necessarily require any ceremony. It was an honor bestowed on a mathematician by his colleagues, with no nonmathematical royalty involved. And it was different from both the European prize and the Fields Medal in another very important respect: it represented recognition of Perelman's singular achievement. He could not be compared with any other recipients, concurrent or past—indeed, there was some likelihood that no one alive today would see another Millennium Prize bestowed.

"I think he might have a plan," Alexander Abramov, Perelman's former olympiad coach, told me. "He may have decided that when he is awarded the Clay prize, he will actually accept it because it will be a sign of total recognition and then he could live however he wants to live and not be dependent on anyone." Abramov paused. "But you see, that's just because one needs to come up with some sort of reasonable hypothesis here." That is, one needed to contemplate happy-ending scenarios for Perelman because otherwise, if one cared about Perelman, one might be scared for him, as Abramov was. "I fear this is a situation that will end badly," he said. "He is too full of stuff and too alone." Abramov was yet another person who gave up on calling Perelman after Perelman had grown abrasive on the phone. Before that happened, Abramov had called occasionally, offering support, both moral and financial. For example, he had suggested that if Perelman wanted no part of prizes, he could write an article for *Kvant*, the popular-science magazine founded by Kolmogorov and at which Abramov was now an editor, and receive money for it. Perelman turned down all offers, including Abramov's offer of his friendship. "He told me," Abramov recalled, "that one of his principles was 'One should not force one's friendship on anyone.' So I asked him if he knew the story of Kolmogorov and Pavel Alexandrov's friendship, and he showed a sudden interest in this topic and we talked about it for about ten minutes. He was most interested in the story of Kolmogorov slapping Luzin" —the time Kolmogorov attacked his and Alexandrov's former teacher after Luzin failed to cast a promised vote to induct Alexandrov into the Academy of Sciences. Happy to locate any common ground with his former student, Abramov offered to send Perelman a book on Kolmogorov and Alexandrov. "I'm not reading anything," said Perelman, using the excuse he used to reject all offers of books, including books on his own proof. Abramov was inclined to see some hope in the exchange he had had with Perelman: "At least he has not lost all interest in all things." But I am inclined to interpret it differently. It seemed that Perelman was then getting ready finally to end his last remaining close personal relationship outside of his mother, that with Rukshin. Sometime in the winter or spring of 2008, Perelman cut off all contact with his former teacher.

But before Perelman stopped speaking to Rukshin, the two spent some time talking about the million-dollar prize, and apparently they jointly worked out their approach to it. Just like the rest of the world of mathematics, they believed, the Clay Institute had betrayed Perelman. Rukshin even suggested to me that Clay had changed its rules along the way, introducing the refereed-publication requirement and the two-year waiting period just to delay giving Perelman the money, or possibly to avoid giving it to him altogether. There is in fact no evidence of any changes being made to the Clay Millennium rules after the prizes were instituted, in 2000. Indeed, someone in Jim Carlson's position might find himself wishing for a way to postpone the decision and the subsequent probable failure to convince Perelman to accept it and then the uneasy publicity that would accompany the award. This series of events would certainly not be the story of mathematical triumph and glory that the Clays had envisioned, and while it would fulfill the stated goal of attracting the public's attention to mathematics, it would hardly qualify as the fairy tale meant to inspire droves of young people to pursue mathematical careers. Jim Carlson might well have wished to put off navigating this tricky terrain. But there is no evidence that he did. In fact, he did everything in his power to speed up the process, driven mostly by the desire to fulfill his weighty mission by helping to affirm Perelman's achievement, but also a little bit by the hope of meeting Perelman himself.

In the spring of 2008, Carlson was planning a trip to Europe. He decided to take a detour to St. Petersburg. It seemed as good a time as any: the controversy had died down, there was no lingering doubt about Perelman's proof, and the moment when someone —probably Carlson himself—would have to ask Perelman to accept a million dollars was very clearly approaching. It was time to start talking to Perelman.

Carlson was perhaps hoping for a conversation much like the one John Ball had had with Perelman—long and in-depth, if fruitless. He had little reason to expect the conversation would end any differently, but he had to hope for this nonetheless.

Carlson called Perelman from his hotel room on his first day in

St. Petersburg. He introduced himself and proceeded to explain the Clay prize timetable to Perelman. He repeated all the things Perelman surely knew—that two years had to pass following refereed publication, and that Morgan and Tian's book had provided the starting point for the countdown. He said the committee would likely be appointed as soon as May 2009 and might report back in August 2009.

Perelman listened politely.

Carlson did not ask whether Perelman would accept the money if offered. "The way the conversation was going," he explained to me, "I didn't think it was appropriate." A wave of shyness, held back for so long, may have broken through. Or perhaps Carlson simply wanted to hold off on asking the question, allowing himself another year of slim hope that Perelman might accept the prize. "I didn't get the sense that the door is completely closed," Carlson told me.

At the end of the conversation, Perelman said, "I don't see any point in our meeting."

The next day, I found Carlson at the Steklov, visiting with his old friend Anatoly Vershik, chairman of the St. Petersburg Mathematical Society and the man who once nominated Perelman for the European prize he later turned down. Vershik and Carlson were having tea. Yau's name came up; he was apparently holding a conference to celebrate his fifty-ninth birthday. "I don't understand it," Vershik grumbled. "I know Gian-Carlo Rota held a conference to celebrate his sixty-fourth birthday, but sixty-four is two to the sixth power—and what is fifty-nine? A prime number!" This was mathematicians gossiping.

Carlson spent the rest of his three-day visit seeing old mathematics friends, practicing his cello—a special, highly geometrical travel model—in his hotel room, and thinking about Perelman and the prize. He concluded that no matter what Perelman decided, the Clay prize could be used for the benefit of mathematics. In fact, it already had been. "It's good to explain to the public that there are unsolved mathematical problems," he told me when we went out for some exotic midday vodka at a café called the Idiot. "Surprisingly, a lot of people don't know that."

It is true, Carlson admitted, that a lot of mathematicians criticize monetary prizes for their superficiality; some find it offensive. His friend Vershik had published a piece criticizing the Clay Millennium Prize on these exact grounds. But Carlson told me he had many conversations with undergraduates who wanted to know what these million-dollar problems were. In a way, the buildup to the prize had brought unexpected benefits: "To spend no money to get mathematics in the public eye is not a bad accomplishment," Carlson boasted. Perelman had been his unwitting accomplice: "There is more interest in the public eye in a person who has no interest in the money."

Carlson was not simply putting on a brave face, though he was certainly doing that. He clearly felt that, in an awkward way, he was helping to draw attention to an accomplishment that deserved it. In all my conversations with Carlson, I never perceived any resentment of Perelman, which set him slightly apart from other mathematicians I interviewed: unlike Kleiner, Carlson had not had to cede any of his professional ambition to Perelman's achievement; unlike Tian, he had not been personally slighted by Perelman. He did not understand Perelman—or claim to understand him. All he had was abiding respect for him.

The only person who not only claimed to understand Perelman but at times seemed to channel him was Gromov.

"Do you think he'll accept the million dollars?" I asked Gromov.

"I don't think so."

"Why not?"

"He has his principles."

"What principles?"

"Because Clay is a nothing, from his point of view—why should he take his money?"

"Okay, Clay is a businessman, but it's Perelman's colleagues who are making the decision," I objected, using a word that in Russian meant both "decision" and "solution."

"Those colleagues are playing along with Clay!" Gromov was very irritated now. "They are deciding [solving]! He has no use for any of their solutions! He has already solved the theorem, what's there left to solve? No one is solving anything! He solved the theorem."

Acknowledgments

I owe a special debt of gratitude to all the sources in this book. Writing about a man who does not wish to be written about is an unusual undertaking, and the decision to talk to me could not have been easy for some of Perelman's friends and teachers. In particular, Alexander Golovanov, Viktor Zalgaller, and Sergei Rukshin went to great lengths to try to make me understand their friend and student, and I hope that this book reflects at least some of their insights. I am also very grateful to Jim Carlson, Sergei Gelfand, and especially Leonid Dzhalilov for doing what they could to ensure I wrote about mathematics in a way that made sense. Any mistakes are, of course, still mine. Finally, many thanks to my agent, Elyse Cheney, and my editors Becky Saletan and Amanda Cook, for making this book much better than it would otherwise have been.

Notes

Prologue

page

viii *Millennium Meeting descriptions and quotes: The CMI Millennium Meeting*, documentary, directed by François Tisseyre (New York: Springer, 2002).

1. Escape into the Imagination

2 *"The mathematician needs no laboratories or supplies"*: A. Ya. Khinchin, "Matematika," in F. N. Petrov, ed., *Desyat Let Sovetskoy Nauke* (Moscow: N.P., 1927).

3 *"Mathematics is uniquely suited to teaching"*: "Sudby matematiki v Rossii," a lecture by Mikhail Tsfasman, http://www.polit.ru/lectures/2009/01/30 /matematika.html, accessed February 1, 2009.

The movement's slogans were based on Soviet law: Alexander Yesenin-Volpin, interview,http://www.peoples.ru/family/children/alexander_esenin-volpin/, accessed January 31, 2009.

4 *His article on linguistics*: I. V. Stalin, "Marxism i voprosy yazykoznaniya," *Pravda*, June 20, 1950, http://www.philology.ru/linguistics1/stalin-50.htm, accessed January 31, 2009.

Stalin personally promoted: V. D. Yesakov, "Novoye o sessii VASKhNIL 1948 goda," http://russcience.euro.ru/papers/esak940s.htm, accessed January 31, 2009.

One of them, Dimitri Egorov: J. J. O'Connor and E. F. Robertson, "Dimitri Fedorovich Egorov," www-history.mcs.st-andrews.ac.uk/Biographies/Egorov.html, accessed December 27, 2007.

6 *Luzin case descriptions and quotes:* S. S. Demidov, V. D. Yesakov, "'Delo akademika N. N. Luzina' v kollektivnoy pamyati nauchnogo soobshestva," *Delo Akademika N. N. Luzina* (St. Petersburg: RKhGI, 1999).

7 *As a result, Soviet and Western mathematicians:* Dennis Shasha and Cathy Lazere, *Out of Their Minds: The Lives and Discoveries of Fifteen Great Computer Scientists* (New York: Springer, 1998), 142.

A top Soviet mathematician: Lev Pontryagin's entire memoir is devoted to the backstabbing and intrigue in which this outstanding mathematician personally took part. Lev Pontryagin, *Zhizneopisaniye Lva Semenovicha Pontryagina, matematika, sostavlennoye im samim* (Moscow: Komkniga, 2006), 134.

"It was in the 1960s": Sergei Gelfand, interview with the author, Providence, RI, November 9, 2007.

8 *Three weeks later, the Soviet air force was gone:* Richard Overy, *Russia's War: A History of the Soviet War Effort: 1941–1945* (New York: Penguin, 1998), 73–85.

9 *The greatest Russian mathematician of the twentieth century, Andrei Kolmogorov:* This work by Andrei Kolmogorov is classified, so the published results, apparently called *Strelyaniy sbornik,* are not available. The information comes from Alexander Abramov, his student and biographer, interview with the author, Moscow, December 5, 2007, and from *Etikh strok begushchikh tesma,* ed. A. N. Shiryaev (Moscow: Fizmatlit, 2003), 355, 500.

by the end of his life he had served as an adviser on seventy-nine dissertations: Mathematics Genealogy Project, http://genealogy.math.ndsu.nodak.edu/id.php?id=10480, accessed January 22, 2008.

it was to promise the people of his country that the Soviet Union would surpass the West: Cited in Roger S. Whitcomb, *The Cold War in Retrospect: The Formative Years* (Westport, CT: Praeger Publishers, 1998), 71.

The effort to assemble an army of physicists and mathematicians: Zhores A. Medvedev, *Soviet Science* (New York: Norton, 1978), 46.

10 *Estimates of the number of people engaged in the Soviet arms effort:* Clifford G. Gaddy, *The Price of the Past: Russia's Struggle with the Legacy of a Militarized Economy* (Washington DC: Brookings Institution Press, 1998), 24–25.

11 *official mathematicians and other scientists could shop at specially designated stores: Etikh strok,* 293, 467.

Sergei Novikov, was not allowed to travel to Nice to accept his award: Pontryagin, 169.

12 *Leonid Levin, describes being ostracized:* Leonid Levin, "Kolmogorov glazami shkolnika i studenta," in *Kolmogorov v vospominaniyakh,* 168–69.

Cook and Levin, who became a professor at Boston University, are considered coinventors: Shasha and Lazere, 139–56; Leonid Levin's homepage at Boston University, http://www.cs.bu.edu/~lnd/, accessed January 29, 2008; description of the P versus NP problem http://www.claymath.org/millennium/P_vs_NP/, accessed January 29, 2008.

13 *One of the people who came for an extended stay was Dusa McDuff:* Dusa McDuff, "Advice to a Young Mathematician," in *Princeton Companion to Mathematics*, ed. Timothy Gowers, June Barrow-Green, and Imre Leader (Princeton, NJ: Princeton University Press, 2008), 1007.

"It was a wonderful education": Dusa McDuff, "Some Autobiographical Notes," http://www.math.sunysb.edu/~tony/visualization/dusa/dusabio.html, accessed March 19, 2009.

14 *Mathematicians called it "math for math's sake":* Vladimir Uspensky, "Apologiya matematiki, ili O matematike kak chasti duhovnoy kultury," *Noviy Mir* 11, 2007.

"If I had been free to choose any profession": Grigory Shabat, professor at the Russian State Humanities University, interview with Katerina Belenkina, Moscow, April 2007.

2. How to Make a Mathematician

18 *Alexander Golovanov:* Alexander Golovanov, interview with the author, St. Petersburg, October 18 and October 23, 2008.

Three other boys beat Grisha in competitions: According to Rukshin, these three were Nikolai Shubin, who went on to become a chemist, and Alexander Vasilyev and Alexander Levin, both of whom became computer scientists.

Boris Sudakov: Boris Sudakov, interview with the author, Jerusalem, December 31, 2007.

20 *he hummed, moaned, threw a Ping-Pong ball against the desk:* Sergei Rukshin, interview with the author, St. Petersburg, October 17 and October 23, 2007, and February 13, 2008; Alexander Abramov, interview with the author, Moscow, December 5, 2007.

he never dazzled colleagues with his geometric imagination, but he almost never failed to impress them: John Morgan, interview with the author, New York City, November 9, 2007; Yuri Burago, phone interview with the author, February 26, 2008.

22 *loudmouthed man named Sergei Rukshin:* Rukshin interview.

23 *I observed practice sessions:* I visited the Mathematics Education Center in St. Petersburg on February 13, 2008.

25 *Mathematicians know this as the Party Problem:* http://mathworld.wolfram.com/PartyProblem.html, accessed March 19, 2009.

the *Ramsey theory, a system of theorems:* Ronald Graham, Bruce Rothschild, Joel Spencer, *Ramsey Theory* (New York: John Wiley and Sons, 1990).

30 *When they grew older, Rukshin hounded:* Golovanov interview.

3. A Beautiful School

34 *Steven Pinker observed:* Steven Pinker, *The Stuff of Thought: Language as a Window into Human Nature* (New York: Viking, 2007), 177.
"A layer or a slab has two primary dimensions": Ibid., 179–80.
words like end *and* edge *are used:* Ibid., 180.

35 *the Möbius strip . . . is among the earliest known objects of topological inquiry:* Richard Courant and Herbert Robbins, *What Is Mathematics? An Elementary Approach to Ideas and Methods,* 2nd ed., revised by Ian Stewart (New York: Oxford University Press, 1996), 235.

37 *His students always wondered why:* V. M. Tihomirov, "Geniy, zhivushchiy sredi nas," in Alexander Abramov, ed., *Yavleniye chrezvychaynoye: Kniga o Kolmogorove* (Moscow: FAZIS, 1999), 73. Tihomirov notes that Ivan Vinogradov, Nikolai Luzin, and Pavel Alexandrov also avoided being drafted into top-secret work but explains that their research had no apparent military application at the time; the same could not be said of Kolmogorov's.
with whom he shared a home starting in 1929: Andrei Kolmogorov, "Vospominaniya o P. S. Alexandrove," in A. N. Kolmogorov, *Matematika v yeyo istoricheskom razvitii* (Moscow: LKI, 2007), 141.
they generally requested academic appointments together: The donation, food for people held in the siege of Leningrad, is described in *Etikh strok begushchikh tesma,* ed. A. N. Shiryaev (Moscow: Fizmatlit, 2003), 332. Issues of joint appointments and accommodations appear throughout the correspondence published in *Etikh strok,* for example, on page 80.
Kolmogorov asked the filmmaker to use Johann Sebastian Bach's Double Violin Concerto: "Posledneye interview," in *Yavleniye,* 205.

38 *"Through the woods or along the shore of the Klyazma River":* R. F. Matveev, "Vspominaya Kolmogorova . . . ," in Albert Shiryaev, ed., *Kolmogorov v vospominaniyakh uchenikov* (Moscow: MTsNMO, 2006), 170.
Another of Kolmogorov's students wrote in his memoir: M. Arato, "A. N. Kolmogorov v Vengrii," in *Kolmogorov v vospominaniyakh,* 31.
a math problem he authored at the age of five: Alexander Abramov, interview with the author, Moscow, December 5, 2007.
two professional mathematicians: These are Alexander Abramov and Vladimir Tihomirov.
In 1922, Kolmogorov: "Avtobiografiya Andreya Nikolayevicha Kolmogorova," in *Matematika,* 21.

The Dalton Plan: http://www.dalton.org/philosophy/plan/, accessed January 23, 2008.

39 *"So every student spent most of his school time at his desk":* "Posledneye interview," 186.

"In just three hours at an elevation of 2400 meters": Vladimir Arnold, "Ob A. N. Kolmogorove," in *Kolmogorov v vospominaniyakh,* 40.

the pair spent the 1930–1931 academic year abroad: Kolmogorov, "Vospominaniya," 143.

all culture, and gay culture in particular: Harry Oosterhuis, *Homosexuality and Male Bonding in Pre-Nazi Germany: The Youth Movement, the Gay Movement, and Male Bonding Before Hitler's Rise* (New York: Haworth Press, 1991).

"Interesting that this idea": Etikh strok, 63.

"The wife will always have pretensions to that role": Ibid., 430.

40 *after Alexandrov's death, Kolmogorov:* A. V. Bulinsky, "Shtrihi k portretu A. N. Kolmogorova," in *Kolmogorov v vospominaniyakh,* 114–15.

At the age of forty, Kolmogorov wrote up a plan: Albert Shiryaev, ed., *Zvukov serdtsa tihoe eho: Iz dnevnikov* (Moscow: Fizmatlit, 2003), 110–11.

In 1935, Kolmogorov and Alexandrov organized: B. V. Gnedenko, "Uchitel i drug," in *Kolmogorov v vospominaniyakh,* 131. Kolmogorov did not invent the format; the first competition actually occurred a year earlier, in Leningrad. He was, however, instrumental in taking the competitions national. See N. B. Vasilyev, "A. N. Kolmogorov i matematicheskiye olimpiady," in *Yavleniye,* 168.

Kolmogorov teamed up with Isaak Kikoin: "Istoriya olimpiady," http://phys.rusolymp.ru/default.asp?trID=118, accessed January 24, 2008.

The Soviet of Ministers issued a decree: Abramov interview.

41 *That August, Kolmogorov organized:* Alexander Abramov, "O pedagogicheskom nasledii A. N. Kolmogorova," in *Yavleniye,* 105.

nineteen boys were chosen: A. A. Egorov, "A. N. Kolmogorov i kolmogorovskiy internat," in *Yavleniye,* 163.

Lectures in mathematics: Abramov, 107.

what he called "a spark from God": Egorov, 164.

a high-school course in the history of antiquity: Alexander Prohorov, interview with the author, Moscow, December 8, 2007.

more hours of physical education instruction: Abramov, 111.

Kolmogorov himself lectured the students in music: Egorov, 165.

He also took the boys on boating, hiking, and skiing trips: Gnedenko, 149.

"And few of us understood the music": L. A. Levin, "Kolmogorov glazami shkolnika i studenta," *Kolmogorov v vospominaniyakh,* 167.

42 *He oversaw a curriculum-reform effort:* A. S. Monin, "Dorogi v Komarovku," in ibid., 182.

Kolmogorov sought to revamp the secondary-school understanding of geometry: Alexander Abramov, *"O polozhenii s matematicheskim obrazovaniyem v sredney shkole" (1978–2003)* (Moscow: FAZIS, 2003), 13.

43 *"These things can provoke nothing but disgust":* Ibid., 40.

authors of the curriculum reform were exposed: R. S. Cherkasov, "O nauchno-metodicheskom vklade A. N. Kolmogorova," in *Yavleniye*, 156.

The New Math movement brought actual mathematicians: David Klein, "A Brief History of American K-12 Mathematics Education in the 20th Century," from James Royer, ed., *Mathematical Cognition.* Preprint version at http://www.csun.edu/~vcmthoom/AHistory.html, accessed January 25, 2008; Patrick Suppes and Shirley Hill, "Set Theory in the Primary Grades," *New York State Mathematics Teachers' Journal* 13 (1963): 46–53.

"the effect of freshening [the student's] eye": Quoted in Klein.

Some of his students believed the illnesses were set off: Abramov, 54; Abramov interview.

his students, who for the preceding couple of years had taken turns: Prohorov interview.

44 *everyone was to be taught the same thing at the same time:* Abramov, 48.

"elite education is not allowable in our society": Egorov, 166.

Moscow's School 2 was apparently the object of many denunciations: Leonid Ashkinazi, "Shkola kak fenomen kultury," *Himiya i zhizn* 1 (1991): 16.

School 239 lost some of its most popular teachers to KGB pressure: Mikhail Ivanov, principal of the Physics in Mathematics Lyceum and former teacher at School 239, interview with the author, St. Petersburg, October 23, 2007.

45 *its principal was frequently reprimanded for admitting too many Jewish children:* Tamara Yefimova, principal of School 239, interview with the author, St. Petersburg, October 17, 2007.

two out of four Leningrad math schools were shut down: Tatyana Hein, education activist and Leningrad School 317 graduate, interview with Katerina Belenkina, Moscow, April 2007.

those parents who were college instructors: Aleksandr Krauz, "Zapiski o vtoroy shkole," http://ilib.mirror1.mccme.ru/2/07-krauz.htm, accessed September 16, 2008.

the school's bulletin boards overflowed with announcements: Ashkinazi.

"What made the school different": Boris Levit, interview with Katerina Belenkina, April 2007.

46 *some schools allowed students not to wear uniforms:* Arkady Tsurkov, Israeli mathematician and former Soviet dissident, interview with Katerina Belenkina, April 2007.

some teachers read forbidden works of literature aloud in class: Ivanov.

"What can be more beneficial at sixteen or seventeen": Mikhail Berg, "Tridtsat

let spustya," http://litpromzona.narod.ru/berg/30let.html, accessed September 16, 2008.

47 *"Because of him, we felt like gods"*: Viktor Kistlerov, Moscow computer scientist, interview with Katerina Belenkina, April 2007.

forge a relationship with a second-tier college: Yefimova interview.

he made no secret of his fear of the secret police: Arnold in *Kolmogorov v vospominaniyakh*, 37; Abramov interview.

48 *in 1957 he was fired as dean*: Arnold in *Kolmogorov v vospominaniyakh*, 45.

He parted with his ideas with famous ease: Prohorov interview.

He claimed little interest in the authorship of solutions: "Posledneye interview," in *Yavleniye*, 191.

51 *I spoke with a Russian Israeli psychologist*: Viktoria Sudakova, phone interview with the author, Jerusalem, December 31, 2007.

52 *her support for a math-club class apparently struck some of the teachers*: Yefimova, Rukshin, Ivanov interviews.

Valery Ryzhik: Valery Ryzhik, interview with the author, St. Petersburg, Russia, February 28, 2008; biographical information retrieved from a website devoted to the memoirs of School 239 teachers and graduates, http://club.sch239.spb.ru:8001/club/htdocs/teach_page/ryzhik/, accessed March 23, 2008.

Students recalled that in ordinary years he picked five top students: Natalya Alexandrovna Konstantinova, recollections, http://club.sch239.spb.ru:8001/club/htdocs/teach_page/ryzhik/words.shtml, accessed March 23, 2008.

54 *he would go to the bakery on Liteyniy Prospect*: Golovanov interview.

what chess players call intuition is in fact the ability to grasp complex systems in a single take: Jonah Lehrer, *How We Decide* (Boston: Houghton Mifflin Harcourt, 2009), 44.

55 *Rukshin focusing more on literature, music, and all-around erudition*: Sergei Rukshin, interview with the author, St. Petersburg, October 17 and October 23, 2007, and February 13, 2008.

Ryzhik on chivalry, honesty, responsibility, and other universal values: Ryzhik interview; Yelena Vereshchagina, a former classmate of Perelman's, interview with the author, St. Petersburg, February 13, 2008.

56 *the student who had slipped his classmate the bomb*: For example, see http://scholar-vit.livejournal.com/159422.html?thread=5221566#t5221566, accessed February 7, 2009.

57 *turned away, apparently because the principal had come under increased pressure to cut the number of Jewish teachers*: Ryzhik, Yefimova, Vereshchagina interviews.

criticized for violating every rule of Soviet teaching methodology: Golovanov interview.

Viktor Radionov was fired amid charges of pedophilia: Yefimova, Golovanov, Rukshin interviews.

impressed students with his willingness to entertain even risky political questions: Vereshchagina interview.

later exposed as a KGB informant: Memoir of 1970 graduate Alexander Kolotov, http://club.sch239.spb.ru:8001/club/HTDOCS/teach_page/ostrovsk /alternative.shtml, accessed March 23, 2008.

58 *patiently explained any math issue to any of his classmates:* Vereshchagina interview.

by the time he was in his last year of school, his fingernails were so long they curled: Rukshin interview.

4. A Perfect Score

60 *Mathmech anti-Semitism:* Valery Ryzhik, interview with the author, St. Petersburg, Russia, February 28, 2008; Alexander Golovanov, interview with the author, St. Petersburg, October 18 and October 23, 2008.

61 *roughly eighty thousand conscripts were serving there at any given time:* G. F. Krivosheev, ed., *Rossiya i SSSR v voynakh XX veka*, website of Zabytiy Polk, http://www.polk.ru/pl/afg1.php, accessed March 27, 2008.

63 *all the boys who took prizes at the Leningrad citywide math olympiad at his grade level:* In 1979 first place went to Alexander Levin and Grigory Perelman; second place went to Boris Sudakov and Nikolai Shubin; all four were members of Rukshin's math club. In addition, Alterman (his first name is unknown) and Vadim Tsemekhman, who had taken first and second place respectively the preceding year, had honorable mentions. Information supplied by Dmitry Fomin, historian of the St. Petersburg/Leningrad mathematics olympiads, in an e-mail to the author, March 14 and 15, 2008.

those who took first and second places in the city olympiad would advance to another round of competition: See http://www.mathcenter.spb.ru/history /fomin.html, accessed March 14, 2008.

Alexander Vasilyev and Nikolai Shubin took first place: Fomin e-mail, March 14, 2008.

65 *He named two people: Perelman and Levin:* Alexander Abramov, interview with the author, Moscow, December 5, 2007.

66 *Alexander Levin had not come to the club that particular day:* Sergei Rukshin, interview with the author, St. Petersburg, October 17 and October 23, 2007, and February 13, 2008; Golovanov interview.

Competition description: Fomin, "Istoricheskiy ocherk."

67 *"Wait!" he shouted:* Rukshin interview.

68 *The solution turned out to contain a serious flaw:* Simon Singh, *Fermat's*

Enigma: The Epic Quest to Solve the World's Greatest Mathematical Problem (New York: Anchor, 1998).

for Perelman it was split into time devoted to solving problems: Yelena Vereshchagina, interview with the author, St. Petersburg, February 13, 2008.

69 *One student recalled waking up in the morning:* Alexander Spivak, 1982 Soviet IMO team member and later mathematics teacher, interview with the author, Moscow, February 7, 2008.

Another recalled arriving by bus in Chernogolovka: Sergei Samborsky, 1982 Soviet IMO team reserve member and later computer scientist, interview with the author, Moscow, February 14, 2008.

70 *Preparedness for Labor and Defense of the USSR requirements:* http://russian-sport.narod.ru/files/norms_gto.html, accessed April 1, 2008.

the only nonperfect grade on his graduating transcript: Yefimova interview.

74 *Both he and Spivak had perfect scores:* Abramov, Spivak interviews.

75 *shortly before the planned trip she was told that her travel documents could not be processed in time:* Abramov interview.

76 *took ninth place with 230 points:* Information from the official IMO website, http://www.imo-official.org/year_country_r.aspx?year=1981, accessed April 7, 2008.

a professor of mathematics at Karlsruhe University: http://www.mathematik. uni-karlsruhe.de/iag1/~grinberg/en, accessed April 7, 2008.

represented Germany at the IMO three times between 2004 and 2006: http://www.imo-official.org/participant_r.aspx?id=7901, accessed April 7, 2008.

"Natalia Grinberg, former number 1": http://www.mathlinks.ro/Forum /viewtopic.php?t=101785, accessed April 7, 2008.

78 *1978 IMO team:* http://www.imo-official.org/year_country_r.aspx?year =1978, accessed April 7, 2008; rumor comes from Rukshin interview.

The students were now on their own: A. Abramov and A. Savin, "XXXIII mezhdunarodnaya matematicheskaya olimpiada," *Kvant* 12 (1982): 46–48, http://kvant.mirror1.mccme.ru/1982/12/XXIII_mezhdunarodnaya_ matemati.htm.; Spivak interview.

The judging process: Abramov, Savin; Spivak interview.

79 *Perelman showed no interest in the sights:* Abramov, Spivak interviews.

80 *Perelman's results:* See http://imo-official.org/participant_r.aspx?id=10481, accessed April 16, 2008.

5. Rules for Adulthood

82 *the group represented a sort of elite learning center:* Alexander Golovanov, interview with the author, St. Petersburg, October 18 and October 23, 2008; Mehmet Muslimov, interview with the author, St. Petersburg, February 27,

2008. (Back in his university and math-club days Muslimov had been known as Aleksei Pavlov, but he later converted to Islam and took a new name, in addition to becoming a linguist.)

in the 1970s Leningrad University had moved its science departments: http://www.naukograd-peterhof.ru/peterhof-history.html, accessed April 17, 2008.

86 *He was, however, unwilling to entertain them:* Muslimov interview.

88 *He was strongly drawn to Viktor Zalgaller:* Golovanov interview.

I interviewed Zalgaller: Viktor Zalgaller, interview with the author, Rehovot, Israel, March 16, 2008.

Zalgaller was a World War II veteran: Mikhail Ivanov, ed., *Sbornik vospominaniy o 239 shkole,* unpublished manuscript.

90 *Alexander Danilovich Alexandrov:* Biography of A. D. Alexandrov at http://www.univer.omsk.su/LGS/#s2, accessed April 24, 2008.

A. D. Alexandrov and graduate school: O. A. Ladyzhenskaya, "Ocherk o zhizni I deyatelnosti A. D. Aleksandrova," in G. M. Idlis, O. A. Ladyzhenskaya, eds., *Akademik Aleksandr Danilovch Aleksandrov. Vospominaniya, publikatsii, materialy* (Moscow: Nauka, 2002), 7.

91 *He was also a member of the Communist Party and remained one:* A. M. Vershik, "A. D., kakim ya yego znal," http://www.pdmi.ras.ru/~vershik/B22.pdf, accessed April 24, 2008.

92 *He managed, almost single-handedly, to reframe it:* Idlis, Ladyzhenskaya, 8–10.

Then one of the mathematicians dared ask Alexandrov: Ibid., 74.

93 *The former student, a very prominent mathematician:* Vershik.

still amounted to exile: Idlis, Ladyzhenskaya.

he wanted to fill a vacant chair in geometry: Vershik.

Alexandrov's hopes of obtaining the chair in geometry were dashed: Ibid.

94 *was generally considered unhirable:* Lev Pontryagin, *Zhizneopisaniye Lva Semenovicha Pontryagina, matematika, sostavlennoye im samim* (Moscow: Komkniga, 2006), 113.

managed to provide him not only with a teaching job: Ladyzhenskaya, "Borba," 75–76.

Rokhlin would see twelve of his students' dissertations to completion: Mathematics Genealogy Project, http://www.genealogy.math.ndsu.nodak.edu/id.php?id=42580, accessed April 24, 2008.

the man who would be largely responsible for introducing Perelman: Zalgaller interview; Jeff Cheeger, New York University professor, interview with the author, New York City, April 1, 2008.

"He would give topics and promising ideas away to his students": V. A. Zalgaller, "Vospominaniya ob A. D. Alexandrove i yego leningradskom geometricheskom seminare," in Idlis, Ladyzhenskaya, 16.

95 *"'So have you proved it?' Alexandrov asked"*: A. V. Kuzminykh, "Pamiati uchitelya," in ibid., 120.

Alexandrov's reaction to a request to write a history of Soviet geometry: M. A. Rozov, "Lev v kresle," in ibid., 155.

he had chosen to become a geometer after hearing another professor's words: Yu. G. Reshetnyak, "Vospominaniya o nashem uchitele: A. D. Aleksandrov i yego geometricheskaya shkola," in ibid., 40.

Alexandrov was said to have made the following comment: O. M. Kosheleva, "My otvetstvenny za vsyo," in ibid., 125–26.

"In the end, through the general interconnectedness of events": Quoted in ibid., 126.

96 *Fedja Nazarov*: Nazarov's faculty page at http://www.math.wisc.edu/~na zarov/, accessed April 27, 2008.

97 *Anna Bogomolnaia*: Bogomolnaia's faculty page at http://www.ruf.rice .edu/~econ/faculty/bogomolnaia.html, accessed April 27, 2008.

Evgeny Abakumov: Directory of French mathematicians, http://wwwmaths .anu.edu.au/people/past_visitors.html, accessed September 23, 2008.

98 *Those banished included Bogomolnaia, Nazarov*: Rukshin interview.

Konstantin Kohas: Kohas's faculty page at http://www.math.spbu.ru/user /analysis/pers/kohas.html, accessed April 27, 2008.

terminology from Laurence Peter and Raymond Hull's The Peter Principle: Laurence J. Peter, Raymond Hull, *The Peter Principle* (New York: Buccaneer Books, 1996), 46.

100 *"He just didn't quite have the temperament"*: Anna Bogomolnaia, telephone interview with the author, April 18, 2008.

6. Guardian Angels

102 *An open letter circulated by a group of American mathematicians*: Khronika tekushikh sobytiy 51, December 1, 1978, http://www.memo.ru/history/DISS /chr/XTC51-60.htm, accessed July 31, 2008; quoted according to G. A. Freiman, *It Seems I Am a Jew: A Samizdat Essay*, trans. and ed. Melvyn B. Nathanson (Carbondale, IL: Southern Illinois University Press, 1980), 87.

103 *Zalgaller and Burago concocted a plan*: Viktor Zalgaller, interview with the author, Rehovot, Israel, March 16, 2008.

104 *Aleksei Verner*: Aleksei Verner and Valery Ryzhik, interview with the author, St. Petersburg, February 27, 2008.

108 *his adviser was Vladimir Rokhlin*: Mathematics Genealogy Project, http: //www.genealogy.math.ndsu.nodak.edu/id.php?id=14999, accessed August 4, 2008.

Gromov . . . despaired of getting a research position: Olga Orlova, "Pochemu ucheniye prodolzhayut uezzhat' iz Rossii," an interview with Anatoly Vershik, http://www.svobodanews.ru/Article/2007/11/22/20071122161321910 .html, accessed August 4, 2008.

So said the university's website: http://www.ihp.jussieu.fr/, accessed August 4, 2008.

As I arrived in the cafeteria: Mikhail Gromov, interview with the author, Paris, June 24, 2008.

110 *Geometry Festival:* http://www.math.duke.edu/conferences/geomfest97 /PreviousSpeakers.html, accessed August 4, 2008.

his first major published work: G. Perelman, Yu. Burago, M. Gromov, "Aleksandrov Spaces with Curvatures Bounded Below," *Russian Math Surveys* 47, no. 2 (1992): 1–58.

Gromov mentioned Perelman to all the right people: Jeff Cheeger, New York University professor, interview with the author, New York City, April 1, 2008.

111 *a French mathematician and historian of science:* Jean-Michel Kantor, mathematician at the Institut Mathématiques à Jussieu, Université de Paris.

7. Round Trip

113 *Gang Tian:* Gang Tian, interview with the author, Princeton, NJ, November 9, 2007.

117 *Lena . . . obtained her PhD in mathematics from the Weizmann Institute:* http: //www.weizmann.ac.il/acadaff/Scientific_Activities/2004/feinberg_degrees .html, accessed August 9, 2008.

Western mathematicians, while suffering from too narrow a focus: Andrei Minarsky, interview with the author, St. Petersburg, October 23, 2008.

Cheeger and his coauthor Detlef Gromoll: Jeff Cheeger and Detlef Gromoll, "On the Structure of Complete Manifolds of Nonnegative Curvature," *Annals of Mathematics* 96 (1972): 413–43.

118 *His paper was four pages long:* Grigory Perelman, "Proof of the Soul Conjecture of Cheeger and Gromoll," *Journal of Differential Geometry* 40 (1994): 209–12.

119 *one of the best American graduate programs in mathematics:* U.S. News & World Report rankings, http://grad-schools.usnews.rankingsandreviews .com/grad/mat/items/45094, accessed August 14, 2008.

Michael Anderson: Faculty page at http://www.math.sunysb.edu/~anderson/, accessed August 14, 2008; Michael Anderson, interview with the author, Stony Brook, NY, November 8, 2007.

120 *Alexandrov spaces at the International Congress of Mathematicians:* G. Perelman, "Spaces with Curvature Bounded Below," http://www.ams.org/math web/icm94/04.perelman.html, accessed August 9, 2008.

fifty-five of the world's top mathematicians: List of speakers at http://www.ams.org/mathweb/icm94/, accessed August 14, 2008.

four Fields Medalists, past and future: Richard Borcherds (1998), Gerd Faltings (1986), Maxim Kontsevich (1998), and Jean-Christophe Yoccoz (1994).

His speech seemed vague and disconnected: Two of the mathematicians quoted elsewhere in this book told me this, but neither one wanted the opinion attributed to him.

geometer Bruce Kleiner: Bruce Kleiner, interview with the author, New York City, April 9, 2008.

121 *the conditions of the fellowship stated explicitly:* Miller Fellowship description, http://millerinstitute.berkeley.edu/page.php?nav=11, accessed August 14, 2008.

123 *Peter Sarnak:* Peter Sarnak's CV at http://www.math.ias.edu/media/SarnakCV.pdf, accessed August 15, 2008.

Sarnak recalled in an e-mail message: Peter Sarnak, e-mail to the author, June 1, 2008.

124 *Perelman told several people at the time:* Jeff Cheeger, New York University professor, interview with the author, New York City, April 1, 2008; Sarnak e-mail.

126 *the European Mathematical Society held its second quadrennial congress:* History of the European Mathematical Society at http://www.btinternet.com/~d.a.r.wallace/EMSHISTORY99.html, accessed September 25, 2008.

Anatoly Vershik submitted Perelman's name: Anatoly Vershik, interview with the author, St. Petersburg, May 24, 2008.

128 *"I did ask him what he was working on":* Bernhard Leeb, e-mail to the author, July 7, 2008.

"I've just read your paper": Grigory Perelman, e-mail message to Michael Anderson, February 28, 2000.

129 *"Dear Grisha":* Michael Anderson, e-mail to Grigory Perelman, February 29, 2000.

He asked if Perelman had looked at his other two papers on related topics: Michael Anderson, e-mail to Grigory Perelman, March 2, 2000.

130 *Perelman responded by saying he could not open the file:* Grigory Perelman, e-mail to Michael Anderson, March 20, 2000.

8. The Problem

131 *"The very possibility of mathematical science seems":* Henri Poincaré, "Science and Hypothesis," in *The Value of Science: Essential Writings of Henri Poincaré* (New York: Modern Library, 1999), 9.

132 *"We know what it is to be in love or to feel pain":* Donal O'Shea, *The Poincaré*

Conjecture: In Search of the Shape of the Universe (New York: Walker and Company, 2007), 46.

"that which has no parts, or which has no magnitude": Isaac Todhunter, *The Elements of Euclid for the Use of Schools and Colleges: Comprising the First Six Books and Portions of the Eleventh and Twelfth Books; with Notes, an Appendix, and Exercises* (New York: Adamant Media Corporation, 2003), 1.

"such as are in the same plane, and which being produced ever so far do not meet": Ibid., 5.

"things that are equal to the same thing are equal to one another": Ibid., 6.

133 *postulate 1 and interpretation:* http://alepho.clarku.edu/~djoyce/java/ele ments/bookI/post1.html, accessed June 18, 2008.

postulates 2 and 3: Todhunter, 5.

postulates 4 and 5: Book I of Euclid's *Elements*, http://www.mathsisgoodfor you.com/artefacts/EuclidBook1.htm, accessed June 18, 2008.

"I had been told that Euclid proved things": Bertrand Russell, *The Autobiography of Bertrand Russell* (New York: Routledge, 1998), 31. (My attention was drawn to this passage by William Dunham's *Journey Through Genius: The Great Theorems of Mathematics.*)

134 *"Since the Euclidean system is rather simpler to deal with":* Richard Courant and Herbert Robbins, *What Is Mathematics? An Elementary Approach to Ideas and Methods,* 2nd ed., revised by Ian Stewart (New York: Oxford University Press, 1996), 223.

135 *The geometry is called elliptic:* Ibid., 224–27.

136 *Euler and the invention of topology:* George Szpiro, *Poincaré's Prize: The Hundred-Year Quest to Solve One of Math's Greatest Puzzles* (New York: Dutton, 2007), 54–56; J. J. O'Connor, E. F. Robertson, "A History of Topology," http://www-groups.dcs.st-and.ac.uk/~history/HistTopics/Topology _in_mathematics.html, accessed June 20, 2008.

140 *proof of the conjecture for seven dimensions or more:* J. Stallings, "Polyhedral Homotopy Spheres," *Bulletin of the American Mathematical Society* 66 (1960): 485–88.

just a year after he received his PhD from Princeton: Mathematics Genealogy Project, http://www.genealogy.math.ndsu.nodak.edu/id.php?id=452, accessed June 29, 2008.

he, however, proved the conjecture for dimensions five and higher: S. Smale, "Generalized Poincaré's Conjecture in Dimensions Greater than Four," *Annals of Mathematics* 74 (1961): 391–406.

extended Stallings's proof to dimensions five and six: E. C. Zeeman, "The Poincaré Conjecture for n ≥ 5," in *Topology of 3-Manifolds and Related Topics* (Englewood Cliffs, NJ: Prentice Hall, 1962).

published a proof essentially similar to Smale's: A. Wallace, "Modifications and Cobounding Manifolds," II, *Journal of Applied Mathematics and Mechanics* 10 (1961): 773–809.

There was also a Japanese mathematician: Szpiro, 163.

141 *John Stallings:* Stallings's website, http://math.berkeley.edu/~stall/, accessed June 29, 2008.

"*I have committed—the sin*": John R. Stallings, "How Not to Prove the Poincaré Conjecture," http://math.berkeley.edu/~stall/notPC.pdf, accessed June 29, 2008.

Michael Freedman published a proof of the conjecture for dimension four: M. H. Freedman, "The Topology of Four-Dimensional Manifolds," *Journal of Differential Geometry* 17 (1982): 357–453.

The accomplishment was hailed as a breakthrough: Szpiro, 169–71.

142 *John Morgan:* John Morgan, interview with the author, New York City, November 6, 2007.

9. The Proof Emerges

153 *He had told Anderson at the outset:* Grigory Perelman, e-mail message to Michael Anderson, November 20, 2002.

He handled the U.S. visa formalities: Ibid., March 31, 2003.

154 *he even added a footnote to that effect to his first preprint:* The footnote read, in part: "I was partially supported by personal savings accumulated during my visits to the Courant Institute in the Fall of 1992, to the SUNY at Stony Brook in the Spring of 1993, and to the UC at Berkeley as a Miller Fellow in 1993–95. I'd like to thank everyone who worked to make those opportunities available to me." Grisha Perelman, "The Entropy Formula for Ricci Flow and Its Geometric Applications," http://arxiv.org/PS_cache/math/pdf/0211/0211159v1.pdf, accessed August 29, 2008.

He submitted the second of his three preprints: Grisha Perelman, "Ricci Flow with Surgery on Three-Manifolds," http://arxiv.org/abs/math/0303109, accessed August 28, 2008.

156 *the* New York Times *published an article:* Sara Robinson, "Russian Reports He Has Solved a Celebrated Math Problem," *New York Times*, April 15, 2003.

157 *an intentional revolt:* Mikhail Gromov, interview with the author, Paris, June 24, 2008.

he was happy to let the organizers: Grigory Perelman, e-mail to Michael Anderson, April 2, 2003.

158 *Perelman's screaming at his mentor had been heard:* Mathematician Nikolai Mnev, interview with the author, St. Petersburg, April 22, 2008.

old enough, wise enough, and woman enough: Alexander Golovanov, interview with the author, St. Petersburg, October 18 and October 23, 2008.

they were incapable of seeing his approach to footnoting as anything but: Gromov interview; Viktor Zalgaller, interview with the author, Rehovot, Israel, March 16, 2008; Yuri Burago, phone interview with the author, February 26, 2008.

159 *"as modest as possible":* Grigory Perelman, e-mail to Michael Anderson, March 31, 2003.

exhibited fantastic clarity in his lectures and unparalleled patience during the discussions: Anderson interview.

the New York Times *published another article:* George Johnson, "The Nation: A Mathematician's World of Doughnuts and Spheres," *New York Times,* April 20, 2003.

163 *"one should never force oneself on anyone":* Grigory Perelman, telephone conversation with Abramov in 2007, in which Perelman told Abramov that this was one of his principles.

164 *to attend a daylong math competition at a physics-and-math school:* Andrei Minarsky, interview with the author, St. Petersburg, October 23, 2008.

He submitted the third and last in his Poincaré series of preprints: Grisha Perelman, "Finite Extinction Times for the Solutions to the Ricci Flow on Certain 3-Manifolds," http://arxiv.org/abs/math/0307245, accessed August 31, 2008.

Kleiner and his University of Michigan colleague John Lott: The product of that website is now posted on the arXiv, http://arxiv.org/PS_cache/math /pdf/0605/0605667v2.pdf, accessed August 31, 2008.

a joint workshop on the first preprint: Allyn Jackson, "Conjectures No More? Consensus Forming on the Proof of the Poincaré and Geometrization Conjectures," *Notices of the AMS* 53, no. 8 (September 2006): 897–901.

10. The Madness

172 *When Perelman spoke to two* New Yorker *writers:* Sylvia Nasar and David Gruber, "Manifold Destiny: A Legendary Problem and the Battle Over Who Solved It," *New Yorker,* August 28, 2006.

174 *The arrangement with camp officials:* Sergei Rukshin, interview with the author, St. Petersburg, October 17 and October 23, 2007, and February 13, 2008.

175 *The entire mathematics contingent broke out laughing:* Boris Sudakov, interview with the author, Jerusalem, December 31, 2007.

it was the Soviet child psychiatrist Grunya Sukhareva: V. Ye. Kogan, "Preodoleniye: Nekontaktniy rebyonok v semye," http://www.autism.ru/read.asp ?id=29&vol=2000, accessed March 3, 2008. Tony Attwood, in *The Complete Guide to Asperger's Syndrome* (London: Jessica Kingsley Publishers, 2006), 36, erroneously identifies the psychiatrist as Ewa Ssucharewa.

Hans Asperger observed that these children's social maturity: Attwood, 13.

British psychologist named Simon Baron-Cohen: Simon Baron-Cohen, telephone interview with the author, February 18, 2008.

"the extreme male brain": Simon Baron-Cohen, *The Essential Difference: Male and Female Brains and the Truth about Autism* (New York: Basic Books, 2003).

176 *When he tested this theory on a population of Cambridge University undergraduates:* Simon Baron-Cohen, Sally Wheelwright, Amy Burtenshaw, and Esther Hobson, "Mathematical Talent Is Linked to Autism," *Human Nature* 18, no. 2 (June 2007): 125–31.

mathematicians scored higher than other scientists: Simon Baron-Cohen, Sally Wheelwright, Richard Skinner, Joanne Martin, and Emma Clubley, "The Autism-Spectrum Quotient (AQ)," *Journal of Autism and Developmental Disorders* 31 (2001): 5–17.

177 *once he had received the information he sought, he had no further use for communication:* Lev Pontryagin, *Zhizneopisaniye Lva Semenovicha Pontryagina, matematika, sostavlennoye im samim* (Moscow: Komkniga, 2006), 22.

Kolmogorov . . . was accosted in a hallway by a man: Alexander Abramov, interview with the author, Moscow, December 5, 2007.

what they called his "temper": Ibid.

"theory of mind": Simon Baron-Cohen, Alan M. Leslie, and Uta Frith, "Does the Autistic Child Have a 'Theory of Mind'?" *Cognition* 21 (1985): 37–46.

178 *a child who sketched a picture:* Attwood, 115–16.

"I suspect that many 'whistle-blowers' have Asperger syndrome": Ibid., 118.

the founders of the dissident movement in the Soviet Union: "Yesenin-Volpin Alexander Sergeevich," *Novoye zerkalo hronosa,* http://www.hrono.ru/biograf/bio_we/volpin.html, accessed February 23, 2008.

179 *a nuisance forced upon them by the incomprehensible world of social mores:* Michelle G. Winner, founder and director of the Center for Social Thinking in San Jose, CA, telephone interview with the author, February 1, 2008.

"He was very patient": Yelena Vereshchagina, interview with the author, St. Petersburg, February 13, 2008.

"weak central coherence": Francesca Happé and Uta Frith, "The Weak Coherence Account: Detail-Focused Cognitive Style in Autism Spectrum Disorders," *Journal of Autism and Developmental Disorders* 36 (January 2006): 5–25.

180 *"The most interesting facts are those which can be used several times":* Henri Poincaré, *Science and Method,* trans. Frances Maitland, unabridged republication of the 1914 edition (Mineola, NY: Dover Publications, 2003), 17.

"jigsaw puzzle of 5000 pieces": Attwood, 92.

181 *socialization seemed to rob the person:* John Elder Robison, *Look Me in the Eye: My Life with Asperger's* (New York: Crown, 2007).

182 *"He didn't think he needed it":* Perelman's last few years at the Steklov described primarily by Sergei Kislyakov, Steklov Institute director, interview with the author, St. Petersburg, April 21, 2008.

183 *he was unable to file his expense report:* Tamara Yakovlevna, Steklov accountant, interview with the author, St. Petersburg, April 22, 2008.

186 *The journal's entire three hundred pages were devoted to an article:* Huai-Dong Cao and Xi-Ping Zhu, "A Complete Proof of the Poincaré and Geometrization Conjectures—Application of the Hamilton-Perelman Theory of the Ricci Flow," *Asian Journal of Mathematics* 10, no. 2 (June 2006): 165–492.
telling Science *magazine that he thought:* Dana Mackenzie, "Mathematics World Abuzz Over Possible Poincaré Proof," *Science*, April 18, 2003.

187 *Yau held a press conference:* Nasar, Gruber.
Yau used the occasion to announce Cao and Zhu's putative breakthrough: Nasar, Gruber; George Szpiro, *Poincaré's Prize: The Hundred-Year Quest to Solve One of Math's Greatest Puzzles* (New York: Dutton, 2007), 238.

188 *"In the last three years, many mathematicians have attempted to see whether the ideas":* Shing-Tung Yau, "Structure of Three-Manifolds—Poincaré and Geometrization Conjectures," http://doctoryau.com/papers/yau_poincare .pdf, accessed October 4, 2008. Date of publication obtained from http: //www.mcm.ac.cn/Active/yau_new.pdf.
Yau rushed the Cao-Zhu paper through to publication: Following much criticism, Yau described the process himself in a letter to the newsletter of the American Mathematics Society. He wrote that he had unilaterally reviewed and approved the paper for publication in his journal. Shing-Tung Yau, "The Proof of the Poincaré Conjecture," *Notices of the AMS*, April 2007, 472–73, http://www.ams.org/notices/200704/commentary-web.pdf, accessed June 13, 2009.
stated clearly, at the outset, that the proof explicated was Perelman's: Bruce Kleiner and John Lott, "Notes on Perelman's Papers," http://arxiv.org/PS _cache/math/pdf/0605/0605667v2.pdf, accessed October 4, 2008.
"for his contributions to geometry and his revolutionary insights": http://www .icm2006.org/dailynews/fields_perelman_info_en.pdf, accessed October 4, 2008.

189 *"It was so much fun":* Sergei Gelfand, interview with the author, Providence, RI, November 9, 2007.
ICM newsletter published back-to-back interviews: ICM 2006 Daily News, Madrid, August 29, 2006.

190 *Yau engaged a lawyer:* "Harvard Math Professor Alleges Defamation by *New Yorker* Article; Demands Correction," press release, September 18, 2006, www.doctoryau.com, accessed September 9, 2008.

192 *The committee drafted a carefully worded invitation:* Jeff Cheeger, New York University professor, interview with the author, New York City, April 1, 2008.

194 *"A Fields Medal is awarded to Grigory Perelman":* International Congress of Mathematics 2006, opening ceremony, http://www.icm2006.org/proceed ings/Vol_I/2.pdf, accessed September 11, 2008.

196 *John Lott gave what would ordinarily have been the laudation:* John Lott, "The Work of Grigory Perelman," talk at the 2006 ICM, http://www.icm2006 .org/v_f/AbsDef/ts/Lottlight-GP.pdf, accessed September 11, 2008.

197 *Two hours later, Richard Hamilton:* ICM 2006 schedule, http://www .icm2006.org/v_f/fr_Resultat_Cos.php?Titol=O, accessed September 12, 2008.

The announcement of this session in the program: Ibid.

The Clay Institute would now use the ICM: James Carlson, interview with the author, Boston, August 27, 2007.

a pdf file started circulating: http://www.cds.caltech.edu/~nair/pdfs/Cao Zhu_plagiarism.pdf, accessed September 12, 2008.

198 *Cao and Zhu claimed they had forgotten they had copied the material:* Denis Overby, "The Emperor of Math," *New York Times,* October 17, 2006.

"In this paper, we provide an essentially self-contained": Huai-Dong Cao and Xi-Ping Zhu, "Hamilton-Perelman's Proof of the Poincaré Conjecture and the Geometrization Conjecture," http://arxiv.org/PS_cache/math/pdf/0612 /0612069v1.pdf, accessed September 12, 2008.

Channel 1 . . . reported that Perelman: "Rossiyskiy matematik razgadal za-gadku, kotoraya muchayet uchenykh uzhe 100 let," transcript of television broadcast, http://www.1tv.ru/owa/win/ort6_main.print_version?p_news_ title_id=92602, accessed September 12, 2008.

he did not have the money to buy a ticket: "Perelman igraet v pryatki," *MK v Pitere,* August 30, 2006, http://www.mk-piter.ru/2006/08/31/022/, ac-cessed September 12, 2008.

Alexander Abramov, his old coach, contributed: Alexander Abramov, "Zagadki Perelmana net," *Moskovskiye Novosti,* September 1, 2006.

"You could say I'm engaged in self-education": http://www.youtube.com /watch?v=jG-DGAdughs, accessed September 12, 2008.

11. The Million-Dollar Question

200 *Jim Carlson:* James Carlson, interviews with the author on numerous occa-sions, including Boston, August 27, 2007, and St. Petersburg, May 24 and May 25, 2008.

207 *he was apparently holding a conference to celebrate his fifty-ninth birthday:*

"International Conference in Honor of the 59th Birthday of Shing-Tung Yau!" http://qjpam.henu.edu.cn/home.jsp, accessed October 5, 2008.

"I know Gian-Carlo Rota held a conference to celebrate his sixty-fourth birthday": That conference was actually organized by Rota's students. A mention is contained in a Rota obituary, http://www.math.binghamton.edu/zaslav /Nytimes/+Science/+Math/+Obits/rota-mit-obit.html, accessed October 5, 2008.

208 *Vershik had published a piece:* Anatoly Vershik, "What Is Good for Mathematics? Thoughts on the Clay Millennium Prizes," *Notices of the AMS*, January 2007, http://www.ams.org/notices/200701/comm-vershik.pdf, accessed October 5, 2008.

Index

11-14-12